THE
SS

ABOUT THE AUTHOR

Robert Lewis Koehl was formerly Professor of History at the University of Wisconsin-Madison. He has researched the SS for more than thirty years and has published widely in the field. He lives in Madison in Wisconsin.

THE
SS

A HISTORY
1919 - 45

ROBERT LEWIS KOEHL

TEMPUS

Cover illustrations: (Front) Massed ranks of Allgemeine-SS at a Nuremburg rally. (Back) Advancing Waffen-SS troops on the Eastern Front. Courtesy of Brian Leigh Davies

First published 1989
This edition first published 2004

Tempus Publishing Limited
The Mill, Brimscombe Port,
Stroud, Gloucestershire, GL5 2QG
www.tempus-publishing.com

British Library Cataloguing in Publication Data.
A catalogue record for this book is available from the British Library.

ISBN 0 7524 2559 5

Typesetting and origination by Tempus Publishing Limited
Printed and bound in Great Britain

CONTENTS

INTRODUCTION

The men in the black coats were, after all, men. Many but by no means all of them donned these coats as other men in other lands and other times might put on ritual masks and join in strange dances, to propitiate a threatening nature. They became 'otherwise' and acted like men possessed. Such persons, both in their own consciousness and in that of their countrymen, acted for others in the German community who therefore did not have to participate directly in the ritual. Thus, they were permitted to torture and kill, to conquer and destroy, and to take part in a theatrical production of immense proportions. Yet this drama and its props remained exactly what it was for other ordinary men, both German and non-German: tinsel and cardboard.

Especially in the *Waffen*-SS (the garrisoned military wing of the SS), in the field-grey of the front, SS men sought later to escape the curse of these same black coats, to become 'just soldiers like the others'. Indeed, in the field-grey uniform also, they were only men. But their SS past, the patterns of soldiering and of German society, as well as National Socialist power politics, thrust many of them into brave exploits, ruthless savagery and thoughtless destruction. An SS unit of the *Wehrmacht* could never be just another military unit, although many of its officers and men were rather ordinary individuals. Tradition, that familiar concept in military annals, had its influence in the SS too and not always as desired by SS commanders – or by SS volunteers – forcing the man to become both more than himself, and a good deal less.

Adolf Hitler experienced this once in the uniform of the Bavarian Infantry. When the overlays of myth surrounding his military service have been removed, he too emerges as an ordinary man, whose Austrian accent was not erased by the uniform and who did not become a comrade or a hero yet nonetheless was stretched (and not merely inflated) into something new. This happened not merely for Hitler but for all the men who had grown up and lived in peacetime. The front generation of 1914–18 was neither more nor less creative than its fathers. Its members made do with what they had, as all men do; and what they improvised out of their emptiness and their very partial fulfilment became their 'messages' to the civilian world to which they were forced to return as arbitrarily as they were forced to leave it in 1914. None of the foregoing was unique to Germany; France, Britain, Italy, eastern Europe, and even Russia and the United States experienced the returned civilian-soldier as an alien if not an enemy, a confused and impatient reformer. Yet to the degree that each country, each environment, could replace what had been lost (or squeezed out) of the war veteran, that man gradually reintegrated himself into the civilian world. Individuals vary due to an infinite, or almost infinite, set of early influences, so that again in Germany as everywhere there were many exceptions. There was, after all, not much of a common denominator to 'front experience'. There was only a potential common denominator of a common uniform, to which the conditions of post-war Europe could then add content: defeat, disgrace, hopeless job conditions, political instability and moral anarchy.

It is a commonplace today that National Socialism was not Germany's inevitable fate any more than Soviet Communism was Russia's. The action and inaction of countless millions, by no means all of them in Germany or Russia, led to consequences of which they themselves were neither the masters nor choosers. But individuals did choose, did plan, did act; and these choices, plans and acts had the consequences of Communism and National Socialism because of complex but not incomprehensible patterns of human behaviour, especially institutional behaviour. German institutions, and especially the processes of change in these institutions, provide the matrix in which individual goals, responses, improvisations and concepts lead to predictable social and political consequences. Popular monarchy could become the Weimar presidency, ready for conversion into dictatorship; the Prussian army could evolve into the 'school of the nation' with potential for becoming a *Volksheer* (people's army) or an elite cadre – or both. Germany evolved into National Socialism without 'choosing' it; individual Germans, faced with overwhelming changes in the framework of their lives, their expectations, their assumptions, their timetable of existence, chose, planned and acted National Socialism.

The *Schutzstaffel* (Guard Squadron) did not spring in a trice from Hitler's forehead. It is remarkable enough how much of the SS did lie embryonically in the minds of Hitler's generation even before 1914. But the reality of the SS could only take shape gradually in the experience which the Nazis had in confronting the political exigencies of post-war Germany, with the naive imagery of pre-1914 youth. Membership of the bodyguard of any leader implies one's own importance: even the power of the strong man is incomplete without the guardsman. Since the academic soothsayers had created an elaborate modern justification for what so many men in different times and ages have craved, a messiah, Adolf Hitler could gradually evolve himself into a magical, quasi-religious *Führer*, the chief of a holy band of crusaders, the political soldiers of a 'super pressure group'. To be his bodyguard was to partake of his charisma, to be important to him. This sense of a special relationship to 'god-on-earth' was a gift of grace Hitler knew very well how to foster among his alienated, *petit bourgeois* followers long before 1933; yet his 'grace' was not limited to the SS. This special relationship was merely there, ready to be elaborated if the opportunity arose, by the right man. All the characteristics of the SS were not inevitable in National Socialism. Himmler, R.W. Darré, and Reinhard Heydrich each made large contributions. Hitler himself started out with the 'bodyguard' idea. Wilhelmine Germany spawned dozens of Teutonic secret societies; eugenic breeding schemes were not limited to pre-war Germany. No one Nazi invented the SS, but much of its design reproduces the mental furniture of post-war Munich and the Class of 1900 – Heinrich Himmler's age-mates. (This term refers to the birth cohort of a given year and is derived from military calculations.)

Many Germans starting with the assumption that there had been a 'natural order' in Germany before 1914 took the conditions of 1919 readily enough to be those of 'a world turned upside down'. If disorder was the result of revolution, then to re-establish 'order' required another revolution, the conquest of power in the interests of all except the 'evil-doers'. Amid much soul-searching, hundreds of groups in Germany decided that they were duty-bound to accept the responsibility of leading this revolution of restoration. Some wished to restore the Kaiser.

Some preferred the Wittelsbach dynasty of Bavaria. Others thought of the Hindenburg-Ludendorff dictatorship of 1916–18. Their common characteristics were a belief in violence, in conspiratorial technique, in whipping up the 'masses' to follow them instead of the 'evil-doers', and in the methods of German militarism. Power was something to be won through conquest, under conditions of extreme instability – politically, economically, socially and psychologically; force, and symbols of force, were most appealing. If 'pressure groups' dominated the political field, why not armed pressure? The armed reformer was the only reformer that seemed to matter in 1923. Amid the multiplicity of armed combat units, the *Stosstrupp Hitler* (the enlarged bodyguard of Hitler on which the SS was modelled) did not stand out. In their field-grey, those Bavarian faces did not look different from those of opponents on the left and right, and their red swastika armbands were not yet memorable. Yet their aggressive propaganda methods gave them a strategic advantage over many another group of armed reformers, although these methods too were hardly unique.

Out of just such elements, by accretion and trial-and-error, the Storm Troops evolved, through the disaster of November 1923 and many near disasters after that until 1934 – with the SS Guard Squadron merely another variety of themselves, a rather silly, even preposterous variety, exaggerating some of the romantic imagery of pre- and post-war Munich lower middle-class youth. What might have been of no consequence except to the play-actors, with their black uniforms and death's heads, became part of National Socialism and thus part of Germany's struggle to adapt itself to the demands of an international machine age, the tremendous juggernaut of destruction for Jews, Poles, Yugoslavs, Russians, and Germans themselves. Even Himmler was quite incapable of choosing and planning for the SS to become all that it was in 1945. How much an SS leader could form and direct what he and his men would become depended on so many factors that at times even the hypnotic *Führerprinzip* (principle of leadership) failed the men in the top echelons, and they admitted that they had lost control. Theodore Eicke, Reinhard Heydrich and Otto Ohlendorf certainly formed and moulded more in the SS than in their own lives, while other SS officers, both named and nameless, created 'refuges' in their corner of the SS bureaucracy for themselves and a few others. But for the majority of officers and men, the SS became a nemesis, a labyrinth in which at first they willingly lost themselves and later from which they could not escape back into humanity, even on furlough. Ironically and significantly, the front was their best camouflage. The *Waffen*-SS remains even today the anonymous, if never wholly neutral, realm of the ex-members of the 'Black Corps' (the name adopted by the SS magazine in 1935).

Modern industrial societies – whether they have been defeated in war or not, whether they are prosperous or impoverished – must improvise new forms of action for their younger generations, must grow and expand in terms of their material output and distribution of that output as well as in terms of their use of resources, both human and inanimate. The NSDAP, the SA (brownshirts or Storm Troops), and the SS, as well as numerous other Nazi institutions like the German Labour Front (a mandatory national union to which employees and employers had to belong and contribute) and the National Labour Service (compulsory non-military service for both boys and girls of a year's duration) must be understood as cruel, wasteful and wrong social efforts, partly conscious and partly unintentional, to do better what had already been done poorly or imperfectly by other processes in the society. Extreme measures of internal and external defence, the organisation of other human beings as tools (rather than as co-workers), the gathering of information and the manipulation of information to control others – all these are the features of most, if not all, modern societies in crisis. That the Germans produced in the dictatorship of 1933–45 so foul and ghastly a combination of features should not tempt non-Germans to any spiritual pride; at best we can merely take warning from the misfortunes of a people. Like all of us, they did not choose their history, but they made many choices. It is to the dialectic of events, the consequences of past choices of specific men, that we must turn if we are to comprehend the SS.

1

PREHISTORY —
THE WILD BANDS

1919–24

When Adolf Hitler and his comrades of the Replacement Battalion of the Second Bavarian Infantry Regiment set about to plan a new kind of revolutionary party in the spring of 1919, they were acting like thousands of other German soldiers who since 1914 had become increasingly resentful at the civilian world. They did not wish to see themselves for what they were – civilians temporarily in uniform – because in civilian life they had been nonentities. Now that the civilian world lay in a shambles, there was no excuse any longer to bow to its outer social or political forms. The new 'party' should be, in brief, not a parliamentary faction but a formation of political soldiers, intent on making good the error of the old army of being 'unpolitical', of following incompetent civilians into defeat. They would bring order into the chaotic civilian world, for were not republicans and Marxists 'merely civilians'? And was their thinking counter-revolutionary? Far from it: theirs was the true German revolution, the revolution of the trench soldiers.

'Soldierly nationalism' in post-war Germany was to take a multitude of forms, many of them contradictory to one another. Before Hitler could become master of this powerful force, it had spawned numerous organisations, each of which became the matrix of a different type of political soldier. Many of these types were later to join together to form the Nazi Guard Squadron. Though it did not come into existence until 1925, and scarcely numbered 300 members five years after that, the SS had its inception and acquired its basic ethos in the social and political maelstrom of the years 1919–24. In these years many Germans experimented with new and revolutionary forms of political and social life; among them were the Nazis, who found meaning and personal fulfilment in their version of the ubiquitous political combat league the SA (*Sturm-Abteilungen*) or Storm Troops, within which grew the future SS.

It is very likely that the stimulus for the formation of the rightist political combat leagues came with the formation of Soldiers' and Workers' Councils and Red Guard (*Volkswehr*) units in the first days of the revolution in Germany. The negative image of these formations is regularly part of both Nazi and rightist literature devoted to the pre-history of National Socialism, always alleging ruthlessness, cruelty and bestial stupidity on the part of these units. Why should not German soldier-patriots of the right turn the device around, against the Marxists, replacing 'anarchy' with the orderliness of the great Prussian military tradition? This appears to be the intention of the free corps (privately organised military and paramilitary units employed by the provisional regime in Germany in 1919 to fight the revolutionary left and Polish insurgents) leaders Märcker, von Epp, Reinhard and some others when the Majority Socialists appealed for military assistance and gave Gustav Noske power to recruit volunteer units to guard the republic. But the very contradiction which was to haunt the relationship between the SA, the SS and National Socialism – the question of whether ultimately the tail would not wag the dog – crept in when the nominally Marxist republicans called back to arms the soldierly nationalists of the right to protect the regime against their revolutionary rivals.

The older exponents of the Prussian militarist tradition were themselves forced to call upon a generation of lieutenants, captains and majors who were far more revolutionary than restorationist. In the guise of units for the restoration of order, junior officers like Ehrhardt, Rossbach and Röhm constructed paramilitary forces – to enhance their own political prestige and power – against the old army clique which had lost the war. Moreover, the trench soldiers such as Hitler, who were after all civilians in uniform, also found themselves in need of the counsel of the professional soldier class.

Thus, Hitler and the German Workers' Party served as agencies of the Munich *Reichswehr* (Reich Defence) headquarters in 1919. Hitler and his comrades were encouraged to enter the miniscule parties of the right and recruit likely candidates for paramilitary units like the Citizens' Militia and the Temporary Volunteers, which acted as auxiliaries for the free corps. The free corps leaders' purpose was always to remain essentially the same, though the aims of the *Reichswehr* leadership changed to the creation of a new model army to whose members soldiering for Germany was a way of life. The pattern for military manipulation of civilian life through patriotic parties had been set by the Fatherland Party of 1917. The north German *Stahlhelm* (Steel Helmet) – a conservative veterans' organisation – and the German-Folkish Protection and Defiance League (an anti-Semitic organisation based around the folkish movement in urban and small-town Germany) were products of the same striving to combine military preparedness with right-wing politics. It is true that the soldierly ideals of Ernst Röhm, the adjutant of Franz von Epp (the conqueror of the left-wing Soviet Republic), scarcely extended beyond counter-revolution and the reconstruction of a usable fighting force. In this Röhm had thousands of military counterparts. For such men any paramilitary organisation of the right would do. However, the political movement which remained for men like Röhm merely a means to soldierly ends soon became for Hitler and his comrades much more than a recruiting ground. Rechristened the National Socialist German Workers' Party (NSDAP), the former civilian conventicle became a soldiers' movement into which Hitler and his friends poured their dreams and their ambitions. Being civilians and thus by no means as narrow as Röhm in their goals or methods, they absorbed the contending tendencies of post-war Germany into their new party and improvised from them something remarkably successful within the circumscribed limits of the Bavaria of 1920–23.

Hitler seems to have realised very soon that the post-war parliamentary regimes rested on the masses as never before. The new age was to be an age of propaganda. Much as the soldier in him detested persuasion, he grasped the dependence of modern states on it. Even before 1914 persuasion had ceased to be the reasonable, refined process of the middle-class press, the public lecture, or the formal debate. The war years had exacerbated the lying style of a yellow press and irresponsible demagogues. Press censorship, bribery and strong-arm squads had made their appearance along with the conspiratorial methods of infiltration, spying, murder and putsch used by Bolsheviks and syndicalists. Without abandoning the elitist ideal of political soldiers as the core of their movement, these civilian soldiers began immediately to consort with quite unsoldierly types who were necessary for the capture of the masses and for conspiracy. Thus, inevitably the first Nazis introduced into their ranks the very contradictions of civilian society which they were fighting, and which were in effect part of themselves. But they went further and created a separate political soldierdom resembling, yet not the same as, themselves (the SA, later the SS) and never wholly subordinate to themselves. On the other hand, the unsoldierly types with whom they had to work, and the civilian masses whom they needed for the power the masses represented, seemed to many far less admirable and indeed often despicable. The ambivalence of German society in the early 1920s toward the soldier thus became a permanent element in National Socialism.

This ambivalence is illustrated in the history of the strong-arm squads of the infant NSDAP. The guards for the founding meeting of the NSDAP on 24 February 1920, in the Hofbrauhaussaal am Platzl were a squad of Temporary Volunteers armed with pistols and clad in the field-grey of the Munich *Reichswehr* to which they were attached perhaps as part of a mortar company. Supplied with the co-operation of Röhm and the rightist Minister of the Interior, Ernst Pöhner, they were composed of younger police officials and students. Such guardsmen might well be sympathetic, but there could be no thought of undying loyalty to the ridiculous little movement.

Certainly Röhm sent a number of the Bavarian *Reichswehr* division, perhaps also some of the Citizens' Militia and especially the young Temporary Volunteers into the party itself. They were often avid nationalists, but their first loyalties lay elsewhere. Hitler describes the very earliest party guards in October 1919 as some of his truest trench companions, probably as usual a more figurative than literal statement but an indication that he preferred his cronies' loyalty to Röhm's assignees. Then in 1920 after the Kapp Putsch in March and the installation of the Gustav von Kahr regime in Munich, the field-grey had to disappear from the NSDAP. Hitler and his comrades had to accept discharges. Röhm found it advisable to disguise *Reichswehr* support of paramilitary and revolutionary activities. The places of the soldier guards were taken by fifteen- to twenty-man *Ordnertruppe* (marshals) in civilian clothing with red armbands on which a swastika was displayed on a white disk. Possibly the use of the swastika symbol of the Ehrhardt-Brigade free corps on marshals' armbands indicates the role played by these veterans of the ill-fated Kapp Putsch as Nazi bouncers in the summer of 1920. In this thin disguise von Kahr and Pöhner permitted Röhm to keep a 'force-in-being' for future use against the Republic.

They were, however, unreliable and even mutinous bands, intrinsically less valuable to Röhm and the Nazis than the members of the well-organised Bavarian *Einwohnerwehr* (paramilitary police force formed by an order of the Prussian Ministry of the Interior) system of Dr Georg Escherich. Organised in towns, counties and regions, these farmers and white-collar workers formed an anti-trade union, anti-Marxist militia, which extended west and north of Bavaria as the *Orgesch* and into Austria as the *Orka*. These were counter-revolutionary bands loyal to Kahr, although they contained revanchist hotheads and conspirators. Röhm tried for some time to capture this organisation. He encouraged Hitler to copy the structure of *Orgesch* and enlist some of its radical membership in his strong-arm squads. Thus, toward the end of 1920 we find signs of a permanent and regular Nazi guard organisation in Munich grouped in *Hundertschaften* (hundreds) like the *Orgesch*. Indeed, they may have often been essentially Nazi 'cells' within *Orgesch* hundreds strengthened with a few free corps men. When Escherich unwisely tipped his hand by an armed anti-French rally during the 1920 *Oktoberfest* and Berlin passed a law requiring troops like the citizen militia to register and/or surrender their weapons, Röhm made preparations to abandon the *Orgesch*, and branched out beyond the NSDAP in several directions, not only forming in Munich a unit of the reactionary National Union of German Officers but also accepting leadership of a Munich detachment of Captain Adolf Heiss's free corps.

While not exactly independent, Hitler began to improvise fighting forces out of his own immediate following, drawing upon other paramilitary groups for leaders and 'stiffening'. In January 1921 he felt strong enough as Nazi propaganda chief to threaten publicly in the large Kindl-Keller to break up 'unpatriotic' meetings with these forces, and in February he was able to put some of them on 'propaganda trucks' which roamed throughout Munich distributing leaflets and posting placards for the first mass meeting in the building of the Krone circus. The success of these methods can be gauged by the continued growth in the size of the mass meetings. They paid off with Hitler's capture of the organisational structure of the NSDAP in July 1921, whereupon he strengthened and consolidated these 'battle units' inside Munich and in the outlying towns of Upper Bavaria where Nazi groups had been founded. However, owing to Allied pressure during the summer, the strong-arm squads had to go through another metamorphosis: into 'Gymnastic' and 'Sport' sections (*Sport-Abteilungen*), which were really camouflaged party troops under the command of an Ehrhardt free corps officer and conspirator, Lieutenant Hans Ulrich Klintzsch.

The dissolution of the *Orgesch* during the summer of 1921, due partly to the Allied pressure and partly to internal dissension, weakened Kahr, so that he fell in September and was replaced by the moderate Lerchenfeld regime which favoured co-operation with the Berlin government and the Allies. Hitler and Röhm nearly parted company for the first time in the autumn of 1921 (an episode to be repeated several more times until 1934), for Röhm now decided to back Escherich's successors, Dr Otto Pittinger and Rudolf Kanzler, whose semi-military and semi-conspiratorial *Bund Bayern und Reich* toyed with a Danube federation and 'temporary' dissolution of the Berlin tie. Röhm's motives were purely opportunistic; he saw no contradiction in simultaneously supporting the Nazis. Hitler, however, saw in Pittinger's group the Nazis' most dangerous rivals. Breaking up its meetings as well as those of the left became the chief function of the SA (*Sport-Abteilungen*). In November 1921 Hitler adopted the term Storm Troops (*Sturm-Abteilungen*) and thus openly alluded to the elitist military ideal of the trenches. This suggested that the movement with military ideals should triumph over both middle class parliamentary parties and conspiratorial cabals. Moreover it implied that it could break away from its dependence on the irresponsible *Landsknechte* (freebooters) of the free corps.

During 1922 the Nazi movement continued to grow throughout Bavaria and penetrate northwards to middle Germany, and with it the Storm Troops, for they absorbed the *Arbeitsgemeinschaften* (semi-secret work-groups) of the illegal free corps and feme societies. Hitler's month of imprisonment in the summer of 1922 at the hands of the Lerchenfeld regime for the use of strong-arm methods against the Pittinger group did the Nazis no harm. In August they displayed six SA *Hundertschaften* among the 50,000-person folkish and conservative-patriotic movements' protest rally in Munich against the new law protecting the German Republic and immediately attracted additional volunteers for more *Hundertschaften*. Under pressure from Röhm, Hitler tentatively made common cause with Pittinger in September 1922 in a putsch plot that failed to come off. By October fourteen SA *Hundertschaften* from Upper

Bavaria were represented (about 700 men) in a demonstration march to Coburg on the Thuringian frontier to join the Third Annual German Day of the *Schutz- und Trutzbund* (Protective and Defensive League). The latter organisation was about to disappear due to the application of the Law for the Protection of the Reich, but its defiant invitation to the Nazis to join it in supposedly 'red' Coburg led to Nazi intimidation of the town after pitched battles with democratic and left-wing groups. In November 1922 Julius Streicher brought *völkisch* Franconia solidly into the Nazi sphere by merging his branch of the *Deutsch-Soziale Partei* (German Social Party) with Hitler's, while in Munich the Nazis were pressed by Röhm into their first temporary alliance, the United Patriotic Societies. In the north scattered bands of Nazis opened up liaison with the new anti-Semitic *Deutschvölkische Freiheitspartei* (German People's Freedom Party) of Reinhold Wulle and Albrecht von Gräfe.

Behind this trend of consolidation lay the strivings of the whole German right and the hopes of the free corps perhaps even of segments of the *Reichswehr* for a German uprising against the demands for reparation. Now the NSDAP received unprecedented recognition by being forbidden by the state governments of Prussia, Saxony, Thuringia and Hamburg. By January 1923 Hitler could summon to his first 'national' Party Day several thousand SA men – a figure swollen by free corps members, of course. Their organisation and outfitting had at this time been turned over to the air ace, Hermann Göring, a fellow student at the University of Munich with Rudolf Hess and Alfred Rosenberg. The first SA uniform of grey field jackets and ski caps was worn by the relatively well-to-do Munich student SA *Hundertschaft* (hundred), led by Rudolf Hess. But most of the SA wore whatever clothing they had, perhaps parts of their First World War uniform, sometimes a helmet with a swastika. Nor should we assume that these were organised 'hundreds' neatly grouped under the four official *Standarten* (standards), literally a Roman 'standard', consisting of a banner with a swastika reading 'Germany Awake!', an old folkish slogan, surmounted by the initials N.S.D.A.P. and the eagle, also bearing the name of the community or unit below the scarlet banner, Munich I, Munich II, Landshut and Nuremberg. Everything was improvised, loose, changing from day to day. Records and rosters were not kept, and SA volunteers were not necessarily listed as NSDAP members either in local files or in the new, incomplete Munich party card file. Many of them were 'members' of two or three defence leagues at the same time. Staunch 'civilian' party members not in the SA were pressed into service for rallies and propaganda marches. Thus, most of the large figures for the early SA in Nazi sources, repeated by many later writers, are misleading.

Misjudging the chances of success, the German right thought its hour had struck in January 1923 with the French occupation of the Ruhr. A state of undeclared war developed between Germany and France, in which the free corps groups again flourished openly and middle-class parliamentary procedures seemed more irrelevant than ever. Hitler himself was swept along with this tide, although not without misgivings. He detested alliances with rival groups, particularly with amateurs, patriotic businessmen and republican politicians. He was afraid of being used by the *Reichswehr* and then cast aside. He had few illusions either about storming republican barricades or about the real intentions of colonels and generals of the old army. Nevertheless, he could not appear merely to want to go on propagandising while patriotic Germans were acting. Above all, his efforts to demonstrate his movement's strength in the Party Day planned for January 1923 in Munich forced him to reveal his dependence on Röhm and Röhm's military sponsors.

Under the influence of the lawless Nazi performance in Coburg and the Fascist takeover in Rome, Bavarian Interior Minister Franz Schweyer and Munich Police President Eduard Nortz forbade the Party Day and other Nazi demonstration meetings as well. Hitler had to promise everybody not to try a putsch; ultimately it was von Epp and the top-ranking general in Bavaria, divisional commander Otto von Lossow, who arranged to let him have his rally: 6,000 volunteers were present from the various friendly combat leagues and the SA. However, in return for saving face, Hitler had to let his 'party troops' slip partly under the aegis of the *Reichswehr*. Röhm joined the SA with other combat leagues to form the *Vaterländische Kampfverbände Bayerns* (VKB) under Lieutenant-Colonel Hermann Kriebel, formerly of the *Einwohnerwehr*; Hitler could not even count on using his SA as he wished, for his men were turned over to *Reichswehr* officers for drill as an element of the secret reserve being formed throughout Germany as part of the Seeckt-Severing agreement to strengthen the hand of the Cuno regime in resisting the Ruhr occupation. The SA was organised more tightly and given a 'general staff' of *Reichswehr* and free corps staff officers. Klintzsch served Göring for a time as head of this staff, withdrawing in the month of

April, since a quarrel with Ehrhardt's *'Wiking'* free corps and OC (Organisation Consul) people in the SA was brewing, precipitated in part by Hitler's double-dealing with them and with the *Reichswehr.*

At this time Hitler designated a squad of twelve bodyguards as a *Stabswache* (headquarters guard), composed of old comrades and individuals personally dependent on himself. He had had a bodyguard or two before, and the idea of forming a headquarters guard out of it probably crystalised gradually in 1922. But now in the spring of 1923, his dangerous policy of double-dealing with the army and with the other combat leagues made him more fearful, and therefore less willing to be dependent for his safety and that of his headquarters on just any 'political soldiers'. The *Stabswache* donned black ski caps with a skull and crossbones.

Hitler still did not really want to putsch. He did want to repeat the Coburg success by destroying the Socialist May Day rally in Munich and demonstrate to his followers and his free corps allies that he still had control over the SA. He would not let Röhm stop him, nor indeed did Röhm dare, for the allegiance of the secret reserves seemed too tenuous. The call went out to the VKB to assemble, and friendly members of the *Reichswehr* assisted them in taking weapons illegally from the *Reichswehr* barracks which they had already used from time to time on manoeuvres with the *Reichswehr.* Hitler did not know whether to believe von Lossow's warnings that he would be fired upon by *Reichswehr* troops and therefore did not join his 6,000 volunteers in battle with the Socialists on the morning of 1 May; indeed confronted at noon with a token show of military force and abandoned by Röhm, he ordered the arms returned. Nobody was arrested, but Hitler had lost important segments of his free corps and student volunteer allies (*Zeitfreiwilligenkorps*).

In May Hitler authorised the formation of a crack military detachment, in part to replace the lost forces, in part to assure himself a fully reliable, mobile reserve separate from Röhm's larger undertaking. With the twelve-man bodyguard as cadre, Hitler created *Stosstrupp Hitler*, a 100-man *Stosstrupp* (*Stosstrupp*, a term carrying the elite ethos of the trenches and referring to small 'shock' or attack units) possibly out of the third Munich SA *Abteilung* (battalion), fully clad and accoutred as soldiers with a couple of trucks for special duty in support of propaganda marches, especially outside Munich and in workers' districts. In the autumn the unit had acquired combat readiness for putsch employment by being divided into three platoons: an infantry platoon of four squads, a machine-gun platoon, and a machine-pistol and mortar platoon. Here Hitler was improvising and characteristically tentative. The *Stosstrupp* was a relatively unpolitical military unit which could be used to support basically political activity or for a putsch. Its formation can best be explained by Hitler's admiration for 'pure soldiering', by his mounting fears of betrayal by both his free corps and *Reichswehr* allies and by his grudging acceptance of the putschist mood of the summer and autumn of 1923.

Although Himmler was not even in this shock troop, and none of its members ever played a decisive part in the future SS, Nazi historians were to point to this diminutive and relatively unimportant formation as the origin of the SS. Nor was this a falsehood or an historical anomaly. The ambiguity of this improvisation of 1923 was transmitted through Hitler himself to the first small Guard Squadron of 1925, from it to the insignificant group of Guard Squadrons throughout the movement between 1926 and 1929, and from 1929 on through the ambiguous Hitler-Himmler relationship to survive the death of *Führer* and *Reichsführer* in the pages of the *Waffen*-SS veterans' magazine, *Der Freiwillige*.

It is incorrect to assume that the Nazis were badly hurt by the May Day fiasco. The VKB continued in existence with extensive weekend 'manoeuvres' in the fields around Munich, Landshut, and Nuremberg. Party membership and participation in the SA grew to an unprecedented 55,000 and 10,000 respectively during that fantastic summer of 1923. The chaotic hyperinflation, the patriotic tension often giving way to senseless internecine street squabbles and ambushes, the widespread expectation of communist revolution led many a rightwing *Spiessbürger* (square) into the ranks of the 'wild and woolly' Nazis. The growth of the SA in 1923 must certainly be associated with its semi-respectability as part of the secret reserves under the auspices of the army. Lack of records makes it difficult to gauge the relative importance of 'professional' free corps men and civilian part-time volunteers among the 10,000 recruits, but a perusal of numerous Nazi personnel records suggests the widespread presence of 'floaters', individuals who were never in one free corps organisation very long, who oscillated between civilian life and the combat leagues from 1919 until as late as 1932. Hitler had good reason to distrust the harvest of discontent which he and Röhm were reaping, but he nonetheless capitalised upon it. He authorised Göring to recruit paid officers with the requisite specialised talents to organise such supporting units for the SA

as medical, motorcycle, cavalry, communications, light artillery and technical battalions. At least temporarily both foreign and domestic monetary
sources were available to pay for these right-wing mercenaries, who had
little interest in Hitler or the Nazi Party *per se*.

The Nazis certainly did not retire from their struggle to be at the centre
of the political arena that summer but used their SA for demonstrations,
propaganda marches, street brawling and intimidation, and for the street-
corner sale of the enlarged '*Völkischer Beobachter*' (the Nazi daily newspaper). It is true that there were severe limits upon their effectiveness. They
could not rule the streets of Munich unchallenged, let alone other comparable cities. Nor could Hitler capture the Austrian Nazi Party at Salzburg
that August, even with Göring's help in taking over the *Vaterländischer
Schutzbund*, the former OT (*Ordnertruppe*) of Hermann Reschny, slated to
become the future Austrian SA. But Berlin seemed to be playing into
Hitler's and Röhm's hands. The Cuno regime had fallen and Stresemann
had failed to win the north German radical right for a policy of less than
all-out resistance. Wulle and Gräfe of the northern *Deutschvölkische
Freiheitspartei* courted Hitler; at the *Deutscher Tag* in Nuremberg on 1–2
September, Ludendorff allowed himself to be made the symbol of an all-
German patriotic union (*Deutscher Kampfbund*). It was a loose alliance, no
better than the former VVV (*Vereinigte Vaterländische Verbände* (United
Patriotic Leagues of Bavaria)) of 1922 and the VKB of the spring. Hitler
did not delude himself that he controlled this ramshackle set up. But there
were many signs of a 'revolutionary situation' in Germany in the autumn
of 1923. There was a total lack of confidence in the established order, into
which even the *Reichswehr* was swept for its failure to support continued
and overt military resistance against the French. Hitler and Röhm believed
with some reason that they could channel the forces of Bavarian sepa-
ratism and hostility to the renewal of a fulfilment policy in Berlin into a
'March on Berlin' modelled on the bloodless coup of Mussolini. They
agreed on their use of Ludendorff as a figurehead, the symbol of an unde-
feated and uncompromising Germany. Röhm, after being transferred out
of Munich by the *Reichswehr*, resigned his commission apparently to cast
his lot finally with Hitler. This act undoubtedly impressed Hitler and many
others, in view of Röhm's uncertain behaviour on 1 May.

There was not a little desperation and a great deal of open rivalry in
the manoeuvring behind the scenes. Many signs existed that the German
right was considering a number of alternatives, none of them favourable

to Hitler. A leading possibility was the formation of a 'directorate' of big business, the landed interest, with representatives of the *Reichswehr*, black-white-red Nationalists of the *Stahlhelm* (Steel Helmet) sort, and the Pöhner-Kahr axis in Bavaria. A less attractive arrangement was the formation of a number of German states independent of Berlin and supported by France, for example a Rhineland federation and a Danubian federation. Stresemann and the moderates were considering a business deal with Great Britain and the United States in connection with stabilising the mark. The more normal, more personally ambitious young men of the combat leagues and the SA, especially the students and white-collar workers, were thinking of taking jobs and getting married. When Wilhelm Brückner, commanding the SA-Regiment *'München'*, told Hitler this, it was already common knowledge. Ludendorff and the free corps leaders certainly knew it. Kahr, Ebert and Seeckt knew it. There was a long risk involved in attempting to tip Kahr's hand, but the times might not be so ripe again.

A number of 'German Days' were sponsored by the *Deutscher Kampfbund* in Augsburg, Hof and Bayreuth to whip up popular enthusiasm for a putsch. To each the Nazis sent their *Stosstrupp Hitler*, to reinforce their local SA and ensure their speakers' prominence and to guard against 'treason' from their comrades of *völkisch* and *vaterländisch* allied groups.

When Stresemann announced the end of the Ruhr resistance on 24 September, Bavaria replied with the reinstitution of the von Kahr dictatorship and moved rapidly toward severing its connections with Berlin. Kahr was supported not only by Pittinger and Ehrhardt, but one of the mainstays of Röhm's plans and of the abortive *Deutscher Kampfbund*, Captain Adolf Heiss's *Reichsflagge*, broke up over the issue of loyalty to Kahr. Röhm quickly reconstituted the south Bavarian contingents as the *Reichskriegsflagge* in which he placed his own trustworthy hangers-on, such as the young Heinrich Himmler. Röhm, and even more so Hitler, was dependent on the willingness of Kahr and von Lossow, who had cast his lot with Kahr, to march on Berlin. When the Berlin regime took over the leftist Thuringian and Saxon administrations, which experimented with workers' militias, and the Rhineland separatist 'movements' turned out to be flashes in the pan, Kahr and Lossow put off action, perhaps intending to bargain with both Paris and Berlin for greater autonomy. Hitler, Röhm and Friedrich Weber, the leader of the *Oberland* combat

league, decided to present Kahr and Lossow with a fait accompli, essen-
tially out of desperation, for Hitler was doubtful from the beginning, and
Röhm knew that the best he could hope for from Seeckt and the
Reichswehr outside Bavaria was neutrality, as in the Kapp Putsch.

The Hitler Putsch consisted of several improvised political demonstrations by persons in uniform, but as a military operation it was woefully
inept. Too much reliance was placed on quick transfers of allegiance,
theatrical shows of force and symbolic gestures of coalition. Seizure of
most Bavarian towns failed because SA, *Bund Oberland* and
Reichskriegsflagge units went to Munich. No serious effort to co-operate
with putschists outside Munich occurred. In Munich, on 8 November
1923, several hundred Munich SA surrounded the Bürgerbräukeller, and
the *Stosstrupp Hitler* escorted the excited would-be revolutionary, Hitler,
to the podium. For a while his bluff worked; uncertainty as to the true
conditions in the Reich and the mutual rivalries and distrust on which
Hitler's movement had fed gave his show of force an initial advantage.
Röhm's *Reichskriegsflagge* and Weber's *Oberland* combat league, however,
contributed more effectively to the atmosphere of a military coup than
the bulk of the SA. Röhm used the *Reichskriegsflagge* to surround army
headquarters. The *Stosstrupp Hitler* stormed the Socialist *Münchener Post*
office. All the other putsch measures failed ludicrously. On the following
morning confusion reigned as to the future of the putsch, but before
either army or police had fired a shot, a few *Stosstrupp* members 'arrested'
the Socialist mayor and the city council. SA men 'arrested' Jews and
prominent Socialists as hostages and held them under guard in the
Bürgerbräukeller. The *Stosstrupp* half-heartedly tried to capture the
downtown police headquarters but gave it up without shooting. Toward
noon about 2,000 armed men in parallel columns of four abreast –
Stosstrupp Hitler on the left, SA-Regiment '*München*' in the centre,
'*Oberland*' on the right – paraded from the Bürgerbräukeller toward the
bridge over the Isar which led to the heart of Munich. They were greeted
by cheering crowds, and they overwhelmed undermanned police
outposts at the bridge, crossing easily. Virtually surrounded now by
excited onlookers and well-wishers, they marched in the general direction of the surrounded army headquarters, through the narrow passage-
way to the right of the Feldherrnhalle. Here they were stopped by police
with rifles held in crowd-control position (horizontally or diagonally),
but they pushed and jostled through this cordon. They were now met by

a second wave of police. There is dispute about who opened fire, but certainly a brief fire-fight ensued. There was some firing from the cover of buildings. Fourteen putschists, one a *Stosstrupp* member, were killed. Another exchange of bullets in front of army headquarters killed two members of the *Reichskriegsflagge* before a surrender was arranged. Groups of *Bund Oberland* surrendered after a brief skirmish. Of the sixteen dead, none were members of the SA. A few SA officers, one of them a *'Wiking'* (Ehrhardt) free corps leader, even proved disloyal at the last minute.

Hitler was forced to recognise that his 'political soldiers' had been worthless as revolutionaries and that alliances with free corps leaders, party politicians and *Reichswehr* officers were fragile in the extreme. His trial early in 1924 was a twenty-four-day sensation which resulted in much favourable publicity for those of his followers who remained outside prison walls; and Hitler permitted himself in his closing speech to extol the 'wild bands' of 'our growing army' which would one day grow into regiments and divisions. But he already had second thoughts, and at Landsberg prison he took little interest or pleasure in the electoral successes of the Folkish-Social Block which had been formed as an electoral coalition of his followers with the northern Freedom Party, or in the growth to 30,000 of Röhm's *Frontbann* into which flowed his SA, as well as many other free corps veterans. Hitler came to see how falsely conceived was the opportunism of Röhm and of some of his own followers, who imagined political soldiering to be merely gathering personnel and driving them forward to the attack as if politics were merely 'going over the top' en masse as in 1916. He resigned the leadership of the *Hakenkreuzler* (men of the swastika) in July 1924, partly for superficial tactical reasons (to get out of jail), partly for deeper strategic reasons: he thereby hoped to avoid responsibility for the disintegration which he foresaw at a time when many of his followers still believed in early fulfilment of the glowing promises of his final plea.

The year 1924 in Germany began radical and ended conservative. The armed bands were very much in evidence in the early part of the year, since unemployment was soaring and wages under the new *Rentenmark* had plunged to a new low after the days of ridiculous shopping bags full of near-worthless notes had come to an end. Political violence continued into the summer, and the May 1924 elections gave the Communists, the far right and the Nazi-Folkish coalition sizeable gains. Distrust of the moderate parties, including the Social Democrats, was correspondingly reflected in loss of seats in the *Reichstag*. Yet by the time Hitler temporarily withdrew from responsibility for his feuding supporters in July, German industry was hiring again, the merchants and bankers were confident enough to arrange future orders and mortgage loans, and the far right (German National People's Party) was swallowing the Dawes Plan to bail out Germany by an international gold loan so the country could resume reparation payments and get France out of the Ruhr. The fellow travellers among the combat leagues gradually drifted off to get married or join the more respectable *Stahlhelm*, although the hard-core *Landsknechte* continued in a hundred different bands loyal to some charismatic captain or major. The business world no longer wanted them around; they were refused handouts, and shakedown attempts began to lead to jail sentences. By December another *Reichstag* election reduced the Nazi-Folkish representation to twelve, the Communists lost their gains of May and the moderates made a small comeback to join with the far right in ruling Germany until 1928. The political soldiers would have to take on the ballot box and show that the struggle could go on in that form too, as long as necessary until they had power to do away with it. The SS was conceived within this new context.

2

THE EARLY YEARS

1925–29

The putsch resulted in the proscription of both the Nazi Party and the Storm Troops in most of the German *Länder* (states). As a consequence, northern National Socialists joined up with Wulle and Gräfe's German Folkish Freedom Party (DVFP), by early 1924 well established except in Munich, Nuremberg and Bamberg. Even in Landshut, hometown of the Strasser brothers, Otto and Gregor, the DVFP spoke for the folkish movement and similarly in Bavarian Coburg and Hof, as well as across the frontier in Thuringia and western Saxony. True, the NSDAP was never proscribed in Thuringia, led there by the religious maverick Artur Dinter. But Julius Streicher, Hitler's old sergeant – Max Amann, and the party orator Hermann Esser, as well as the party's philosopher and link with radical right conspirators, Alfred Rosenberg, founded a substitute organisation, if not precisely a political party, the Greater German Folk Community. Having collaborated electorally with the DVFP in the May 1924 elections as the Folkish-Social Block, the ultra-loyal Hitlerites reversed themselves when Ludendorff seemed to threaten to replace Hitler in the leadership of the National Socialist Freedom Movement in the summer of 1924. This folkish unity ploy failed because Hitler saw it headed for putschist adventures along with Röhm's *Frontbann*. Another initiative from the north was the National Socialist Work Community, formed of pro-Hitler locals who refused to join the Freedom Movement. Each of these factions was associated with paramilitary bands, each professed loyalty to Hitler, and each would contribute divergent tendencies to the reconstructed NSDAP of 1925, causing suspicion and fear in the Munich leadership for which the future 'ultraloyalist' SS was supposed to be a remedy.

Hitler's loss of the field to Röhm and Ludendorff in the heyday of the folkish movement – the summer of 1924 – necessarily led to a loss of influence on the SA membership, which was compounded by the official illegality (even if only nominal) of the Storm Troops and the adhesion of many newcomers to the Hitler movement to the northern folkish wing with its parliamentary ambitions. Röhm's *Frontbann* was a loose confeder-ation of disparate combat leagues which retained their individual identity throughout 1924 and into 1925. Organisations like the black-white-red *Stahlhelm* that Hitler hated were welcomed by the *Frontbann* as allies, and SA units camouflaged as sport and hiking societies often frater-nised extensively with non-Nazi paramilitary 'clubs' like the *Jungdeutscher Orden, Tannenbergbund*, and *Blücherbund* (armed, right-wing clubs whose political goals were opposition to co-operation with the victors and opposition to the Republic). Formal responsibility for the SA slipped from hand to hand, from Walter Buch, former commander of the SA-Regiment *Frankenland*, to Wilhelm Marschall von Bieberstein, free corps leader and commander of a Munich SA batallion, and thence to his adju-tant, Emil Danzeisen, in the winter of 1924–25. Röhm utilised Hitler's passivity to press SA men into the *Frontbann*, while Captain Gerd Rossbach and his young associate, Edmund Heines, sought to seize the SA from the faltering hands of quarrelling and despondent party bosses and merge it with their brownshirted combat league, *Organisation Rossbach* and *Schilljugend* (a youth contingent organised on a local basis by Heines).

According to a secret handbook of the *Frontbann*, that organisation was to be divided regionally into three types of units: Storm Troops (not necessarily the Nazi units of the same name); reserves, made up of inac-tive veterans willing to serve in emergencies and to drill once a month; and a *Stosstrupp*, a 'police unit and model unit (of company strength) for the support of military propaganda, composed of the best personnel'. The organisation was divided nationally into three almost independent commands, *Gruppe Nord, Gruppe Mitte*, and *Gruppe Süd* (North, Central and South divisions). Theoretically, each *Gruppe* was divided into sectors and each sector had one of these *Stosstrupps*. In fact, except for staff units, most of this organisation was on paper, but it was to leave its mark on the Nazi SA and SS.

The *Frontbann* was well designed as the paramilitary ally of an author-itarian, rightist revolution from above in which the parliamentary National Socialist Freedom Party could have co-operated with the *Deutsch-Nationale Volks-Partei* (DNVP) and the *Reichswehr*. But the tide of revolution receded in the summer of 1924, and the demagogic with-drawal of the *Freiheitspartei* from a *Reichstag* which approved the Dawes Plan with the aid of black-white-red votes was not the trumpet summoning the paramilitary forces to a popular revolution to free Hitler from prison or place Ludendorff in Berlin as dictator. In fact, the day of the folkish parties was waning fast. While the combat leagues remained and the formal framework of the *Frontbann* was to persist and thus complicate the task of reconstructing the SA, the rapid disintegration of the *Freiheitspartei* even before its defeat at the polls in December 1924 paved the way for the victory of the ridiculously parochial splinter 'party' created by Streicher, Amann and Esser in Munich, the *Grossdeutsche Volksgemeinschaft* as the unadulterated embodiment of Hitlerism.

After a short delay, due to the putschist manoeuvrings in both north-ern and southern echelons of the *Frontbann* – squashed by a series of arrests including that of the SA leader Wilhelm Brückner in Munich – Hitler was released from Landsberg prison in time for Christmas 1924. Hitler hastened to assure the Bavarian regime of his legalitarian change of heart; neither they nor many of his followers could quite believe it. Hitler did not know exactly how he was going to come to power – but he knew how he was not going to make it, which was a good deal more wisdom than that possessed by Röhm and most of the *Frontbann* leaders. Röhm tried to hold on to the *Frontbann* throughout the spring of 1925, although Ludendorff had already abandoned it as a lost cause (only to take up his wife's fanatical anti-clericalism). Röhm and Hitler completely failed to understand one another. Hitler still hoped to subordinate Röhm and a future SA to the role of a *condottiere* of propaganda troops at the beck and call of party leaders who were political soldiers, with the accent on political. Röhm still imagined that political soldiering was a good in itself and that he and his confederates should be on even terms with 'civilians'; they were political soldiers with the accent on soldiers. Finally, in May 1925 it was Röhm's turn to vacate the field to Hitler. He turned the *Frontbann* over to the commander of its Central *Gruppe*, Count Wolf von Helldorf (who would become a leading Storm Troop commander in Berlin, then the Police Chief of Berlin, and finally a conspirator against

Hitler) and, like Rossbach and Ehrhardt, withdrew into a semi-private life to conduct intrigues as a part-time amusement.

Hitler succeeded in getting the rival Nazi factions to join him in refounding the National Socialist German Workers' Party in February, and slowly throughout 1925 the local political organisations reformed and separated themselves from the folkish groups with whom they had been merged or allied. Patiently the business manager, Philipp Bouhler, repeated to local party officials that the question of the SA was not yet settled. Organisation, clothing and leadership would be decided upon soon. He urged them to make out as best they could in 'self-defence' with whatever personnel was available. There was no national SA, and even in Munich, Nuremberg and Landshut the SA was not clearly separate from the *Frontbann* and the other combat leagues. Legally the SA was still forbidden throughout the Reich, where it did exist as a separate, distinctively Nazi organisation, and in view of the number of persons under eighteen in such groups, it was often little more than a social club of young roughnecks.

Already in March 1925, in the course of the re-establishment of a party headquarters soon to be located at Schellingstrasse number 50, Julius Schreck, one of Hitler's drivers and a veteran of the earlier *Stabswache*, reformed the headquarters guard detail with the other drivers, the personal bodyguards of Hitler, and a few of the *Stosstrupp Hitler* who had been in prison with Hitler, numbering twelve in all. In April 1925 eight of these men served as torchbearers in the funeral for Ernst Pöhner, killed in an automobile accident. During the summer, when it became clear that Röhm was not going to assist in the reforming of the SA, Hitler decided to recommend to local party leaders the formation of small guard details on the model of the *Stabswache*. They were to be known as *Schutzstaffeln* (Guard Squadrons) a term entirely new, subject to no old prohibitions, not identified with sports or free corps traditions, connoting if anything, a *garde mobile*, since *Staffeln* were widely identified with cavalry, motor and air squadrons. It was stipulated that they should be about ten in number, selected from the most reliable of the party members of an *Ortsgruppe* (party local). They were to wear black caps with a skull and crossbones, the insignia of the old *Stosstrupp Hitler*.

The call for the formation of Guard Squadrons was issued by driver Schreck on 21 September 1925, 'with reference to the approval... by Herr Hitler and the Party leadership', along with a set of guidelines for the men

named as leaders of the new groups by *Gauleiter* or the leaders of independent party locals. The names of the designated leaders, who must unre-
servedly subscribe to the guidelines, were to be submitted to the High
Command of the Guard Squadron (*Oberleitung der Schutzstaffel der*
NSDAP). In order to keep things tightly under control, membership cards
could be obtained only from the High Command (*Oberleitung* or OL),
which would supply application forms. Applicants had to secure the
endorsement of two local party members – one of them prominent – be
registered with the police in their locality for five years, be between
twenty-three and thirty-five years of age and be of powerful physique.
Dues were to be 1 mark a month, and the items of the uniform cost altogether 16 marks, all of which was to be sent to the OL. Furthermore,
special cards were to be distributed for use in collecting donations for the
Guard Squadrons, but only a quarter of such collections might be retained
locally, along with a fund to transport the unit to Munich and back. The
units were to be employed as salesmen for the *Völkischer Beobachter*, of both
subscriptions and advertisements for which prizes were to be offered for
the highest sales. Members were to clip all references to the movement in
other papers and magazines and send them in for the archives of the OL
and were also to collect data on embezzlers, confidence men and spies in
the movement for the OL. That this was no imaginary problem is indicated
by the large number of such tricksters reported in 1925 by the outlying
party headquarters and also a report by Schreck to Munich headquarters
on 24 September of a denunciation of Hermann Esser at a local meeting in
Neubiberg, which Schreck thought should be looked into.

The rush into the Guard Squadrons was not overwhelming.
Numerous local party chapters were getting along by using some combat
league or other. Hamburg was using the adolescents from the conservative *Blücherbund*. Berlin was using the *Frontbann* with Hitler's blessing.
Cuxhaven was using the right-wing *Stahlhelm*. The Ruhr had formed its
own SA already in 1924 under free corps leader Franz Pfeffer von
Salomon. Amid three-cornered rivalries, such as existed in Saxony
between Helldorf's *Frontbann*, *Organisation Rossbach/Schillbund*, and an
SA that would not recognise the official *Gauleitung*, there was little
personnel left over for a new guard unit. Schreck complained to the
Munich Party headquarters on 27 November when the '*Völkischer
Beobachter*' innocently reported that day a ludicrous 'founding' of a Guard
Squadron in Neuhausen at a family evening between musical and

theatrical numbers, which was in fact merely the rechristening of some fifteen former SA men by a self-styled SS officer from Schwabing of whom Schreck had obviously never heard. Schreck also forwarded a complaint in November to the party headquarters at 50 Schellingstrasse from a travelling party speaker against the SS leader in Silesia, who was in fact the business manager of the region, for drunkenness, molesting women, small thefts, etc. Letters Schreck wrote to Viktor Lutze, the SA leader in Elberfeld (who would become Röhm's successor as chief of the SA; he never liked the SS) requesting assistance in forming a *Schutzstaffel* remained unanswered. Nevertheless, on the second anniversary of the November putsch, the Guard Squadron was officially proclaimed in Munich in a ceremony at the Feldherrnhalle and in the *Völkische Beobachter*, so that in later years the SS traced its founding to this date and commemorated the occasion in a far more elaborate ceremony of oath-taking at the Feldherrnhalle (a monumental shrine-like museum honouring Bavaria's generals before which fourteen of the Nazis were shot on 9 November 1923).

In later years it would also be alleged that the Guard Squadron had been formed especially for use in Thuringia and Saxony because public meetings there, while supposedly legal for the NSDAP, were so threatened by 'red' hecklers. There is some evidence of an early SS in Thuringia, where meetings were indeed legal; in Saxony where they were not, there were serious *Saalschlachten* (battles for the hall) that the Nazis lost in 1925, and one of the earliest Guard Squadrons was founded in industrial Plauen. Nevertheless, the legend probably developed after the extensive Nazi electoral campaigns in these two states in 1926, in which SA were used fully as much as the Guard Squadron, a curious relic of the early, and recurring, argument about the proper role of SS and SA. The SS claimed that it could and should guard party meetings, having been created for that purpose; the SA felt that this was its prerogative. In places where there had been no SA (Thuringia) or where the SA was in a disintegrated state (Saxony), the SS got a head start; but the Guard Squadron was not created for these areas alone, nor as a permanent substitute for the Storm Troops. Something of a temporary substitute while Hitler regained control of the SA, the early SS must have been big bruisers of the traditional stormtrooper variety. However, from their initiation they were supposed to form local units for special tasks of security where a small number of men were sufficient and for intelligence purposes.

Most of the seventy-five Guard Squadrons in existence at the time of the Weimar Party Day in July 1926 were formed in the spring of 1926. Heinrich Himmler, the business manager of the *Gau* (region) of Lower Bavaria, was just getting the Guard Squadrons organised in April and May, and as late as July wrote urging the Munich party headquarters to order the 'gentlemen of the Guard Squadrons' to hurry and send 100 application forms, a characteristically over-optimistic number. Already in February 1926, however, the *Oberpräsident* of the Prussian province of Hanover sent out a notice to the Prussian district chiefs regarding the formation of the Guard Squadrons, which he correctly described as opposed to members carrying arms, maintaining weapons caches, or belonging to combat leagues. Even more, he identified the motives of the party leadership as separation from the folkish and *Wehr* (defence) organisations. In contrast to the secrecy of these other groups – especially the *Frontbann* – the Nazis probably welcomed this 'revelation', especially since they were as yet far from achieving their purpose of freeing themselves from dependence on such groups for protection. The SS-OL was personally responsible for guarding the anniversary meeting of the party on 25 February 1926 in Munich, an indication that as yet the Munich Guard Squadron and the High Command (OL) were one and the same. The Munich Guard Squadron had its baptism of fire alongside the SA in civilian clothes at an anti-Communist meeting jammed with leftists on 31 March. The 'hall guards' of the NSDAP of Danzig Zoppot in March consisted of the chairman, his brother and two others, who all applied for SS membership. The next month when a meeting was called to found an SA, forty-five Nazis who had just been expelled from the Danzig citizens' militia for forming 'cells' signed up. By July there were seventy-five SA men outfitted personally by the Danzig *Gauleiter*, and twenty *Schutzstaffelleute* (SS people), led by the assistant *Gauleiter*.

The High Command of the Guard Squadron, though diminutive, was not without its intrigues that spring. A certain Ernst Wagner went with the assistant chief of the Guard Squadron, Erhard Heiden, to Philipp Bouhler (general office manager of the Nazi headquarters) and Franz Xaver Schwarz (treasurer of the NSDAP) and later to Hitler, to request that Joseph Berchtold, who had returned to take over the Munich SA – left leaderless by the refusal of Wilhelm Brückner to continue without Röhm – also take on the Guard Squadron, heavily criticising Schreck. While Bouhler and Schwarz resented this attack on Schreck, Hitler did in fact give the SS to the old commander of the *Stosstrupp Hitler* in April, who began by sacrificing the intriguer to Bouhler and Schwarz. Although Wagner had just returned from organising trips to Heilbronn and Esslingen, he was excluded from the High Command headquarters.

Berchtold's greater initiative was responsible for a recruiting campaign for the SS in the *Völkische Beobachter* and in local recruiting evenings set up by the *Gauleiter*. He also re-wrote the guidelines for the SS and founded an ancillary organisation of SS sponsors (*Fördernde Mitglieder* – these 'sponsors' were not members of the SS, but they received numbered tiny silver SS pins for their lapels) to raise funds, all before the Party Day in July 1926. He stressed that the SS should be a collecting centre for front veterans while insisting that it not be a combat league. He reduced the dues but made life and accident insurance compulsory – 'bouncing' and street fighting were dangerous to life and limb. Uninsured SA and SS men's relatives sought to sue or otherwise collect from the party. He gave the local party chairmen the power of expulsion but reserved the right to hear appeals and claimed the exclusive power to name Guard Squadron leaders. He ordered that the Guard Squadron must consist of at least ten men (never really observed until 1929) and that they meet twice a month as units. Monthly membership rosters must be submitted. Above all, he denied that the SS was subordinate to the SA. In his early appeals in the form of personal letters to SS sponsors, he stressed the need for transportation costs to bring the scattered Guard Squadrons together for effective service at the time of visits of major party speakers and at meetings of the party leaders, quite frequent in 1925–26. He clearly did not want the Guard Squadrons to degenerate into local bands, enforcing the petty wishes of small-time party bosses. He fought bitterly with the *Gauleiter* of Halle-Merseburg in June for disbanding an officially authorised Guard Squadron because it did not agree with his political direction, apparently successfully, since the *Gauleiter* soon left the NSDAP to form a more radical, leftist National Socialist splinter party. Similarly, Berchtold wrote sharply to Viktor Lutze in Elberfeld in April scolding him for neglecting the SS.

At the party congress in Weimar, Hitler rewarded Berchtold for his energy by bestowing on him, as self-styled *Reichsführer* of the Guard Squadron, the *Blutfahne* of 9 November 1923 – the flag stained with the blood of Andreas Bauriedel. Of the alleged 'thousand' SS membership, only a fraction was present at the National Theatre for the ceremony.

Probably the transportation funds were not sufficient. The SA is supposed to have sent 3,000 in their new brown shirts, purchased from Heines's mail order house, the *Sportversand Schill*. Heines soon replaced Berchtold as SA commander in Munich, bringing into the SA the Bavarian *Organisation Rossbach* and *Schilljugend*, the original 'brown shirts.'

Very likely many of the 'SA' at Weimar were these very units, just as many of the SS present were Berchtold's old Munich companions of the *Stosstrupp Hitler*. Though the break with the past was thus still not complete, Hitler had won major battles in the party organisation over the insubordinate northern faction of Goebbels and Strasser. His charismatic consecration of eight SA standards by simultaneously touching the *Blutfahne* and the new banners symbolised not only his own central position but also the clear intention to continue the SA, as well as the SS. By September 1926 the police already had heard that Hitler had decided on Pfeffer von Salomon as Supreme SA Leader (*Oberster SA-Führer*), although Gregor Strasser had wanted the post. This was to prove a fateful decision! Pfeffer, whose Ruhr SA had been a model of *Hitlertreue* (Hitler loyalty), would become a lesser Röhm, while Strasser's new job as propaganda boss was to advance his assistant, Himmler, from the regional office in Landshut to the Munich headquarters as deputy propaganda chief. The SA, although nominally politicised, was handed back to the soldiers; and the future *Reichsführer* SS (from January 1929) began to make political contacts throughout the movement but especially in Munich.

Hitler's 'good behaviour', his repeated admonitions to SA and SS alike to stop playing soldiers and the peaceful recovery of Germany that made putsches unthinkable disposed nationalistic bureaucrats to permit the Storm Troops to organise and march openly in the autumn of 1926. Thus, the Guard Squadrons were no longer so vital to the protection of public meetings and electioneering street-corner assemblies. Nor was the absolute loyalty of the SS to Munich and to Hitler so decisive after the *Frontbann* dissolved or swung behind Hitler, and as Goebbels and then the Strassers gave up the effort to depose 'the Munich Byzantines'. Berchtold uneasily acknowledged the suzerainty of Pfeffer in the autumn of 1926 and was 'confirmed' as *Reichsführer* by Pfeffer on the anniversary of the formal founding of the SS, 9 November 1926. But Berchtold rapidly lost interest and relinquished his office in March 1927 to Erhard Heiden, the unimaginative second-in-command under both Schreck and Berchtold. The latter turned his talents to writing for the *Völkischer*

Beobachter while maintaining a connection with the SA, believing perhaps that the Storm Troops held, after all, the promise of political soldiering which for a time the Guard Squadron had seemed to offer.

In his fourth SA order (SA-*Befehl*, SABE) of 4 November 1926, Pfeffer statcd that the *Oberster* SA-*Führer* had the power to name the *Reichsführer* of the SS, to designate which communities were to have Guard Squadrons (only the larger ones) and to regulate temporary situations where well-organised Guard Squadrons existed without a comparable SA structure. Normally the SA commander of an area was to be responsible for the commitment of the SS. SABE 4 goes on to emphasise that the SS was to consist of men especially hardened to individual employment (*Einsatz*) in contact with opponents, in contrast to the SA – which could expect to be used en masse. Thus was preserved a sort of elitism, although no mention is made of a requirement that the members be party members as well. It would be safe to say, however, that the local SS commanders in the period 1925–29 were usually party officials, such as the business manager of the local branch; they rarely appear as officers in the SS officers' lists of the 1930s. A dozen or so 'founders' of local SS-*Staffeln* finally made it to *Sturmführer* (second lieutenant) in 1933 or 1934, as a retrospective recognition. Another sixteen men clearly have officer rank before 1929, including Berchtold and Heiden, but neither Berchtold nor Heiden were listed in the SS during the 1930s. Rudolf Hess, although he was never assigned an SS number, may certainly be regarded as an SS officer during this period, as revealed by many old photographs of him in SS attire. Clearly, the status of SS officer (*Staffelführer* or squadron leader) was uncertain and of variable importance as compared to positions in the party and even in the SA. To judge from the records of very early SS 'privates', they only needed a party card and a good physique.

Preserved in a magazine called *Die Schutzstaffel*, of which only the second issue of the first year (December 1926) is known to the author, are accounts of joint propaganda activities by small SS and SA units in Saxony, Thuringia and Danzig. The methods of the Salvation Army are enthusiastically recommended along with torchlight processions, bonfires and wreath-laying. Combat 'manoeuvres' are also described, apparently without weapons and in very small proportions (squads). An atmosphere of boyish earnestness survives in the accounts. Police and newspaper records suggest more dangerous and bloody pastimes whenever the police were absent or passive. No differences between SS and SA are ever mentioned. Pictures from the years 1926–29 rarely show ten SS men together, although they are clearly distinguishable in their black hats and sometimes black riding breeches. They are intermingled with numerous Storm Troopers, though often in positions of prominence, obviously bodyguards for Hitler or some other party speaker.

As early as 13 November 1926, Himmler, signing for the *Propaganda-Leitung*, sent out a warning to propaganda officials of the regional organisations based on secret intelligence information on *Stahlhelm*, Ehrhardt and Rossbach activity sent in by *Gauleiter* Hildebrandt of Mecklenburg to the *Oberleitung* of the SS. The SS was beginning to function as an intelligence unit in close collaboration with propaganda. It was not long before Himmler was made second-in-command of the SS in September 1927 under Heiden, a logical combination with the former's propaganda work. Himmler's own experience in raising and organising the SS of Lower Bavaria gave him an added advantage. As deputy propaganda chief, he had the problem of arranging speakers for the *Gaue*, which inevitably brought with it the question of 'protecting' them from catcalls, broken-up meetings and occasionally physical harm. The existence of a small Guard Squadron guaranteed that protection – at least at a minimum – was available.

Hitler was indeed pursuing an uncompromising path of legality. The work of the party was one of organisational consolidation under the absolute authority of the Munich headquarters while at the same time it entered every public debate, as well as municipal and state elections, and sought to reach the unpolitical masses by street-corner rallies, beer hall gatherings, meetings in the tenement backyards and tens of thousands of leaflets, as well as the *Völkischer Beobachter* and a slowly increasing number of other magazines and newspapers. While Hitler never repudiated violence as an aid to propaganda, and it was rarely absent from news of Nazi activities in the years 1926–29, he did not expect to destroy his opponents by force – only to hold them at bay while the movement went about its missionary work with the German people. Hitler had no different intentions for SA and SS in this respect, although their employment might vary. In times of middle-class comfort and modest optimism, the Nazis could not afford excesses of rowdyism or the amoralism of the free corps. In May 1927 Heines, an unsavoury figure, was dismissed from the Munich SA leadership and Pfeffer strengthened the discipline and chain of command in the SA. As never before, the party organisation became lower middle class through and through, and Heinrich Himmler, the deputy SS leader, was a perfect example of the type.

Himmler was well educated not only by Nazi standards but even in the context of post-war Germany: he was the graduate of a *Technische Hochschule* (Institute of Technology) with a diploma in agronomy. His father was a university-educated high school teacher who had tutored a scion of the Bavarian Wittelsbach dynasty for a time. In fact, Heinrich Himmler was named after the tutee. Young Himmler wanted to be a soldier but was twice cheated of real service – first in 1918, when he spent the year in Officer Candidate School without ever going near the war, and in September–October 1923, when he briefly belonged to a unit of the 'Black *Reichswehr*' known as 'Werner Company' organised to crush the leftist Saxon and Thuringian regimes. It was formed out of Captain Heiss's *Reichsflagge* combat league, which Himmler had joined with some of his friends from the *Hochschule* and from his job at a fertiliser factory. When 'Werner Company' was dissolved by the Bavarian regime as unreliable (the Berlin government had liquidated the leftist regimes in Saxony and Thuringia), Röhm put Himmler and his friends into *Reichskriegsflagge*, where they camped around the Munich *Reichswehr* headquarters and Himmler got his picture taken with the unit flag. He was not even arrested. He joined Röhm's folkish officers' league (*Deutsch-Völkischer Offiziersbund*, Himmler was theoretically a second lieutenant, retired) and looked for a new job in desultory fashion. In July 1924 he became the secretary for Gregor Strasser in Landshut, then *Gauleiter* of the Lower Bavarian National Socialist Freedom Movement. He bought a motorcycle and began speaking at local rallies. In May 1925 when Strasser joined the new NSDAP, Strasser was still *Gauleiter* of Lower Bavaria, but he now designated the twenty-five-year-old Himmler as his deputy and business agent. It was in this capacity that Himmler organised the SS in Lower Bavaria. In September 1926 he moved with Strasser to the Munich party headquarters in the propaganda section. Now in 1927 he became engaged to a thirty-five-year-old nurse who had her own clinic in Berlin. They planned to buy a small farm in nearby Waldtrudering and raise chickens!

The effect of Himmler's firm hand and his taste for detail are revealed in SS Order No. 1 of 13 September 1927. While praising the Guard Squadrons for having 'passed the test' of the Nuremberg Party Day, in which they had functioned as honour and bodyguards of the *Führer*, he also orders a tightening of uniform regulations to avoid a repetition of the motley effect of *Lederhosen* (short leather trousers), coloured sports apparel, etc. Black sports breeches, black neckties and black leather equipment must accompany the brown shirt and the black hat. The Guard Squadrons were to have four activities every month: to attend the first discussion meeting of the party local in uniform but not to engage in the discussion, to hold two training meetings where drill and singing were practised, and to carry out a propaganda march or a meeting with a neighbouring SS – in case the fourth occasion had not already been provided by 'protection' duties at a public meeting. The SS commanders were urged to make systematic intelligence reports on the following as the basis for the formation of an intelligence service: (1) unusual activity among opponents, (2) names of prominent Freemasons and Jewish leaders, (3) special events in the community, (4) secret orders of the opposition and (5) press clippings about the movement. The command- ers were reminded to stay out of intra-party politics but to report improper conditions to the High Command (OL) of the SS, to have their squadron on a twelve-hour alert basis, and to get their dues, insurance premiums and monthly rosters in on time. SS members with official positions in the SA and in the party were to be reported, as well as those still incompletely outfitted.

There were probably fewer than seventy-five active Guard Squadrons between 1927 and 1929. Official membership seems to have fallen from 1,000 to 280. But it would be wrong to say that the SS was re-absorbed by the SA at this time or that it fell into inaction. The first and subsequent SS orders breathe a spirit of hard-bitten vigour and slow, if not steady, growth. If Aachen and Danzig are scolded by name for their inactivity, Frankfurt-am-Main is praised for its initiative in dyeing its uniforms and selling the most copies of the *Völkische Beobachter*. Plans are made for 'motorization' of squadrons by collecting information about drivers' licences, access to vehicles, etc. Berchtold's clever scheme of SS sponsors to supply the SS with funds above and beyond its dues was rigorously applied and perfected during these years. Unlike the SA, which since the summer of 1926 was supported by a ten-pfennig per member tax on the general NSDAP membership, the SS was without party subsidy, indeed its members sometimes paid the SA subsidy. The SS lived very frugally, without an expensive overhead or staff organisation, such as the SA soon developed. No one seems to have devoted himself full time to the SS, not even Heiden or Himmler, though Himmler accomplished more for the organisation in time taken from his propaganda activities than Heiden – who seems to have become a fifth wheel, hanging around the offices of the *Beobachter* as a survival of an earlier free corps type, now more a hindrance than a help. Himmler must have found many SS officers less business-like than he was in view of the earnest scoldings issued for reports sent in on scraps of paper, false reports, clippings sent without identifying newspapers, recruits under age and size, failure to salute SA officers, disrespect of party bosses, and so on.

Besides the reborn SA, the SS had other rivals. In Berlin, for example, Reinhold Muchow's reports to the Munich party headquarters tell of not only a *Zivil-Ordnungs-Dienst* (civilian marshal service), but also the formation of a *Freiheitsbund* (freedom league) – 300 strong, founded by the new *Gauleiter* Goebbels to finance and staff a Special Duty combat unit, 'the future noncommissioned officers of the new state'. Kurt Daluege, the head of the old Berlin *Frontbann*, was serving as Goebbels's deputy, as well as both SA and SS chief and leading a very vigorous, indeed vicious, around-the-clock attack on 'reds'. The early SS officer (Kurt Wege) who was his subordinate could never be anything but an appendage; Daluege's position was the important one, and throughout the Reich there were a dozen Nazis like him, none of them SS men.

It was in the years 1927, 1928 and 1929 that so many of the colourful local Nazi leaders emerged from the brown mass of lower middle-class *Vereinsmeier* (club enthusiasts). The men over forty, i.e. older than Hitler, were thanked for their services and thrust aside to make room for the 'Front Generation', more ruthless, better organised, lacking the veneer of pre-1914 Germany. Men like Erich Koch in East Prussia, Karl Kaufmann in Hamburg, Fritz Sauckel in Thuringia and Josef Bürckel in the Palatinate were in many respects the embodiment of Hitler's conception of the political soldier. They did not 'play at soldiering' nor did they indulge in the 'paper wars' of an older generation of *Stammtischhelden* (beer club patriots) and amateur parliamentarians. They set about the business of organising propaganda on a modern mass scale in their communities, and they used whatever methods came to hand, including conspiracy and violence. They often found that the SA members were initially more readily ordered about than the party 'civilians' and so local party leaders used them for many tasks (so unremittingly, indeed, that they protested). Although the average SA man in his twenties was himself a civilian, with increasingly less in common with the old free corps veterans, he prided himself on his soldierly obedience, his aggressiveness and his *esprit de corps*, in contrast with party bigwigs and callow fellow travellers. Thus, the Storm Troops gradually developed a sense of superiority and resentment against the Political Organisation (PO), while the rising generation of younger *Gauleiter* demanded manageable cohorts, not 'equals' who had to be consulted about policy. It is not surprising that the SS men of these years are faceless nonentities who did not rise to prominence even later, since it was just such individuals who could be employed without any later kickback. By 1929, faced with a contumacious SA, Munich would rediscover the SS and start it upon the road to independence of the SA and of the *Gauleiter* also.

The year 1928 may well be regarded as a turning point in Nazi fortunes. A few electoral victories in 1926 and 1927, and the slow restoration and surpassing of the old membership figure of 55,000 in 1927 were crowned by their passing the 100,000 mark in membership and the acquisition of enough seats in the *Reichstag* (12) and in the Bavarian and Prussian *Landtage* (9 and 6 respectively) to raise the possibility of coalition politics. In the comfortable year of 1928, the Nazis were becoming a respectable part of the political right. Gregor Strasser had given up the propaganda leadership to Hitler personally before the spring elections and was paid off with the organisational leadership, which needed tightening. After the elections Hitler characteristically divided the authority for propaganda between Goebbels in Berlin and Fritz Reinhardt in Munich, with Himmler assisting Reinhardt.

The Political Organisation was also divided in such a way that Strasser got control over the party and its affiliates – an apparatus for attacking the existing order (although he lacked control over the SA and the two propaganda centres), while a kind of general staff or 'shadow cabinet' began to form around the former *Reichswehr* colonel, Konstantin Hierl. This was more than a division of labour; Hitler was dividing his forces, not only to prevent being overwhelmed by a coalition against himself at the moment of a possible temporary coalition with others of the political right, but also to make possible the courting of other groups like non-Marxist workers in Saxony and the farmers of Schleswig-Holstein.

In view of party leaders' quarrels with the SA, what more obvious extension of this policy could there be than the expansion of the SS under its efficient deputy, *Reichsführer* Himmler? Amid charges in the

Social Democratic press that Heiden was being sacked as a venal police spy, which Hitler denied, Himmler was made *Reichsführer* SS on 20 January, 1929, retroactive to 6 January, and charged with consolidating the scattered fragments (280 men, according to tradition) into a mobile police task force with its strength in the thousands. However, Himmler was not relieved of his major propaganda secretarial duties and he was able only to make a few trips during 1929 to get things started, on time taken from speaking engagements. Only because he was a very energetic, indeed compulsively self-driving, young man of twenty-eight was he able to accomplish anything for the SS that busy year of the 'battle against the Young Plan'. Himmler increased the roster to about 1,000 men in fewer than 100 squadrons.

Pfeffer was willing to see the SS grow a little because by the spring of 1929 he was contemplating a massive SA, between the 100,000 in Hitler's mind (perhaps modelled on the *Reichswehr*) and 250,000. In reality, the twenty-five SA *Standarten* of early 1929 probably did not exceed 10,000 men. But the notion of the SA as cadre of a future *Volksheer* certainly antedates Röhm's return at the end of 1930. The SS was to be accorded its own 'higher officers' corps' – until then there were simply SS-*Führer* and no noncommissioned officers, although the SA already had *Standartenführer* (regimental commanders, i.e. colonels), *Gauführer* (regional commanders) and *Oberführer* (superior or senior colonels), as well as *Gruppenführer* (squad leaders or lieutenant-generals) and (*Stoss-*) *Truppführer* (platoon leaders). Whereas each larger town or rural county was to have its SA (*Sturm-Abteilung),* made up of several SA-*Stürme* and corresponding to a battalion made up of companies, the SS retained temporarily the term '*Staffel*' for the local unit. The designation of the local SS commander as a *Sturmführer,* however, indicated the tendency to assimilate the SS to the SA structure, which was to become even stronger under Röhm in 1931–32. The official use of the plural term *Schutzstaffeln* continued long after the local units became SS-*Stürme,* however. Although purely on paper in 1929, the SS was given a *Standarten* (regimental) level in some of the more active *Gaue* (Franconia and Upper and Lower Bavaria), and each *Gau* was supposed to have a *Scharführer* (*Gau* SS leader). Hess, incidentally, was made *Scharführer* of Upper Bavaria, an indication that high party position rather than full-time SS service was demanded. This soon changed, however, when Sepp Dietrich (a favourite of both Hitler and Himmler, who eventually rose to become a five-star general of the *Waffen*-SS) replaced him; in Franconia too Johan ('Jean') Beck, a long-time SS (and SA) veteran who somehow could get along with *Gauleiter* Streicher, was appointed.

But in fact there were not that many higher SS officers in 1929. Most of the SS growth took place as prescribed in the SA Basic Order VII of 12 April 1929: local SA commanders selected five or ten SA men to form a Guard Squadron and often named the commander also. In Dessau the party district leader was also the local SA leader. When at the request of the SS-*Oberführer Ost* (regional commander East) in Berlin (Kurt Wege), the leader named seven men, they were subsequently rejected by Munich because it was discovered that the commander was also the *Gau* business manager, and 'the SS should be independent of the political organisation'. The *Gauleiter* Wilhelm Löper complained that all this was going on under his nose but without his being asked – the *Gau* did not have that much personnel for so much decentralisation. Many of the early SS officers, whose records were studied by the author, also had held positions in the Political Organisation and the SA. They did tend to give up their SA and party positions in the course of 1930, however, though returns to the SA in 1931 were also common.

Hitler gave the SS their first ten *Sturmfahnen* (company banners) at the National Party Rally in Nuremberg on 4 August 1929. They had arrived with only one – the original *Blutfahne* borne by the Munich Squadron I. The diminutive size of the SS is revealed by their lack of *Standarten* – the SA had forty at Nuremberg – and the existence of only ten company-size units (*Stürme*) eligible for flags. When Heinrich Himmler took the salute alongside Hitler from a supposedly 1,000-man strong SS contingent bringing up the rear of the SA, he should have had the satisfaction of knowing that 95 per cent of the SS had come to Nuremberg. They were only a fraction of the SA present that day, supposedly 30,000 strong (perhaps really 10,000!). The true significance of the SS was to show up later, when on 5 August after the main programme was over, the party, SA and SS units had dispersed to roam the town and quench thirsts aroused by marching and shouting in the hot weather. Rowdies in SA and party uniform – perhaps assisted by a few imposters – began to pick fights, molest Jewish businesses and generally upset the atmosphere of patriotic camaraderie in the town. Gradually the party and SA personnel were sent back to the local quarters with the help of the quickly assembled SS. Functioning as a kind of paramilitary police, they prevented the rally from ending in chaos. The violence and disturbance was still a nine-day sensation in the democratic and Marxist press, leading Pfeffer to issue an SABE urging that the SS be built up to handle just such emergencies before they got so large. Ironically, one result of the Nuremberg rally was the dismissal of Himmler's first SS adjutant, Hans Hustert, another unsavoury free corps veteran like Heiden. Retired for 'health reasons', he was charged with no specific shortcoming. He was simply bad for the image of the new SS.

The five years 1925–29 had brought Germany a taste of prosperity, a modicum of international respectability and a little practice in parliamentary give and take. By 1929 a severe agricultural depression beset the rural areas and capitalist rationalisation had already begun to drive small businessmen to the wall. Hitler and his henchmen had whipped the Nazi Party into an entirely new shape as an electoral machine, which had begun to pay off in 1928, though not handsomely. The propaganda line had been shifted away from an urban 'German socialist' appeal to non-union workers (which had failed) to a call for nationalistic anti-class folk solidarity, which made inroads on the frightened middle class. Hitler carefully disentangled support for unruly 'anti-System' (anti-democracy, anti-capitalism and anti-reparations) farmers in Schleswig-Holstein and Lower Saxony from revolutionary National Bolshevik firebrands (free corps types, who combined chauvinist and militarist convictions with an essentially non-Marxist liking for Lenin-like revolutionary organisation). Through it all the paramilitary bands, though shrunken, had never disappeared. The SA retained contact with them, and by 1929 could march with the more respectable versions (no manoeuvres!) and even the 'reactionary' *Stahlhelm* could be seen at party rallies. Pfeffer hoped to expand his SA from these sources. Hitler kept his eye on Pfeffer, but he also dreamed of absorbing the German right as the world depression approached. The SS would have a special appeal to the 'respectable' right – businessmen, medical men and the university community.

THE FORMATIVE YEARS

1930–32

Already in the year 1929, when the miniature SS tripled and quadrupled in size, there was a sense of uneasiness in Germany, as if the good times were already over. However, the coming years provided a much clearer argument for Nazi radicalism. The SS grew in 1930–32 within the matrix of a rapidly expanding SA and party membership. The SS engaged in rigorous combat in the streets with Socialists (*Reichsbanner*), Communists (*Roter Frontkämpferbund*) and Nationalists (*Stahlhelm*), and in numerous party headquarters with rivals and opportunists. To experience rapid growth while fighting on a double front was not without its disadvantages – many members joined and left – but it provided for a process of 'natural selection' from which arose some of the best cadre of the future officers' corps.

SS growth in 1929 was still part of the need to expand the effectiveness of the party's propaganda instrument, which the SA itself had represented since 1926. The recruits were accordingly merely the bolder, more determined and perhaps more intelligent SA men. By 1930 the increasing possibility of political coalition and political responsibility required a greater discipline in the party as a whole and in its political soldiers in particular. A military elitist, Pfeffer desired this discipline as much for the purged SA as Himmler desired it for the SS. However, Pfeffer had not only to work with the kind of unruly men available but depended on their organised independence for the realisation of his own ambitions *vis-à-vis* those of other SA 'top brass' like Walter Stennes. Himmler, on the other hand, having little to begin with and certainly no powerful local SS leaders, could select a new type of officer, no less bold, determined, or intelligent than the seasoned veterans of countless SA and SS propaganda missions, but more interested in discipline, self-education, the social virtues and ideas. Himmler could and did recruit SA officers and men for the SS, but he was never restricted to the SA.

As the SA expanded by leaps and bounds in the hard winter of 1929–30 and the spring of the new year, it tended to grow out of the hands of Pfeffer and even of Hitler. Pfeffer in 1927–28 had set up an elaborate system of regional staffs to control the old centrifugal tendencies of the regional combat leagues, yet already in 1929 these staffs themselves became the subject of much bitterness and altercation with the *Gauleiter* and the Munich political office headquarters. Hitler had purposely reduced the size of the party *Gau*, even dividing some into sub-*Gaue* to correspond with electoral districts; thus no *Gauleiter* would become independent enough to challenge Hitler as Strasser's northwest alliance of 1925–26 had done. However, Pfeffer had insisted on creating seven large SA regions (*Oberführer-Bereiche*): 'North', 'East', 'South', 'Centre', 'West', 'Ruhr' and 'Austria' – headed by former officers of the First World War. In 1929 he made five of these men his deputies downgrading the party-oriented Lutze in the Ruhr and Reschny in Austria. These intermediate SA staffs concentrated SA talents and syphoned off SA income from lower levels, leaving units dependent on the goodwill of district and local party leaders. In 1929–30 as the old SA units expanded and new units were formed – often by the remains of some older combat league coming over as a unit – the need for funds for clothing and equipment brought bitter recriminations from unemployed SA men against the still comfortable *Spiessbürger* (square) of the NSDAP, whom they accused of niggardliness. Occasionally they also blamed Munich 'corruption' – but only rarely their own top-heavy staffs. Pfeffer himself complained about 'civilian interference' and did his best to support the regional staffs' requests for ever more funds for their expanding local units, so that a local SA usually felt more loyal to its own higher headquarters than to its local party. Furthermore, all of the regional SA leaders and many regimental commanders were ex-free corps officers and practitioners of charismatic leadership composed of camaraderie, paternalism and self-dramatisation. Such was Walter Stennes, whose revolt against Goebbels first threw the SS into the limelight in Berlin on 30 August 1930.

Walter Stennes had served as a battalion commander of illegal Black *Reichswehr* units and had played a part in the abortive north German putsch of September 1923. Already in August 1928 he is supposed to have 'gone on strike' against the Munich Party headquarters to obtain funds in his eastern SA region, including Brandenburg, Mecklenburg, Pomerania, Danzig, East Prussia and Silesia. Supported by Pfeffer, he had got what he wanted and the local Berlin SA were his most loyal adherents. In July 1930 funds were short again, but there were other grievances. Lawlessness was increasing, and so was the appeal of Communism or at least of anti-capitalist radicalism. In this setting the breach between Otto Strasser's '*Kampfverlag*' and Munich Party headquarters over the right of Saxon workers to strike gave rise to the well-founded suspicion among unemployed Berlin SA men that the party, which had joined hands with the ruthless and reactionary press tycoon Alfred Hugenberg, was abandoning them. This impression seemed confirmed when Hitler refused Stennes and several eastern SA leaders places on the Nazi list for the *Reichstag* elections at a time when it looked as if anyone on the Nazi list in Berlin could win. Paramilitary leaders of *Reichsbanner* (Social Democrat), *Stahlhelm* and Storm Troops all sought *Reichstag* seats in order to get unlimited train passes (and salaries) to enhance their organising capacity, and probably in the case of the Storm Troops to 'take over' the 'gossip-club' (*Schwatzbude*) by spectacular theatrics. Pfeffer was not averse to intimidating the party people and even forcing Hitler's hand. But Hitler refused Stennes's demands, and his delegation of Berlin SA men were refused a hearing in Munich on 23 August. Stennes's staff resigned on the spot. Pfeffer temporised with Stennes's clique even after about thirty SA men raided the Berlin district headquarters and beat up the NSDAP business agent on 28 August. Two days later Stennes called a 'peace' meeting at the headquarters, but the discovery of an SS 'spy' at the meeting led to the forcible removal of seven SS guards from the building, two of whom received head injuries. Goebbels flew off to Munich and on 1 September brought Hitler immediately to Berlin, which was in a complete uproar. A police riot squad arrested the rebels, releasing them when Goebbels refused to press charges. Hitler had to brave hisses and catcalls at the SA taverns and clubs (SA-*Heime*), but his charisma was still effective. The *Führer* rallied the mutinous bands of SA men with promises of more paid SA posts, more funds for the units and better relations with the Political Organisation. He did not remove Stennes or the SA regional leaders who had joined him, but on his return to Munich he removed Pfeffer. He even placed a few SA officers on the Nazi ballots, though none from Stennes's group. Not all of them were elected, but Heinrich Himmler, *Reichsführer* SS, was.

Pfeffer had made efforts to bring the SA under stricter control in 1930. In June he had created a general inspectorate under the retired Lieutenant-Colonel Kurt von Ulrich, formerly SA Commander 'West', whose new job was to inspect and regulate local SA and SS units. Pfeffer had also brought in as *Stabschef* (Executive Officer or Chief of Staff) Otto Wagener, once a captain in the German General Staff and now a disciple of small business advocate Gottfried Feder. Wagener hoped to develop a classless social and economic order of *Stände* ('professional estates') within and through the SA. Nor were Pfeffer's military ambitions putschist in character – they were merely preparatory to forming a people's army after a legal victory. Finally, Hitler did not yet know whether Röhm, who had returned from Bolivia, would accept the SA leadership on Hitler's terms. In fact, Pfeffer had actually offered his resignation to Hitler as early as 12 August, following Hitler's refusal of the *Reichstag* seats for the SA. Hitler announced it on 2 September. Pfeffer's offer to manage affairs temporarily was not accepted. Instead, Hitler made himself Supreme SA Commander, keeping Wagener on temporarily as *Stabschef* to manage affairs. Thus did Hitler prevent a wholesale desertion of SA officers before the national election, a move indirectly threatened by Pfeffer in his formal letter of resignation of 29 August. The remarkable electoral victory of 14 September 1930, to which SA and SS propaganda teams contributed much, helped to convince Röhm that the Nazis were indeed on the road to victory. Heinrich Himmler had also done his part to bring Röhm back with a steady flow of correspondence to his old *Reichskriegsflagge* commander. The SS would not be neglected if Röhm did return. Indeed, Röhm had promised Himmler money for the SS 'if he ever had any'.

With about 150 numbered SS *Stürme* brought into existence by the end of 1930, overhead costs were bound to mount even if little or nothing was paid to several hundred 'full-time' officers and NCOs. Like their SA counterparts, the SS units as yet usually paid no rent for their meeting places, utilising a back room in a local public house owned by a party member or sympathiser. They paid their rent with their purchase of beer 'after duty'. SS men were expected to pay for their own outfitting, black cap, pants, tie, belt and shoulder strap, brown shirt, etc. If a 'paper *Sturm*' was ever to advance much beyond its original *Staffel* character of seven to fifteen men, at least one man had to be freed from the burden of full-time employment elsewhere to devote himself to the unit or at the very least he could not be expected to pay for printing handbills, licences, telephone bills and gasoline for his motorcycle. The pride with which a *Sturm* of twenty-five to thirty men was reported in 1930 indicates that few even reached this weak 'company strength'. Although officially commanded to do so, not all SA commanders bothered about setting up SS units and few cared to part with the best ten SA men in a community, much less to devote time and money to seeing that once created a *Sturm* went on existing. Nonetheless, nineteen of the thirty-five SS officers of 1930 were from the SA.

It was fortunate that Himmler was able to locate a number of reasonably competent *Gau-SS-Führer* in the course of 1930, and even to set up three ('East', 'West' and 'South') Regional Commands (*Oberführer-Bereiche*) on the model of the more numerous SA areas of the same name. The system of *Standarten* – two or three per *Gau* – was filled out somewhat on paper by designating two or three *Stürme* as a *Standarte*, numbered I–XXX, but the SS could not really afford the luxury of so many staff levels. At the *Gau* level, soon to be designated as SS-*Brigaden*, there was usually an adjutant-and-business manager and a treasurer; often the former had some accounting experience and the latter was a small businessman. To replace Hustert, Himmler acquired as an adjutant (later *Stabsleiter*) Josias von Waldeck und Pyrmont, a nobleman with some university education; Himmler picked up a business manager and a treasurer as well. The local business managers handled the rosters, reports and correspondence, while the treasurers looked after the collection of dues and contributions from supporting members and 'active members' and also made disbursements. Often in the absence of a treasurer, the 'adjutant' was supposed to do everything, and the books were often in slovenly condition or non-existent.

The 1930 revolt of Stennes and his SA cohorts in north and east Germany ushered in a period of SA-SS jostling for position and favour in Munich and in local communities. If the seven 'unknown SS men' in Berlin had accomplished little else in August 1930, they had underscored the value of SS units independent of SA dominance. While Hitler did not dare displace Stennes and the SA commanders in Pomerania, Silesia, etc, he very much needed 'objective' reports on local conditions; that is,

reports written from the point of view of the movement as seen with
eyes loyal to Munich, not from the local party headquarters. It was hoped
that the SS could begin to collect this information. Naturally, especially
in Berlin, Mecklenburg, Pomerania, East Prussia and Silesia, the Storm
Troops would have nothing to do with the SS, regarding any new local
units as 'wild and unauthorised'. It is perhaps not accidental that we have
no record of *Gau-SS-Führer* at this time for Mecklenburg, Pomerania
and East Prussia. In Silesia the blueblooded Udo von Woyrsch took over
this function in open opposition to the SA. Above all, Himmler, now one
of the 107 Nazis with an unlimited train pass, was finally relieved of his
propaganda duties to devote himself full time to setting up the SS as 'fully
independent of the SA'.

In a circular letter to the OSAF (*Oberster Sturm-Abteilung-Führer*,
Supreme Commander of the Storm Troops) deputies, now including
Lutze, Chief of Staff Wagener on 3 October described the SS as a police
unit inside the movement, with the duty to guard against infringements of
government regulations. He stressed the need for the SS to be
independent of the SA, especially in recruitment, according to special
standards which had been given to the *Reichsführer* SS. He gave the SS a
quota of 10 per cent of the SA strength, a figure often repeated thereafter,
but stated that an SS unit should not be formed until an SA company in
the area had reached fifty members. The SS was not to recruit among SA
members. These regulations were regularly disregarded, though they were
given lip service for several years. The SA was to turn away from propaganda, guard duty and the solicitation of funds to prepare for its role as the
future reservoir of the national army, while the SS would presumably take
over these duties and serve as the personal guard of the leader, analogous to
Royal Guards. A belief in the imminence of the National Socialist accession to state authority is likewise reflected in an order of OSAF Deputy
August Schneidhuber of Munich in November. He stressed military training, the formation of motorised and medical SA units, the combing out of
opportunists, the geographical analysis of recruiting to fill up gaps and the
creation of a *Standarte* staff level. In an earlier memorandum of September,
Schneidhuber had called for equality between the district SA leader and
the *Gauleiter,* as well as the use of SA corps commanders with tactical and
not merely administrative authority over the district SA leader. Thus,
before the reappearance of Röhm on the scene, the SA showed many signs
of empire-building as a preliminary to taking over the state, in addition to

ominous claims to independence of the Political Organisation. It even decided to create its own SA headquarters' guards to provide security, a move which would free them from reliance on the SS.

Some of Schneidhuber's organisational proposals were indeed carried out by Röhm in 1931 and were copied by the SS; but the SA did not gain independence of the Political Organisation, and therefore the SS did not gain independence of the SA. Himmler's announcement on 1 December 1930 that the SS's final separation from the SA had occurred was followed six weeks later on 14 January 1931 by the order of Hitler clearly subordinating the SS to the SA. Röhm's new position as chief of staff was carried through a meeting of SA leaders at Munich on 30 November, only after considerable difficulty and by Hitler's will. Both before and after 30 November, Stennes and his SA leaders in the north and east resisted party efforts to reduce them to submission; Stennes seemed to try to enlist Röhm on his side. Röhm cleverly steered a middle course that favoured SS strength but bound the SS to the SA, insisting, for example, that SA cadres continue to be furnished for the formation of new SS units. That this winter (1930–31) saw a serious struggle for power is shown by the appearance of Göring, already a potential rival of Röhm, as an 'official mediator' between SA, SS and the *Gauleiter.*

Conditions for the recruitment of several thousand relatively competent 'political soldiers' for the SS improved steadily as unemployment mounted to 4 million that winter and early spring. Soup lines and lines for unemployment pay attracted Communist and Nazi recruiters. The political atmosphere darkened; and revolutionary tendencies, banished since 1923, reappeared. The police increasingly failed to protect life and property. Street battles, political brawling in public places, 'raids' on 'enemy' headquarters and murder by political thugs enhanced the desire of the more educated activists of the right to join 'protection units', such as the SS represented. Still very much 'strong-arm squads', SS units tended to be better prepared for each confrontation, better disciplined *vis-à-vis* the police and subject to control. While it is doubtful that all the 4,000 numbered identity passes of the SS were really in the possession of that many active SS men by December 1930, it is clear from SS personnel and organisational records that the six months following the great electoral victory did see a wave of SS recruitment at the higher (officer) ranks as well as rapid promotions to officer from within existing units, in order to staff the newly created SS units of late 1930.

Under Röhm the SA also grew very rapidly, attaining sometime in 1931 its first 1 million men. The forty SA-*Standarten* became several hundred; Röhm reorganised the SA regionally into ten 'Groups' (the corps recommended by Schneidhuber), each composed of several sub-groups, the former *Gaustürme* (regional companies). While the powerful OSAF-deputyships were done away with, a vast staff network was created, whereby brigades of several *Standarten* were formed to manage the auxiliary formations being set up, and the term *Sturmbann* (battalion) was improvised to take the place of the old *Sturm-Abteilung* designation for a local tactical unit. Many of the German lower middle class, fright-ened by the return of all the violence of 1919–23, were led to don uniforms and assume military ranks, which permitted them to dream of a future position of honour and respect in a restored national army reserve. Hitler helped out by publicly reissuing orders to SA and SS units alike against carrying military weapons or creating weapons depots. Citizens need not fear involvement in a putsch.

Many of the 'straight' middle classes took offence, however, at the rough and blatant disregard of their morality in the ranks of the Storm Troops, especially as a number of old free corps veterans and even adven-turers were attracted back to the SA with Röhm's return. Hitler saw fit to issue an impatient warning, not to the malefactors but to their accus-ers, pointing out that the SA was no 'school for girls' and promising expulsion for disloyalty for tongue-wagging, letter-writing party members. While there was no dearth of roughnecks in the SS at this time, certain traces of prudish, middle-class morality began to appear in 1931, which may reflect a cultivated sense of superiority on this issue in terms of discipline. The SS never recruited groups of the old combat leagues; Röhm did so precisely at this time, partly to offset the Stennes faction in the north and east. Röhm and Hitler could wink at homosex-uality, pimping, petty thievery and heavy drinking, but they would not tolerate insubordination. Pfeffer's institution of the general inspectorate (GISASS) was retained and widened to include regional inspectorships. One of the major duties was the removal of controversies between SA and SS units, to save Röhm's organisation from internal interference by the Political Organisation and especially by Hitler's 'official mediator', Göring.

Early in 1931 the SS was kept busy changing and rechanging its unit designations to keep up with the elaborate tables of organisation constructed by Röhm and his staff. The SS-*Stürme* had scarcely been given Arabic numbers when the Arabic numbers, locally often the same ones, had to be reassigned to *Standarten*. Weak SS companies thereby became even weaker SS regiments; thirty weak SS regiments formerly designated with Roman numerals became SS brigades. This forced-draft cadre system taken over from the SA, which of course was aping old familiar military procedures and practising for the rapid buildup of a citizen army, both helped the SS to expand more rapidly than many local SS leaders would have preferred, and also challenged the ingenuity and constructive ability of many new SS men recruited for command purposes. The brigade system (five *Standarten*) was soon abandoned again, for the SS really was not large enough for as many levels as the SA; and light, purely administrative units known as *Oberführer-Abschnitte* (sectors) were interposed between about forty *Standarten* and the *Reichsführung* SS. As in the SA, however, the effect was to destroy the special position of the SS-*Oberführer* as favoured 'Deputies of the *Reichsführer* SS', although the term lingered on in 1931, and Sepp Dietrich and Kurt Daluege may have exercised this function even later.

Sepp Dietrich was already termed the commander of the SS in the south by a police report of December 1930. While Himmler was in Berlin at the *Reichstag*, it was certainly the hearty charisma of the ex-truck driver rather than the new SS bureaucracy of the palatial Brown House in Munich which helped the SS grow in Bavaria. Kurt Daluege in Berlin had been displaced earlier by Stennes as SA leader; Hitler set Daluege to watch his rival by having Himmler make him *Oberführer Ost* in place of the less effective SS veteran Kurt Wege. Daluege set up his SS headquarters at the corner of Lützow Strasse and Potsdamer Strasse near the Sportpalast, across from Stennes's SA offices. This 'intelligence centre' utilised links between SS and SA, as well as with government workers and businessmen to keep Hitler and Himmler abreast of the political currents of seething Berlin. Daluege was also instrumental in the spring of 1931 in setting up fledgling SS units in the traditional SA territories of Brandenburg, Pomerania and Mecklenburg. Thus, the northern SS leader and his cohorts were able to alert party and State Police authorities against Stennes when Hitler was ready to goad him into a second fruitless 'revolt'. Foreshadowing the plot against Röhm, Hitler's tactics with Stennes included an intensive wooing to catch him off guard, an effort to divide his followers among themselves and from him, a sudden manoeuvre to place him in the wrong and afterwards a vilification campaign. Just as in the previous August, only a few SS personnel seem to have been involved in the preliminaries, but the subsequent removal of virtually all the ranking SA leaders in the northeast by resignation and expulsion put the SS, at least temporarily, in the position of 'protecting the movement', so that a legend could be created out of the 'Stennes-Putsch' of Easter Sunday, 1 April 1931.

Hitler began by offering Stennes the Ministry of the Interior in the state of Brunswick, opened to the Nazis by their September electoral victory and collaboration with the Nationalists. When Stennes refused, Hitler began to remove Stennes's appointees as *Gau-SA-Führer*. Stennes did not remain inactive, stirring up his SA against *Gauleiter* and the Brown House for their showy inefficiency. But Stennes's plotting only united his enemies, inside and outside the party, without being decisive. Hitler precipitated the 'revolt' on 31 March at a party meeting at Weimar called to patch up the differences with the Nationalists in Thuringia; repeating his orders to observe the strictest legality, he announced that Stennes, a thorn in the side of the right, would be transferred to Munich as Röhm's chief executive officer – not an unworthy move but disruptive of Stennes's connections. Stennes had not been consulted, but five SS men were warned by telephone during the night of 31 March of the move, which then appeared in the morning papers. Stennes's district SA leaders wired Hitler in protest, Stennes wired his refusal to come to Weimar to parlay with Hitler (at Hitler's request), and Berlin SA forces took over the party headquarters and the *Angriff* (Goebbels's paper) as a kind of public protest. It was an act of despair, for the SS had alerted party personnel of Hitler's intentions to observe strict legality. The police cleared away the stubborn SA minority in the next days amid charges and counter-charges of betrayal.

Daluege and his men had acted in the interests of Röhm, as well as of Hitler, but Röhm put another ex-free corps officer, Paul Schulz, in charge of what was left of the northeast SA. Friedrich Wilhelm Krüger, the SS lieutenant who had been Daluege's courier to Röhm, became SA Staff Leader for the region. When later Schulz himself turned against Röhm, Krüger took his place, leaving the SS and ultimately rising to a high staff position close to Röhm. Nevertheless, he was to return successfully to the SS in 1935 as an *Obergruppenführer* (General). Daluege subsequently issued a card of thanks in Hitler's name to the SS of the

Berlin *Abschnitt* Sector III bearing the inscription, 'SS-*Mann*, *Deine Ehre heisst Treue*' ('SS man, Your honour is your loyalty'). Changed to, 'My honour is my loyalty', Himmler would adopt it as the inscription for the SS belt buckle in the tradition of the '*Gott mit uns*' ('May God be with us') on the buckles of German First World War uniforms.

The summer of 1931 in Germany with its bank collapse was traumatic for the German middle class. All illusions about the previous year's supposed 'bottoming out' were swept away as more and more white collar men joined the bread lines. For the Nazis the chaos was the confirmation of their world view. Although many of their membership had supposed they would already be in power by that time, the Nazi leadership experienced the impasse in the parliamentary system as a confirmation and justification of the party's doctrine. These men carried on their bombardment of the public with rallies, propaganda marches, handbills, new party newspapers, undaunted – indeed stimulated – by ineffectual police measures against them. The SS emerges at this time in the speeches and orders of its leaders as remarkably full blown; though it would be long years before they could realise their ambitions for the SS, its ideal contours appear remarkably complete by the summer of 1931. While the reasons for this emergence remain obscure, it is likely that by then all the conditions which had given rise to National Socialism had had time to express themselves fully and the potential role of the SS as political soldiers of this movement was now clear, at least to an inner core of Hitler's followers. That this role was in fact permanently bifurcated – intrinsically so, due to the contradiction between soldiering and politics – was much less clear then than it now appears to the historian's eyes.

No less a person than Hitler himself that summer defined the SS in its dual aspect as: (1) a police service and (2) an elite troop. Neither Hitler nor Himmler, then or later, regarded these as mutually exclusive or even opposing functions. The police task is described in the speeches and orders of the summer of 1931 as security service and regulative service, concepts borrowed from German police practice. The former consisted of counter-intelligence and protective service. The regulative functions were carefully distinguished from the more inclusive SA 'protection of meetings'.

The SS responsibility was to prevent party and SA personnel from threatening public order – a counter-revolutionary, or perhaps more accurately a regulative, role of preventing the revolutionaries from going off half-cocked and thus jeopardising the long-term revolutionary ambitions of the leadership. The commonest concrete example of this function was searching SA men for concealed firearms, not surprisingly a source of great bitterness. Counter-intelligence activities were of course not as yet limited to the SS, but the anti–Stennes operations in the north and east were undoubtedly a strong argument and incentive for investing the SS with this role. Its smaller size and selective character offered more possibility of secrecy and protection against spies and *agents provocateurs*. Reinhard Heydrich, who joined the SS in 1931, did not have to introduce the idea of a security service. SS regiments and even battalions and companies had 'I-C officers' ('I' represents troop commander's staff and 'C' represents intelligence) by 1931, as of course did many SA units, by analogy with the intelligence staff officer system of the German army. The protective functions of the SS were distinguished from those of the SA by this time: the personal defence of the *Führer*, all speakers, functionaries and invited guests, as well as protecting special gatherings of party leaders. Last of all, there was a general category of 'special tasks' which was kept purposely vague. Emphasis was placed upon the absolute reliability of the individual SS men involved, including commitment to murder.

The concept of the SS as a mobile unit, a storm battalion for employment at a point where it would throw the balance to the side of National Socialism, was as prominent a theme as the police duties. Whereas the Storm Troops were to be foot soldiers, whose early motorised formations had been detached to form the independent National Socialist Motor Corps (NSKK), the SS was encouraged to create its own motorised companies. Moulding together the tradition of the *Stosstrupp Hitler* and the November 'martyrs', Hitler had already conferred on the SS the status of a *Garde*. It was Himmler, however, who insisted in the summer of 1931 and ever afterwards on transcending police traditions and copying the traditions of the guardsmen of the old army. 'We are not wiser than the men of two thousand years ago,' said Himmler at a meeting of the SS leaders in Berlin in June. 'Persians, Greeks, Romans and Prussians all had their guards. The guards of the new Germany will be the SS.' The use of members of elite guard units as personal bodyguards for heads of state was of course traditional; the SS's role as Hitler's bodyguard was reinforced as Sepp Dietrich and a few hand-picked aides accompanied him everywhere.

The SS was described ideally in 1931 as the 'Core Troops of the Movement' and 'the most active fighters of the party', reflecting the initial concept of 1925–26; but SS speeches and orders made amply clear that the Political Organisation was something apart, just as appeals to be 'good comrades to the SA' while setting them an example suggest a similar sense of separation. In fact, the SS was supposed to become the very best paramilitary troop in Germany, so it would attract by its very nature the best of the front veterans, replacing the *Stahlhelm* in the public eye. The future guardsman of the future national army should be recognisable anywhere in civilian clothing: his bearing, build, outlook – indeed his biological heritage – would show his SS membership. There were to be no Slavic or Mongoloid faces in the SS, said Himmler. The SS was to become a blood community, the bearers of the blood of the Nordic race. The future SS officer should have his family and background thoroughly investigated, for it was supposed that when the fatal decisions must be made, only the purest of the pure could act without hesitation, 'on principle'. Recognisable here are the values of the old officer caste translated into Nazi racism.

Himmler did not stop with this, however. The task of the SS did not lie primarily on the battlefield but in the homeland. In war it must be the instrument which at the most difficult moment decides the battle – the last reserves. The year 1918 – that terrible trauma – should never be repeated. Instead of faint-hearted or mutinous rear-echelon protectors of the home front, mobile storm battalions would be at the state's command to crush Bolshevism, to close a gap in the defences, to thrust home the victory. 'We are called to lay the foundations upon which the next generation will make history,' said Himmler. He foresaw in the summer of 1931 a future ring of 200 million Nordic farmers around Germany, an impregnable wall against Bolshevism, the enemy of the Nordic race and thereby of civilisation. Thus, the shadow of Richard Walter Darré, author of *Farming as the Life Source of the Nordic Race*, was cast on the SS that summer, soon to dominate its ethos, if not its ultimate purposes.

Himmler, Sepp Dietrich and Kurt Daluege clearly visualised a future SS officers' corps at this time, perhaps by contrasting their current difficulties with SA and Political Organisation leaders, especially with the Stennes clique. Absolute obedience to Hitler, modelled on the supposedly traditional soldier's unquestioning loyalty to the Prussian king, was to be combined with the 'Prussian' or perhaps 'Germanic' conception of voluntary self-subordination of independent personalities to constituted superiors in the interest of a higher good. To maintain the authority of the party against the interests and will of dissident minorities, to handle mob situations independently and responsibly, and to stamp their personality upon their followers, SS officers were to have implanted within them an indestructible *esprit de corps*. They were to be welded together as one body of interchangeable units and yet capable of replacement from below by men of merit. The future corps would be made up of thoroughly trained men in all branches of SS discipline; there were to be no mere specialists nor professional branches to engage in service rivalries. Himmler did not want any SS book-keepers or SS doctors: all were to be political soldiers. Parade-ground drill, dressy uniforms and marching bands were to be better in the SS than in the SA or Political Organisation but only to impress SS superiority on the public and on SS men themselves – never as an end in themselves. The SS officer must be the type to understand this and not love the show for its own sake, just as he must want his men to understand their training and purpose, rather than desire their ignorance and consequent subordination and inferiority to himself. He must know his men as individuals, their jobs and their family conditions. The SS officer was to be a practitioner of middle-class virtues – again not for themselves but for their influence upon the German community. The future SS officers' corps was to become the treasury of the 'best human material' in Germany left over after the supposed terrible 'decline in human heredity' during the past century.

The summer of 1931 ended with a new outbreak of Nazi violence in Berlin against the Jews on the occasion of the Jewish holidays, but it was becoming increasingly clear to the German right that Hitler was in control of his strong-arm squads and that he really intended to come to power legally. Hitler's problem was to make this conviction stick, without being forced to come into a government on terms other than his own. The Harzburg meeting (a huge rally of all the rightist groups in Germany), the demonstrations in the *Reichstag*, the SA and SS rally of 1 million members at Brunswick, all in October 1931, were designed to hold this balance between reassurance and intimidation. It was no longer merely or mainly a problem of agitating the populace; the economic catastrophe was now apparent. The inflow of members was also becoming a matter of course. In fact the problem rather was to maintain control of local and regional Nazi activists, and to prevent the invasion of the controllable membership by such masses of new 'human material', so that *agents provocateurs* (real and fancied) could not destroy Hitler's bargaining power.

The Storm Troops were still the most vulnerable area in this respect, although the Political Organisation was not altogether impregnable. A temporary coalition of Otto Strasser and Walter Stennes, involving Erhardt and some 'National Bolsheviks', plus the spectre of infiltration from the KPD (Communist Party) created a spy scare among the Nazis, which produced numerous 'intelligence bureaus' in the SA, SS and Political Organisation. That the SS's intelligence operations were more trusted by Hitler than the others' and ultimately were more successful is doubtlessly due to Reinhard Heydrich; yet if the SS had not had an 'edge' with Hitler in late 1931, it is doubtful if the opportunistic ex-naval officer would have bothered to insinuate himself into Himmler's good graces. Himmler may also have been looking for someone for the Munich office, to offset the threat of Daluege's intelligence centre in Berlin. He is supposed to have set Heydrich up as the SS-PI-*Dienst* (Press and Information Service) that autumn in a Munich apartment with Himmler's card files on individuals and newspaper clippings assembled over the years in the *Propaganda-Abteilung* with the aid of his correspondents at *Gau* levels. It was to be some time, actually only in 1933 and 1934, before Heydrich was able to assert clear authority over the 'I-C personnel' in SS regional and local headquarters, not to mention Daluege's apparatus. However, in early 1932, with the official formation of the *Sicherheitsdienst* (security service) *des Reichsführers* SS, Heydrich made a beginning by designating some new SS members from professional and academic circles as his local agents, who were to remain outside the regular SS formations.

The Political Organisation and SA were beginning to resent the SS for its still vague pretensions of superiority, more and more enhanced by the predilection of the better educated and the bluebloods to its ranks. Probably for this very reason Hitler allowed Himmler to develop his own connections in the business and professional world at this time and also to develop a special SS ideology to distinguish his units even further from SA and Political Organisation. This ideology was furnished by Richard Walter Darré, whose first connections with the NSDAP dated back only to 1930. Darré's educational background in agronomy was similar to Himmler's. Darré had begun in the party by helping Konstantin Hierl organise a farmers' wing of the NSDAP but was not satisfied or comfortable as a rabble-rousing political organiser. He was attracted by the elitism of the SS, which he proceeded to give ideological footing by tying Himmler's vague racism with Darré's own theory of a Nordic race of aristocratic farmers. The SS was to restore a mythical golden age of rural splendour by rigorous self-selection, mate selection and re-training its members as future aristocrats of the soil. This romanticism was tinged with right-wing reformism, which opposed the 'impersonal cash nexus of the market' with a familistic, personalistic corporativism. The idealised East Elbian *Junker* was contrasted with the absentee Jewish landlord. The old *Junker* could not be restored, but the SS aristocrats would take their place. In the meantime Darré was a drawing card in the SS not only to landed and formerly landed bluebloods but to a good many businessmen and bank clerks who had dreamed of owning a little farm some day. He also drew to the SS the leaders of his Farm Policy Apparatus – the well-to-do farmers of north Germany, who were not so much Nazis or racists as rebels against low prices and high interest rates. Late in 1931 Himmler made Darré head of a new Racial Office within the SS and put him in charge of approving the marriages of SS men. The already married were not, however, subject to review.

Both Himmler and Röhm turned more and more to the professional classes at this time, forming not only a medical branch, cavalry and flying corps, but also signal and engineer units – a complete paramilitary infrastructure. Himmler's units were somewhat more homogeneous, both within themselves and in relation to the larger body of which they were a part. The SS had always been largely white collar, lower middle class in character, while SA doctors, directors, lawyers and college students too often found themselves rubbing shoulders with SA bricklayers, farm labourers, head waiters and newsboys. It became increasingly necessary in the Storm Troops to make rank distinctions above and beyond functional and command distinctions – and the practice spread immediately to the SS. All the old army ranks reappeared, and persons with education and social standing began higher and rose faster. Noblemen were given commands. In the 10,000-man SS of December 1931, the original 200 or 300 had been bypassed. Even the 'founders' of 1929 were being swamped. Formalities expressed by stress on proper uniforms, numerous printed forms, coloured stamps, elaborate filing systems, forms of address, precedence at public functions, clearance for publication, and so on were irritating SS and SA men alike that dismal winter of 1931–32; but they divided the SS less than the SA, uniting it both with the SA top brass and with the German middle class outside the Nazi movement.

'What is Hitler waiting for?' was repeatedly asked in German circles – especially within the SA, where putschist sentiment for a march on Berlin was heightened by the suffering of their own families, and within circles of conservatives expecting Hitler to come to them with an offer. The existence of an increasingly better disciplined SS scheduled to grow to 22,000 by spring of 1932 helped to keep Hitler's hand steady in dealing with firebrands in the SA and Political Organisation, and with impatient negotiators from the right. Stennes and Otto Strasser, ex-free corps commanders Buchrucker and F.W. Heinz, Himmler's former adjutant Hustert and eastern regional SA commanders Tietjens, Lustig and Kremser formed the National Socialist Combat Movement with contacts to National Bolsheviks, such as Ernst Niekisch. They managed to subvert hundreds of SA men in the northern half of Germany. Not merely to combat this internal 'plague' but to stiffen the resistance to it of the national SA leadership was the role of the now-favoured SS. Doubtless some white-collar unemployed chose the SS unit in their community to avoid contamination by 'red' SA units.

In a sense, Hitler was not waiting at all. He was forming his cadres for the administration of the Third Reich within the party, the Storm Troops and the SS. He was fanning the fires of political revolution in Germany, thereby building up social pressures, which he hoped to thrust him and his party into power. He was training his cadres in the art of graduated terror and counter-revolutionary repression while he cultivated reckless violence in the streets and seemed to permit his followers to prepare for a putsch. The leak of just such a putsch plan occurred in Hesse in November 1931, the so-called Boxheim Plot. But Hitler had the Italian Fascist example of 1922 clearly in mind: he would not putsch. He was waiting to be invited. He would make himself and his movement acceptable – even attractive – to businessmen, military leaders and conservative state officials, he would not beg. In another sense, Hitler did not know what he was waiting for – what conditions he would find acceptable. From the electoral victory of September 1930, to the Harzburg Front era of late 1931, through to the presidential campaigns of March and April 1932 and beyond, he was improvising, trying to build up popular pressures behind his cause, for he did not know just how he would come to power.

For this reason he fostered every imaginable sort of political, social and economic affiliation; he allowed all sorts of professional and ideological groupings to develop as part of the 'movement', with fantastic and self-contradictory promises and programmes. The SS in 1932 was at once (1) an odd grouping of white-collar reformers; (2) a collecting centre for professional men, business leaders and landowners; and (3) a surveillance and control group to channel useful tendencies in the Nazi movement toward the Munich leadership and harmful tendencies away from the centre of the political arena. Thus, a year before Nazis came to power, the SS took on most of the organisation and the attributes of their subsequent history.

With 350 officers and 10,000 enlisted SS men as cadre, Himmler and his top-ranking lieutenants rapidly expanded the SS in the early spring of 1932 to a figure of 432 officers and 25,000 enlisted men in April at the time of the official dissolution of SA and SS by the regime. When the effort at dissolution was cancelled as a failure in mid-June, there were 466 officers and 41,000 men. This four-fold expansion could take place without an extensive officers' corps because the original staff organisation had been built up in 1931 in the form of approximately forty regimental staffs, consisting of a regimental commander and an executive officer and two or three similar pairs for the battalions in each regiment. Companies were regularly entrusted to noncommissioned officers, sometimes even to brand-new SS men on trial. Some thirty SS officers with the rank of colonel, or higher, staffed the eight regional commands, the newly created SS-*Oberstab* (top staff) and the oldest and strongest regiments. Most regiments were commanded by newly created SS majors and even captains, many of whom were transferred in from the SA, while the battalions often had to get along with new SS lieutenants lacking even SA experience, although many had had free corps careers. The growth took place by the filling out of the 'paper' or 'skeleton' units created in 1931, the further breaking up of battalions to form new ones and the formation finally of a dozen new SS regiments in virtually undeveloped areas: Mecklenburg, Pomerania, Danzig, East Prussia, Silesia? Austria, Württemberg and the Mosel valley. The practice of transferring SS officers to new regions to organise a fresh unit or re-inspire a somnolent one was begun at this time. Rapid growth continued to take place in the SS, and with it the expectation that the Nazis would soon come to power. Even before the period of illegality, which interfered with record keeping, the Munich headquarters had fallen far behind in the registration and acknowledgement of new SS members. This breakdown in record keeping would continue into 1933.

A real SS headquarters had begun to take shape in 1931, after several years in which Himmler had tried to operate almost without staff due to hatred for bureaucracy, lack of funds and a naive estimate of his own ability to do everything. In 1932 under the influence of a proliferation of SA bureaucracy, more funds, the expectation of many new tasks associated with early Nazi victory and the availability of men with the technical skills, Himmler began his *Oberstab*. It was to be constructed along German staff lines, with five sections numbered I–V, each made up of a half-dozen *Referate* ('desks') staffed by *Referenten* (specialists), lettered a-b-c-d-e-f, etc. Modifications, of course, occurred to serve the political soldier's goals, such as Darré's Section V (Race). Technical experts rather than the seasoned SS commanders were recruited. Daluege, with whose Berlin office Himmler came increasingly in contact due to his *Reichstag* post, supplied several candidates for Section I (Leadership), already also known as the Leadership Staff. There was, however, nothing permanent about this *Oberstab*. Himmler seems never to have accustomed himself to bureaucratic institutions, though he was ultimately responsible for a great many of the worst sort. Although service on Himmler's staff was soon much sought after, for much the same reasons as in other military organisations (nearness to power, rapidity of promotion, future prestige), already in 1932 it became a riskier venture than setting up a new unit or cementing ties with a jealous *Gauleiter*. Himmler was most difficult to satisfy, since his ideals were at one and the same time both vivid and yet vague; on top of this his concrete requirements were both highly specific and also unreasonable. Of the early *Oberstab*, only Heydrich really kept Himmler's confidence; Darré kept it for several years; but most of the lesser figures disappeared within a year or two. Himmler reserved most of his confidence for SS officers whom he kept or who remained by choice in field commands: Sepp Dietrich, Fritz Weitzel, perhaps Kurt Daluege (although he and Himmler were virtual rivals) and a dozen or more younger officers. Even after 1939, when Himmler had found a number of congenial and capable staff officers, he did not succeed in retaining them; he usually drove them away albeit inadvertently. He was a far cry from the charismatic Röhm or indeed Hitler himself, both of whom he admired. He could be pleasant and he could be harsh, but if there were such a thing as negative charisma, Himmler possessed it.

In the year 1932, however, the political, social and economic chaos drove able and aggressive men toward all the Nazi formations in a mood symbolised by the phrase, 'We have tried everything else'. Less known and therefore less stereotyped in the public mind, the SS appealed to many middle-class people as a relatively unstructured elite in which they could accomplish their own reformist notions. Its tight discipline, its relative reserve in relation to the public, its incipient quasi-mythical undertones could only recommend the SS to a generation sick of disorder, noisy demonstrations and false sentiments. At a time when both the Storm Troops and the Nazi Party appeared to pass beyond the original elitist dreams of their founders to become mass-movements, the SS seemed to retain and embody the ideal of selectivity now enhanced by the elaborate rigmarole of 'racial' qualifications for admission and for marriage partners of the members. For all these reasons Himmler did not require positive charisma, which is not to say that local commanders could do without it. The SS of 1932 did possess some charismatic leaders, though perhaps fewer than the SA; at the staff and technical levels, the SS tended to have rather colourless personalities. But like the party itself, the much larger Storm Troops had more poor local leaders and more stuffed-shirt bureaucrats at intermediate levels than the SS.

In the elaborate power game which Hitler played, it was both necessary and very dangerous that the Storm Troops under Röhm should court the *Reichswehr*, that the National Socialist Factory Cell Organisation (NSBO – essentially an anti-union 'cell' for Nazis in factories) should court the workers, that Darré should court both the small and the large farmers, that Frick, Ley and Göring should court bankers and business leaders. Himmler's SS provided a device for checking up on each of these 'partnerships' on the inside and also a potential checkmate against disloyalty. Yet the SS was not so strong as to be itself a serious challenge to SA, party, or Hitler. Himmler's undoubted personal loyalty to Hitler entirely coincided with the interests of the SS, which could easily have been destroyed in 1932 by either the party or the SA. Indeed the increased contacts between Himmler, Göring and big business interests in 1932 suggest that Himmler was both insuring a flow of funds to the SS independent of Röhm and F.X. Schwarz, the party treasurer, and aiding Hitler to move in the political direction which he wanted against the wishes of a very large segment of his own party. The role of adjunct to Göring – though perhaps distasteful – was profoundly wise, since it enabled Himmler to outmanoeuvre Daluege, virtually independent in Berlin.

Röhm sought to subordinate the SS to the SA and partially succeeded in 1932, in that the major preoccupation of all the paramilitary units in Germany was street combat and preparation for civil war, necessitating at least minimal co-operation between allied units. Röhm's – and probably Hitler's – ambition to win a partnership with the *Reichswehr* in a future *Volksheer* also held out valuable compensation for many ex-soldiers among SS officers in the form of a re-established military career. Thus, in 1932 the SS held the same kind of weekend manoeuvres as the SA, often jointly with them. Street and beer hall battles were common tactical operations often planned in detail by SA and SS officers. Propaganda marches of SA were in turn 'guarded' by car-loads of SS in advance and at the rear of the columns, as well as on motorcycles and along the line of march. Indeed, many of the quarrels that year turned on how much protection the SA needed; leaders complained of getting none at all or else of being guarded too ostentatiously. The SS in turn resented the 'luxurious' SA-*Heime* (a combination of a clubhouse and headquarters) which increasingly appeared throughout the more Nazi sections of the country, while the SS usually still had to hold their weekly *Appell* (roll call) at a tavern. However, both kinds of units were guilty of gangster-like 'shakedowns' to obtain money. For example, the FM (Sponsors) records of the Munich SS regiment I for the spring of 1932 include the names Hirschmann, Goldschmidt, Levi, Rosenzvet and Rosenberg.

For world-war veterans in the SS and SA, the year 1932 began to look more and more like 1918: battle after battle, victory after victory, but the final battle still unfought. Victory, momentarily expected, remained elusive. The nervousness of the 'holding on tactics' of the trenches permeated the whole Nazi movement, but the action-oriented Storm Troops took the successive false alarms of 1932 the hardest. They had been placed on an alarm footing in March before the first presidential elections; special detachments (*Alarm-Bereitschaften*) were assigned the task of preventing a *Reichswehr* coup against the party. Even those not directly involved in either planning or operations at this level had great expectations. Hitler's acceptance of the SA-SS prohibition without a coup was hardest for the newest Storm Troopers, but even the *Altkämpfer* (Old Fighters) were perplexed when their triumphs over Gröner in May and June, leading to the electoral victory of 31 July ran off into the sand. The 'condition red alert' of the first weeks in August was virtually a repetition of their experience in March. It was in great part preparation for a *Machtergreifung* (seizure of power) accompanying Hitler's being appointed to the chancellorship, but it was also intended as a 'clean-up' of the Communists and the Social Democrat *Reichsbanner*. Berlin was encircled; SS and SA units in every community made ready to secure train stations, ammunition depots and police headquarters. Then came two weeks' leave, followed by orders to prepare for new propaganda marches, new *Reichstag* elections and another *Hungerwinter*. Small wonder that Communist agitators began to disrupt SA roll calls and ex-SA men multiplied on the platforms of SPD and KPD rallies. Röhm had again reorganised the SA, reducing the geographic scope of the SA *Gruppen* and increasing their number to eighteen, and returning to five SA corps' areas. What he had begun as a response to tremendous growth and increased optimism only added to the confusion and resentment in the months of uncertainty ahead. The publication of new, more complicated and restrictive SA service regulations in October seemed to mock SA impotence.

Even the SS began to show signs of losing its momentum in the autumn of 1932. The recruitment was slowed down by efforts to establish the identity of all new candidates. The eight SS *Abschnitte* (sectors) had proliferated into eighteen to correspond with the SA divisional *Gruppen* and was topped by five SS-*Gruppenkommandos* (division headquarters): 'North', 'South', 'West', 'East' and 'Southeast'. SS men also began to feel remote from higher headquarters. Certain units, who requested to help the SA collect money to keep their soup kitchens in operation, rebelled or collected the money for themselves. Other SS units took part in 'mutinies' against *Gauleiter*, 'against Goebbels', or 'Munich'. In Halle SS men joined SA in jeering at Hitler when he asked for their continued loyalty. However, other SS men descended on the rebels, SS and SA alike, beating them with truncheons and brass knuckle-dusters. Sustained from the ranks of the unemployed, the SA did not collapse in the lean winter months. Moreover, accession of unemployed white-collar workers to the SS stiffened the loyalty of the Black Corps to the middle-class party leadership when men like Ley, Streicher, Frick, Goebbels and Göring were attacked by more Nazi 'renegades' like Stennes and even Gregor Strasser. Unlike many of the SA, the average SS officer had no sympathy with rebels, working men, or the down-and-out.

Himmler's appearance with Hitler in the home of the banker Kurt von Schröder on 4 January 1933, along with Wilhelm Keppler and Rudolf Hess seems to have been primarily symbolic. Himmler and the

SS were not yet so important to Hitler that they should have been granted a voice in the counsels of the mighty. Himmler stood, however, for the absent Röhm in a double sense, both as a reminder of the armed masses who stood behind the demagogue Hitler and as an alternative. Hess too represented the party, as a reminder of the absent Strasser whom he had defeated and also of Röhm, his less palatable rival. It is not unlikely that Himmler and Hess were also there to watch each other, and to help Hitler reassure his followers later that he had not 'sold out'. In any case, this portentous promotion of Himmler had been well earned, or if it had not yet, soon would be.

The world depression, much more than the treaty of Versailles, withered the tender seedling of German democracy. Republicans-of-the-head had outnumbered republicans-of-the-heart in Germany for most of the time since 1919. It no longer seemed rational to favour a parliamentary system that was powerless to cope with the suffering, the mindless violence, and the political division of families and communities. The Catholic Centre Party and the Social Democratic Party had sought to save the pieces; the core of their support was still intact when the German right, heavy industry and banking, the *Reichswehr* leadership, and the conspiratorial politicians around Hindenburg began to 'tame' the Nazi wolves by introducing them into the sheepfold. The Communist cadres too were intact, with their masses of supporters in German cities ready to engage in a civil war on orders from Moscow. Hitler needed the threat of the Storm Troops to force the right to the bargaining table and later to convince it that he could handle the Communists. He needed the Storm Troops to engulf the police and intimidate the supporters of the Centre Party and SPD, while he carried out the 'revolution from above' which the German right had preached since 1920. But he also needed the SS, to absorb the right, destroy its positions of influence and impregnability, and channel the constructive and destructive potential of the 'Conservative Revolution' so long heralded in Germany. And ultimately he needed the SS to watch the SA, that kaleidoscopic and centrifugal mass of political soldiers swollen with the poor and the hungry, the greedy and the psychopaths, the *Landsknechte* and the crooks. The next eighteen months would see the total transformation of Germany but also of the Storm Troops – and the SS.

4

THE AGE OF OPPORTUNITY

1933

Torch-bearing SS units marched under the Brandenburg Gate on the night of 30 January 1933, indistinguishable in the dark from their more numerous SA comrades. In the moment of victory, rivalries and organisational differences were forgotten. National Socialists of every branch – Political Organisation, SA, SS, NSKK, HJ, *Altkämpfer* and newcomers of last summer – were united in the determination to make a revolution. After so many disappointments and false starts, they were determined to seize and hold power. The spirit of a unifying, national renaissance which permeated the ranks of many a non-Nazi organisation in the coming months, and penetrated even to foreign observers, did not obscure the purpose of the political soldiers, whether national party official, SS regimental commander or SA man: to wrest the whole power from their conservative allies and to crush any counter-revolution, from the middle-class right as well as from the Marxist left. No one knew how, where, or when this challenge would be faced; opinions differed as to method and timing. But within the movement there was a deep reservoir of faith and confidence replenished by victory, upon which Hitler and his lieutenants could draw.

In spite of the quarrels and the partial differentiation of tasks among party, SA and SS since 1929, the years of combat side by side, the steady hammering out of a propaganda line, the common denominators of class, education, region and above all world war and free corps memories gave nearly all those who were Nazis in January 1933 a functional similarity which is best expressed in the term 'political soldier'. Out of the amorphous and romantic resentment of 1918 had come into being a functioning reality: 'a political instrument'. Just as the actual soldier – be he private or general – must possess will and intelligence in order to be a good instrument, thereby opening up the possibility of insubordination and error, so the political soldiers of National Socialism were not automatons. Their disagreements and quarrels, like those of the Communists but unlike those of most other political factions, concerned means exclusively, not ends. They agreed in their image of themselves as instruments. The rise of the SS, particularly in this period but also later, at the expense of SA and party can be explained by its more rapid and efficient adaptation to the Nazi ideas of political soldiering. The party and the SA did not wish any less to be political soldiers; indeed they were, each in their way, quite successful. But their size, structure and composition ultimately militated against 'perfection'. Of course, the SS never became a perfect instrument, and the party was to be at least partially rehabilitated years later by Bormann's skill.

Hitler had evolved his revolutionary methods in the practical, day-to-day political conflicts of the past decade. His political soldiers of every branch were (1) tools of conquest, (2) cadre, (3) control apparatus and (4) devices for exercising pressure. For Hitler conquest meant the seizure of power, from below in the streets, from above in parliaments, cabinets, executive offices and bureaus. Cadre meant a reservoir of indoctrinated, reliable personnel. Control apparatus meant a two-way communications network, directed outwards toward the opponents, toward state authorities and foreign countries, and toward potential allies and members, as well as inwards toward lower ranks and different branches of the movement. Pressure devices meant instruments of propaganda and terror for the purpose of holding and using power, which were directed against the masses, counter-revolutionary opponents, allied groups, foreign countries and various branches of the movement. While differentiation among the Political Organisation, SA and SS began at this level, all three were equipped in all the above areas.

While the exercise of force was in some respects left to the SA and SS, the emphasis on legality and persuasion in the movement meant that all three branches had developed as propaganda organisations. The SA and the SS were accustomed to holding forth as rabble-rousers and expected to join in the conquest of parliaments, cabinets, executive posts and bureaus. The party stalwarts were in the SA and the SS; they had personally dealt out violence and terror, and filled the streets with their membership for elections and alarms throughout 1932. Except in the military area, there was little to distinguish the SA and SS from the party in aspiration toward responsible positions in the state and the economy. All three branches were attractive to the ambitious on the Nazi lower rungs of professional success. There was a multitude of intelligence services, and every branch sought to infiltrate the state, the economy and the other branches with confidential agents. Since the exercise of pressure had been the chief means for conquering power before 30 January, all parts of the Nazi movement were equally conscious of their importance as pressure groups in holding and exercising power thereafter.

Where, then, did the seeds of future antagonisms lie? Not – as might too readily be surmised – in the powerful ambitions of the SS officers' corps. Of the three branches, the SS was the least hungry for a monopoly of power. The difficulty lay with the nature of the victory of January 1933 and with the subsequent revolution of that year. Hitler had only barely won power. The door had been opened to him because he was noisy and dangerous, but he had not captured the power as yet. While not intact, the powers of the German state, the army, the economy and the social institutions were immense. If these institutions, their flanks once turned, could have been seized by direct frontal assault, it is unlikely that the SS would have been elaborated beyond party and state – although an SA-State formed from the most revolutionary elements of the NSDAP, the SA and the SS is quite conceivable. Hitler, Göring, Goebbels, Hess and Himmler, as well as many *Gauleiter*, gradually discovered that to conquer a whole modern society requires time and technical ability. Amazing as the extent of their subsequent victory was in the struggle for hegemony in Germany, the Nazis were not prepared for frontal assaults upon all the entrenched power of political, military, economic and social institutions. They feared absorption by the conservative inertia of a professional army, a skilful bureaucracy, a tough capitalistic elite and the German masses. To have cast their lot with the radicals, a far from insignificant minority in their own ranks and throughout Germany in 1933–34, might have brought an earlier success, but the shadow of 9 November 1923, and even more of November 1918 – when internal factionalism weakened Germany in the face of her enemies – thrust them all almost against their will into the solution found after 30 June 1934; a silent revolution in permanence. For this revolution the SS was best equipped or could become so earlier than the other factions.

It is erroneous, however, to carry back to early 1933 the deep antipathies (SA-SS and ultimately party-SS) of later years. Even the party-SA polarity, prominent in the Stennes case and as late as May 1933 in Pomerania, emphasised differences among flamboyant personalities and quarrels over money rather than ideological principles. The party in 1933 was not well disciplined, and it was not conservative. Röhm held the SA remarkably well in hand right until his demise; its atrocities were more or less intentional. Hitler was in the habit of using both SA and Political Organisation as power-political instruments as a kind of one-two punch, whereby it was wholly incidental which fist flew first. Both were to expand rapidly in 1933 (as indeed the SS did too), far too rapidly. But whereas the party's newcomers were civilians who admired the success of political soldiering, the SA's growth came from the *Stahlhelm*, who were ex-soldiers. Furthermore, the structural weaknesses of the NSDAP hierarchy, marked by localistic *Gauleiter* and the wound left by the Strassers, were greater than those of the SA due to Stennes and other *Landsknecht*-figures, for Röhm had built a formidable command structure. Thus, the party was more quickly overrun by opportunists than the SA, more easily persuaded to adjust to a long, drawn-out conflict with existing institutions, and ultimately ready to accept the substitution of the smaller, better disciplined and apparently more subordinate SS for the SA as its instrument of force and violence. However, before all this could occur, the SA was to gather unto itself all the prerequisites of a state-within-a-state, to foreshadow the SS-State to come, indeed to form the matrix in which the SS ripened.

No small part of the SA's power came from the survival of the notion in nationalist, militarist and conservative circles that the SA contained 'good human material' which could be exploited in rearming Germany. Coupled with the loose thinking of men like Schleicher and Papen that the Nazis could be tamed and harnessed was the plan to use the SA domestically against the Marxists without involving the 'unpolitical' *Reichswehr*. There was thus just enough acceptance by Hitler's Nationalist partners of both a domestic terror role and a share in defence responsibilities for the SA to permit Röhm to penetrate rapidly in 1933 not only into police and defence activities but the operations of numerous administrative bureaus at national and regional levels. While party personnel proceeded to enter state positions of all kinds with equal rapidity, the SA tended to set up a kind of secondary governmental framework beside the state authority. In all these operations, Himmler and the SS played a supporting role. The SS had few if any unique activities in the seizure of power and the co-ordination; everything it did, SA units did too. Yet by the winter of 1933–34, older differentiating tendencies – particularly with regard to police activities – combined with reawakened antipathies and new political alliances had thrust the SS into the front ranks of the defenders of the National Socialist edifice, while Röhm's power system, of which the SS was still a part, threatened to secede. Not the act of secession (the non-existent putsch) but the credibility of SA secession and belief in the seriousness of the consequences, due to the extent of the SA-State, led Hitler to strike on 30 June. The top leadership of the SS was to contribute to the notion of the danger – out of motives of ambition, loyalty to Hitler and a conviction that the SS was better equipped to fulfil the tasks Röhm had set for the SA – anti-capitalist, anti-clerical, above all, anti-Semitic – which it held to be as vital to National Socialism as did the men the SS killed.

The peculiar blend of random lawlessness and calculated political crime found in the SS murders of 30 June–3 July 1934, can be discovered in the performance of the *Hilfspolizei* (Auxiliary Police) as early as February 1933. Indeed, the strange pedigree of the June 1934 'night of the long knives' traces back to the Feme murders of 1921–23. There too a bloody amateurism was combined with cool, ruthless *Realpolitik*. There was nothing peculiarly SS in the Auxiliary Police arrangements; yet from this short-lived institution grew two of the most characteristic SS organisations, the *Totenkopfverbände* (Death's Head units) and the *Verfügungstruppe* (Special Duty troops or VT).

The Nazis' main concern in February was the elimination of the maximum number of their rivals in the coming election. They wished to come as close as possible to a monopoly of influence over public opinion before 5 March. In a sense, all they needed to do was to expand their 1932 techniques of electioneering propaganda and terror. Often in 1932 the police had failed to do them either much harm or much good; the Nazis' real concern was the paramilitary organisations of the *Reichsbanner* and *Roter Frontkämpferbund* (Social Democratic and the Communist left). Most of the 'martyrs' of SA and SS died in brawls or ambushes at the hands of their opponents, not from the police, who were forbidden to use firearms. After 30 January it was certainly not the police who accounted for the many deaths and injuries among SA and SS, beginning

with Hans Maikowski in Berlin returning from the torch procession. The
Nazi effort to capture the police, seen first in Prussia on 11 February with
the creation of a Superior Police Leader 'West' by Göring as Prussian
commissarial Interior Minister, was not defensive but offensive – to
procure tools of repression. Furthermore, it was tactically important to
moderate the civil-war atmosphere which pure SA and SS repression
would have created, not only in behalf of the elections but to lull Social
Democrats and other future victims into a postponement of serious
resistance until it was too late. The designation of only specified SA and
SS units as Auxiliary Police, with special armbands, had a triple advantage: (1) the reluctance of some veteran police officials to use violence
against the left could thereby be bypassed, (2) the authority of the police
was maintained for future use and (3) the revolutionary radicalism of
some units could be controlled. It is not surprising that the first auxiliary
police were in effect a kind of SA and SS *Streifendienst* (Military Police)
created on 15 February. Individuals and groups of SA and SS men had to
be prevented from molesting innocent persons and alerting the leftist
parties by unco-ordinated raids on their headquarters. On 17 February
Göring ordered the Prussian police to use their firearms freely, and a
week later on 22 February he issued orders for the creation of an
Auxiliary Police force of 50,000, a doubling of the existing Prussian
police force of 54,712. They were to carry firearms and to remain in
intact units of SA, SS and *Stahlhelm* in the proportion of 5:3:1 (25,000,
15,000 and 5,000), wherein the SS was greatly over-represented and the
Stahlhelm under-represented. Their actual employment was reserved for
the Interior Ministry of Prussia and its subordinate police officials, who
only gradually and incompletely were replaced by SA, SS and party
personnel by 5 March. Their commanders were to be police officials. The
first official Auxiliary Police in Berlin were a direct forerunner of the
garrisoned SS-*Verfügungstruppe*. On 24 February 200 hand-picked SS
men were especially armed and garrisoned under Wolf von Helldorf,
commander of SA-*Gruppe* Berlin-Brandenburg. The remainder of the
subsequent Auxiliary Police in Berlin were SA volunteers, operating in
detachments from their regiments and battalions. They were supposed to
work with the regular precinct stations of the police.

  Auxiliary Police appeared in February in such National Socialist
strongholds as Brunswick and Thuringia, but detailed negotiations were
still necessary in Brunswick on 25 February to win approval of a specific

action desired by an SS commander. The men were not permitted to wear their uniforms, and authority was withdrawn again after a specific action. In several *Länder* (Hessen and Saxony), there were no Auxiliary Police, due to Socialist interior ministries. Nevertheless, even before the excuse of the *Reichstag* fire and the Emergency Decree of 28 February 1933, Auxiliary Police units of SA and SS were engaged in terroristic acts. Especially in the Rhineland and Ruhr areas with their intense 'class war' atmosphere, SA and SS Auxiliary Police rounded up workers and labour leaders as alleged Communists and beat them in the police prisons. While in Hanover province – still briefly presided over by the Social Democrat Gustav Noske – the police retained the upper hand, Göring's purge of the police system in the Ruhr and Rhineland led to the overrunning of the regular police headquarters by 'auxiliaries' who were without central direction and control.

The Emergency Decree of 28 February created the conditions necessary for the future SS–State to flourish, yet it appears highly improbable that the SS had anything to do with starting the fire in the *Reichstag*. While it is less certain that the SA can be as definitely excluded, it now seems that if young Marinus van der Lubbe did receive some help, this came from the Berlin SA, with or without Göring's knowledge and not as part of a Hitler conspiracy among Göring, Goebbels, Röhm and Himmler – as is still sometimes alleged. Röhm and Himmler were in Munich, as was Heydrich although not Daluege. Daluege and Helldorf rapidly mobilised SS and SA-*Hilfspolizei* to aid hand-picked, regular police units in their arrests before morning on 28 February. There is no question that all units worked from lists prepared long in advance, yet neither their alacrity nor their thoroughness are proof of a plot to burn the *Reichstag*, but rather of a plot against civil liberties, which was already suspected by astute political observers. On the basis of Frick and Gürtner's 'Decree for the Protection of People and State' of 28 February, the Auxiliary Police when acting 'on orders of the National Government' were empowered to arrest persons; stop public meetings; raid homes, businesses and meeting places; seize property and printed matter; and intercept mail, telegrams and telephone calls. Their influence was no longer confined to Prussia and Nazi strongholds but could be applied anywhere in the Reich by the Hitler regime. A wave of arrests, beatings and even killings followed in which former Communists and suspected Communists were included with card-carrying ones. SA, SS and *Stahlhelm* units were rushed into service as guards at public buildings, power plants and frontier outposts. An atmosphere of public emergency was created for the election day, aided by Göring's pronouncement that he would fight Communism not with the State Police but 'with those down below there' – the SA and the SS. Intimidation extended well beyond the ranks of the Communists through the SPD (Social Democratic Party) to the Centre Party and even against the erstwhile Nazi allies, the DNVP.

Nevertheless, in spite of true stories of SA and SS 'supervision' of the voting on 5 March, the election must be recorded as the last German one in which secret ballots and genuine alternatives could not be successfully counteracted by implied or actual threats of retaliation. The Nazis received exactly 43.9 per cent of the votes despite all their repressive tactics. They still needed the votes of the Papen-Hugenberg bloc to govern legitimately. Clearly, the revolution had not gone far enough. The street-terror techniques of 1932 had proved insufficient, and the capture of the state apparatus had scarcely begun. Instead of having won, the Nazis had their biggest battles still ahead of them. But now they had regained their own momentum, while their opponents were rapidly to lose theirs. The task of the coming months was obviously to create chaos and then to 'liberate' the German people from it while simultaneously reorganising society along the lines desired by the 'order-bringers'. This general conception was shared by widely divergent supporters of the new regime: conservative revolutionaries in Papen's circle; business and military leaders of the right like Schacht and Blomberg; party theorists such as Hess, Goebbels and Rosenberg; the practical politicians Hitler and Göring; and Röhm's SA leadership just as definitely as by Himmler's SS officers.

As early as 5 and 6 March, groups of SA and SS men entered public buildings and raised swastika banners on the flagpoles. They were not always Auxiliary Police with white armbands, nor were they always successful at first. When they met resistance, they called for reinforcements and sometimes ended by destroying property, notably records and furniture. 'A revolution is, after all, a revolution, even when it comes to power legally,' wrote Goebbels in his diary. This was a revolution by command. A show of violence was needed to help topple bureaucracies and vestiges of local autonomy. Thus, on the one hand, the Auxiliary Police now made their appearance everywhere, symbol of the revolutionary people's justice, while on the other hand, mobile details of 'unauthorised' SA and SS perpetrated acts of savagery and licence. In Liegnitz the press building of the SPD '*Volkszeitung*' had been under guard by SS Auxiliary Police. On 10 March it was 'seized' by SA Auxiliary Police under the leadership of the police; during the following night an SA squad from Breslau led by an *Oberführer* broke in and destroyed or stole much of the equipment. Here and elsewhere the blame was put on Communists in SA uniform – just like the accomplices of van der Lubbe, according to Göring.

One of the chief Nazi concerns was the possible development of centres of armed resistance in Hamburg, Saxony, Hessen, Bavaria, Württemberg and Baden. The SA and the SS played a vital role in the skilful *coups d'état* in these areas. Formations of SA and SS gathered in front of government buildings, demanding the raising of swastika flags and the formation of Nazi regimes. Local police, not wishing bloodshed and possible retribution, refrained from dispersing them; the *Reichswehr* refused to intervene. Thereupon Frick, acting on the basis of paragraph two of the 28 February Emergency Decree, appointed Reich Police Commissars 'to maintain peace and order'. Intimidation of local regimes, who resigned out of fear of bloodshed and civil war involving an overestimated Communist threat, was thus combined with actual bloodshed and violence, which justified the intervention of Berlin against the autonomy of the *Länder*, more or less in the spirit of the Nationalist right's ideal of *Reichsreform*. No Reich Police Commissar was an SS officer. Dietrich von Jagow in Württemberg and Manfred von Killinger in Saxony were SA-*Gruppenführer* and former free corps leaders; some police commissioners were party leaders like Robert Wagner in Baden, discharged from the *Reichswehr* for his support of the 1923 putsch. In Bavaria the free corps general Ritter von Epp, a strong exponent of the Nazis since 1923, assumed this role and assigned Himmler the post of Munich's Commissarial Police President. These Reich Police Commissars gave way quickly to so-called Reich Commissars (occasionally, as with Epp, the same person), who created commissarial cabinets to replace the collapsed regimes. Thus, irrespective of the majorities in local parliaments, the Nazis were able to form majority cabinets in which the interior ministries controlling the police always fell to them. This made the use of Auxiliary Police a matter of course. It also opened the way to replace police officials outside Prussia with SA and SS officers. Moreover, these Reich Police Commissars and Reich Commissars were authorised to commandeer the party and its formations in case of serious armed resistance. This resistance never came, and the post of Reich Commissar was eliminated. Instead, in a matter of weeks Hitler had named eleven leading Nazis, mostly *Gauleiter*, as *Reichsstatthalter* (Viceroys of the Realm) with Hindenburg's approval. They were in effect local dictators.

There was little difference in the employment of the SS and the SA in the months of March and April. Since there were far more SA than SS members, the latter were perhaps already slightly more dependable as executors of official policy in contrast with the SA's more numerous private vendettas and general hell-raising. This might account for the relatively greater employment of SS as auxiliaries, as much as any pre-1933 plan to use the SS primarily as police while the SA developed as a people's militia. Indeed, it was the SA rather than the SS which laid claim to the offices of police president and police director. SA and SS men alike were frustrated by their failure to capture the local police apparatus wholesale in March. They formed their own Battalions for Special Purposes at this time, whose headquarters rapidly became jails and torture chambers – the so-called Bunker. While the Berlin variety were notorious, they appeared elsewhere and simultaneously with the first concentration camps, located in deserted barracks, factories, wharves, etc. The purpose of both Bunker and concentration camp (KZ or KL) was dual: to have a place for enemies other than the jails controlled by conservative officials, and to have secret dens where prisoners could not be found by the police or by their friends. There was nothing uniquely SS about either phenomenon; at all times there were also SA and SS auxiliaries as guards in official jails. Significantly, however, SA and SS men seem to have been always separately assigned and not mixed in jails, bunkers and camps. Not yet a result of antipathy in most cases, this was rather an expression of the difficulty of asserting authority over the groups except through their own personal leaders. In fact, it is likely that Röhm and Himmler in Munich were temporarily in a poor state of communication with their regional commanders, who behaved like local despots alone or in collaboration with the party leaders who had become commissarial ministers. In Brunswick an anti-Semitic and anti-*Stahlhelm* terror exploded prematurely in March on the authority of Minister President Dietrich Klagges and the leadership of SS battalion and regimental commanders. Yet Klagges and the SS could actually be restrained better than many *Gauleiter* and SA-*Gruppenführer*; this terror was 'cancelled'.

Kurt Daluege beat Himmler to access to State Police authority by becoming Prussian Special Commissar in Göring's Ministry of the Interior on 6 February. Göring's political sense, like that of his master, told him not to concentrate all the police power in one man's or one agency's hands. He used the select battalions of Nazi Police Major Wecke in Berlin for his personal security. He made Rudolf Diels Chief of the Political Police (IA-*Chef*) under a Police President (Admiral Levetzow) who was neither an SA nor SS officer; and he placed Daluege as a watchdog in the police section of the ministry while he selected as Permanent Secretary a business-oriented, practical bureaucrat, Ludwig Grauert, to replace the monarchist Herbert von Bismarck. Helldorf, the dashing SA-*Gruppenführer*, he kept at arm's length, with only the police presidium in Potsdam for a prize. Daluege was of course Göring's liaison with the SS, and to some extent with Himmler. However, Daluege and Himmler, though *Duz-Freunde* (privileged to use '*Du*'), were nearly open rivals in the spring months of 1933. Daluege seems to have understood his function in the Prussian police primarily in terms of his old intelligence role in the Potsdamer Strasse. He expanded his liaison 'bureau' into a clean-up detail and was rewarded by being put in charge of the police section of the ministry while he went on collecting incriminating information from IA-files, from denunciations, from SS commanders, and by watching the intrigues of party, state and business leaders in Berlin. He preferred to court the SA, Göring, businessmen and state officials, rather than Himmler, his nominal superior.

Himmler was just as interested in securing a state position, however minor, as a foothold. He was swept into office along with Röhm and the old Party Guard of Munich. In the critical weeks before and after election day, Röhm and Himmler, the Bavarian SA and SS, were assigned the special task of checkmating any efforts at a Bavarian secession with possible international repercussions. Probably this chimera was born of the 1919–23 era, like the much-feared, but largely illusory, Communist uprisings in Berlin and the Ruhr. However, it must be emphasised that just as Röhm did not even receive an executive position, having to return to the old staff relationship with Epp of 1919, so Himmler became the subordinate of *Gauleiter* Adolf Wagner, commissarial Bavarian Interior Minister. Heydrich modestly entered state employment as chief of the political bureau of the Munich police. Himmler's promotion to the newly created post of *Politischer Polizeikommandeur Bayerns* on 2 April did not change his subordinate status, though it widened considerably the area of his and Heydrich's legal influence over the police apparatus. Himmler and Heydrich created a 152-person office out of 133 transfers from other police posts (including some of the most notorious old undercover cops like Heinrich Müller, Franz Josef Huber and Friedrich Panzinger). Some nineteen temporary appointments were probably SS personnel, possibly I-C (SD) in some cases. Himmler was forced, however, to give up his post as Munich police chief to August Schneidhuber, the SA-General. Röhm was collecting offices for the SA, becoming a Permanent Secretary in the Bavarian government in charge of the so-called *Sicherheitspolizei* (Security Police) – actually just the Auxiliary Police (SA, SS and *Stahlhelm*). He also commanded the various SA commissars in local communities, as he did in Prussia and elsewhere. Yet Daluege's shift to the command of the Prussian *Landespolizei* (State Police) – a comparable move – would turn out to be of more lasting import for Daluege and the SS. Röhm did not move to consolidate SA power over the state apparatus as did Himmler, Heydrich and Daluege. The apparent strength of the SA 'beyond party and state' led Röhm astray.

The differentiation between the SA and the SS that set in with the autumn of 1933 had its origins in the spring. When the membership of the two organisations were turned loose on the German population after the elections, Hitler expected 'abuses', 'injustice' and 'excesses'. These he regarded with a cynical relativism as valuable lessons to his enemies and even his friends. He expected to 'correct' some of them, but in the majority of such cases in the past, he had merely made a show of punishment – or if he were personally irritated, had made an example of one or two luckless devils. From the very beginning he carried on an ambiguous, on-again, off-again policy of restraints on the SA to confuse his allies on the right. Over a period of many months, he succeeded in this; he also succeeded in confusing the SA. The ultimate failure of the SA to resist its own emasculation in June 1934 was an important result of the very same process that led a significant proportion of officers and men in the Storm Troops to lose faith in Hitler, in the revolutionary slogans and promises of the *Kampfzeit* (the time of struggle: pre-1933), and in the ideal of political soldierdom. Their confusion as to what was expected of them was perhaps no greater than many in the SS, but Himmler weaned the SS away from the spontaneous radicalism and violence of the resentful *déclassés* and gave it leaders who understood how to mould it into an instrument of revolutionary terror and control that did not become confused by tactical shifts in state policy. The SA was not intrinsically incapable of discipline and training. Had it been a smaller organisation and therefore forced to restrict its ambitions – as was the SS, for example – to the police or to absorbing the *Reichswehr*, Röhm and his top leaders could not have been tempted to try so many avenues to power and fail in all of them.

The theatrical character of the 'legal revolution' which appears in the Potsdam Day ceremony, the passage of the Enabling Act by the *Reichstag*, the 'quiet and bloodless' pogrom of the *Judenboykott* of 1 April, and the celebration of May Day as a Day of National Unity conceals from modern-day observers the violence, confusion and spontaneous radical-ism of the Nazi seizure of power. Few persons living in the Reich in March and April 1933 could cherish the illusion that soon all would be as before. The contrary illusion, that soon everything would be different and much better, was in the atmosphere. It was felt that the violence and the terror must be short-lived and quickly restricted to enemies of the state. Genuine efforts to restore order on the part of countless members of the right in the old state apparatus, and even among the new officials such as Rudolf Diels in his newly created Berlin *Geheimes Staats-Polizeiamt* (Gestapa) in the Prinz Albrechtsstrasse, lulled Germans into accepting Nazi theatrics as a New Order – even while the Storm Troops and *Schutzstaffeln* poured out the resentment of two frustrated genera-tions upon the defenceless bodies of their victims at Dachau and the Columbia Haus, Kemna, Durrgoy and Oranienburg concentration camps.

Not the least significant phase of Nazi radicalism in March and April 1933 was the onslaught against the business world – industrial and commercial. While SA and SS often formed the vanguard of 'committees' and 'flying squads', party rank-and-file of distinctly middle-class origin made up a goodly proportion of the scarcely veiled shake-down and blackmail enterprises which intimidated and infuriated businessmen and managers. Numerous cases occurred where boycott actions against chain and department stores leading to violence and plun-dering were initiated by functionaries of the NSBO (National Socialist Factory Cell Organisation) and Adrian von Renteln's Combat League (*Kampfbund*) of the Commercial Middle Class – and then executed by SA and SS. However, the SS were themselves initiators though not the exclusive executors of programmes to recruit paying supporters or sponsors among both 'Aryan' and 'non-Aryan' managers of large firms, the enforced 'contributions' of automobiles, motorcycles and trucks to the SS, and the forcible requisitioning of Masonic and Jewish community buildings as SS headquarters. The SA was, of course, not inferior to the SS in these exploits. Its speciality was the naming of commissars and even directors to local firms, who were obliged to pay them a salary for the privilege of not being interfered with. The heavily arranged boycott of Jewish businesses on 1 April may be understood as a technique of Goebbels and Hitler to concentrate the attention of foreign observers and native Germans on the Jewish issue, to divert them and perhaps minimally even the Nazi radicals from the unrestrained expression of Nazi envy and hatred against all the propertied class. The success of this manoeuvre, at least domestically, demonstrated the superior advantages of disciplined units, whether of SA or SS, over self-constituted 'committees' in which SA or SS men fulfilled the function of executors of random mob violence. During the coming year the SS was more effectively subjugated to this ideal than the SA, though never completely.

We have already seen that Goebbels's and Hitler's conception of manipulating staged events for dramatic effect made excellent use of the SA and the SS as symbols of Revolution and Order. For several years already uniformed platoons of SA and SS men had paraded into the churches, to underscore the Nazi appeal to Germans who were both pious and nationalistic. These demonstrations reached their height in 1933 during the struggle for a National Church. Similarly, on 21 March the Potsdam square was lined on one side with *Reichswehr* and on the other with SA and SS in shiny new uniforms, all in perfect order. Again, on 23 March the outside of the Kroll Opera was surrounded with SS in formation, while the inside was lined with SA, arms akimbo, against the walls of the corridors and in the chamber around the benches of the SPD and the Centre Party. Already in the *Kampfjahre* (1918–33, years of struggle) the pictures show a change from a scattering of black-capped SS in a confused crowd of civilians and brownshirts surrounding the speakers to a rigidly aligned platform squad of six or eight SS men in black caps and breeches, with the SA stationed at entrances and in rows at the back and sides of the audience. Intimidation was becoming massive and shifting to a demonstration of potential terror rather than outright violence. In the boycott action of 1 April and again in the seizure of the union headquarters on 2 May, SA and SS were employed essentially to prevent random violence and destruction by enthusiastic and venal participants from the NSBO and von Renteln's *Kampfbund*. That individuals and units of both SA and SS in April and May 1933 too readily joined in gratuitous abuse of persons whom Goebbels, Göring, Ley or Frick would have spared, or stole properties belonging to national-minded individuals or to the German people, was indeed a temporary inadequacy – which Hitler and the rest were prepared to overlook, provided Himmler and Röhm could bring their men into line when it seemed absolutely necessary. In fact, Röhm never lost the ability to do so, even if Himmler did outshine him in this matter of commanding discipline. The ultimate crime of the SA was not radicalism and indiscipline, but too much overt ambition. Himmler and the SS leadership learned better to keep silent and to wait.

After the passage of the Enabling Act on 23 March, the essential task of party, SA and SS became the piecemeal conquest of the remaining centres of resistance. The maintenance of disorder as a technique for dissolving old obligations and loyalties had to be balanced by the ability to cut off disorder at any time and place that demanded and was ripe for *Gleichschaltung* (co-ordination). Co-ordination was accomplished in two or more stages – never at one dramatic swoop. First came infiltration, often based on a few persons already in a bureau; meanwhile Nazi agitation for massive changes and even non-compliance with the bureau's measures could go on. Next there arrived one or more commissars, often SA, occasionally party officials or an SS man, to supervise the top leadership. With semi-official status, these commissars collected 'information' with the help of the other Nazis in the agency, interfered with operations they thought deleterious to the revolution and arranged for the employment of friends and relatives and members of their SA, SS, or party formation. Later, in most cases by the summer of 1933, the office or agency would receive a Nazi chief, a Nazi majority – or minimally, as in the cases of the *Reichswehr*, the Foreign Office or big business firms, a collaborating leadership. At this time open resistance to the agency's acts had to cease, although undercover acts of disobedience and policy twisting might continue where 'non-National Socialist' survivals still had to be tolerated. Here the older conflicts within the Nazi system resumed their force: party, SA and SS struggled for priority and 'leverage'. Furthermore, since the tougher resistance to *Gleichschaltung* came from their rightist partners rather than from the supposedly dangerous Marxist and liberal 'November criminals' (the revolutionaries of 1918) in the state apparatus, the task of the Nazis remained that of dissolving the old authoritarian structures without destroying the instruments of control and conquest which they wished to conquer. It was no mean accomplishment of Hitler and his lieutenants to have preserved the *Reichswehr*, the Foreign Office, and the conglomerates and banks from the onslaught of his radicals and the rivalries of *Gauleiter*, without succumbing wholly to the inner purposes of these institutions. Naturally, their powers of resistance – enough to preserve them from total destruction or subjugation for many years – were nonetheless limited by short-sighted estimates by their leaders of such factors as Communism, world opinion, and above all of Hitler and his chief lieutenants, including Röhm and Himmler.

Hitler's concept of the SA as political soldiers and Röhm's concept of political soldiers were not diametrically opposed, but the potential differences between the two possibilities became exaggerated during 1933, so that after a year of 'plastering over the cracks', Hitler destroyed the SA's chances for either alternative. The SS then occupied the former role, only to develop the same alternative emphasis on soldiering in the *Waffen*-SS of 1940–45. Thus, the path of development taken by the SS was laid down for it by Hitler and Röhm and to some extent by the *Reichswehr* leadership. It was the short-sighted decision of the *Reichswehr* leaders in 1934 to drive the devil (Röhm) out with Beelzebub that placed Himmler's SS squarely in the path of the conservative generals between 1938 and 1944.

Confronted almost immediately by Hitler's policy of co-operation with the *Reichswehr*, Röhm developed an octopus-strategy of seizing a maximum number of power positions for the SA in the new regime. He sought to develop a monopoly of force outside the *Reichswehr* and to outmanoeuvre 'the old codgers' for whom he had a free corps captain's contempt. We have seen that the SA had made steady progress in the capture of the police systems in the *Länder*, even in Göring's bailiwick. Similarly, through the device of *Kommissare* z.b.V. (Commissars for Special Duties) responsible to himself and scattered throughout all levels of administration, Röhm secured leverage and listening posts. His most important coup, however, was the piecemeal absorption of the *Stahlhelm* between April and September 1933. He accomplished this with Hitler's help, for indeed it was in the Nazi interest to deny to its allies of the right an independent paramilitary arm. However, Röhm was also denying the

Reichswehr a valuable ally, he believed, forcing them to come to him for the 'good material' with which to build a great army. Starting in June with the transfer to Röhm's authority of the *Jungstahlhelm* – the 'replacements' from post-front generations – as well as their youth groups to the *Hitlerjugend*, the *Stahlhelm* was further hollowed out in July by the transfer of *Wehrstahlhelm* (all men under thirty-five) as a separate formation to Röhm's command. On 31 October 1933, the separate formation was done away with inside the SA, adding 500,000 men to the SA regulars. On 1 December the remaining *Kernstahlhelm* was split into a 450,000-man unit known as the SA-Reserve I (men between thirty-five and forty, mostly veterans) and another larger group of 1.5 million known as SA-Reserve II. Ultimately this spectacular SA victory not only drove the generals into the arms of Himmler and Heydrich but weakened the SA by watering down its revolutionary character. The SA of July 1934 that took its own emasculation lying down might be said to have been destroyed by the very 'middle class rot' which Röhm had preached against for so long.

Yet this was not the picture Röhm, Hitler, or the *Reichswehr* had of the SA at the Bad Reichenhall conference (near Berchtesgaden) on 1–3 July. The army had just completed its three-month pilot project ('short course') in SA training and was ready to undertake a full-scale training programme, as well as the systematic integration of the SA into the border and customs defence systems as part of an overall militia-defence network. Röhm intended to and partially did create an SA elite of 250,000, the *Ausbildungswesen* (AW), or 'training system', under the former (and future) SS officer F.W. Krüger, to tap the talents of the *Reichswehr* while he prepared to lay down the cadre of a future German People's Army in the SA units assigned to the Border Defence. Blomberg and Reichenau had given up on the *Stahlhelm* and Seldte; in fact they now hoped to woo 'the best part of the SA' away from the party while quickly building up a strong militia to protect Germany from a preventative war. Although they feared the radicalism of the SA, they admired its vitality; they hoped to bring it under constant surveillance and ultimately military discipline. Hitler made it perfectly clear that the *Reichswehr* and the SA were of equal status:

> This army of the political soldiers of the German Revolution has no wish to take the place of our army or to enter into competition with it… The relation of the SA to the Army must be the same as that of the political leadership to the Army.

Hitler's ambiguity of language paralleled the regulations for the AW, which gave them a Reich budget beyond the reach of the *Reichswehr* but prohibited their acquisition of weapons outside *Reichswehr* channels. In F.W. Krüger's file notes for July 1933 lie the elements of the SA of 1935, a veterans' organisation and pre-service training unit for high school and college youths; yet these same notes reveal an ambitious SA programme of penetrating the *Reichswehr* with its ideologically selected trainees from the high schools and universities. Indeed, the men close to Röhm in the summer of 1933 were moving toward a conception of the SA as a future military elite with its members in all-important parts of the social and political system, a people's *Junker*-dom with its own inner elite in the form of an officers' corps composed of free corps commanders, former *Reichswehr* officers, political soldier-statesmen, administrative wizards, revolutionary intellectuals and artists, and university students as cadets. There was no special status of any kind for the SS.

To realise this conception, it was necessary to avoid unnecessary clashes with potential allies. The revolutionaries of yesterday had to become outwardly respectable. Although serious efforts along these lines were made by Röhm and throughout the SA – many of them ridiculous, some of them fairly successful – generally the speed and complete success of the initial seizure of power had given the average SA man, or SS man for that matter, little time to prepare himself psychologically for the slower upward pull to respectability. Accustomed to self-help and a goodly portion of eye-winking at their foibles by superiors, the majority of men still engaged in brawling with a vengeance. The result was a wave of protests from *Reichswehr*, SS, party and citizens, with some efforts at repression. Expulsions from the SA and the SS became the order of the day. With the summer a gradual selection process began to take form in both the SA and the SS whereby those persons who could not conform to regulations and take out their violence on official victims were gradually removed from positions of prominence and increasingly disciplined.

In this context the struggle for a separate SA jurisdiction and the creation of a special SA *Feldpolizei* (Internal Police Force), represent a self-correcting mechanism, as well as an escape from the control of lingering survivals of the rule of law. As early as 28 April 1933, a law was passed creating a disciplinary authority for the services (*Dienststrafgewalt*) in the SA and SS whereby unit commanders received state authority to punish crimes committed by their subordinates. The reintroduction of the 1898 code of military justice in the *Reichswehr* on 12 May 1933 gave rise to SA efforts to achieve the same complete severance from civilian authority. On 31 July Röhm cautioned SA members that non-service-connected acts of violence against opponents were not yet covered by SA justice and could be prosecuted by the police. Kerrl, the Prussian Minister of Justice, ordered his *Feldgendarmerie* not to prosecute SA and SS members unless caught *in flagrante delicto* without first getting the approval of their commanding officers. Röhm decreed in October that arrests of SA members be made only by the newly created *Feldjägerkorps*, accompanied by ordinary police. The law of 1 December 1933 for the securing of the unity of party and state expressly confirmed the principle of separate SA justice where derelictions of duty were involved, while the Service Discipline Order of 12 December 1933, limited the authority of the commanders to service-connected acts.

The SA-*Feldpolizei* were formed by Göring out of the toughest SA personnel of the Hedemannstrasse and General-Pape Strasse 'bunker' in Berlin. Actually dating only from the summer of 1933 and restricted to the Berlin-Brandenburg-SA district, they were soon replaced by the Prussia-wide *Feldjägerkorps*, whose cadre they became as of 7 October. The latter were formed in groups of 65–100 known as *Bereitschaften* or *Hundertschaften* (police terms also adopted by SS units set up at this time for riots and other emergencies), to co-operate with Rudolf Diels's Gestapa. Subsidised by private sources, these SA police troops spread throughout the Reich before their dissolution in 1936. Göring did not trust the *Feldjäger*, however. He sponsored the development of his own armed police regiment under Major Walter Wecke, the *Landespolizeigruppe* 'Hermann Göring', which played a significant role in the purge of 30 June 1934, and also survived until 1936, the date of Himmler's complete police monopoly.

We have insisted that the SS in its make-up in 1933 was not intrinsically more disciplined or respectable than the SA. Nevertheless, from Himmler's closing of membership in April 1933 to the introduction of the SS's special oath to Adolf Hitler on 9 November 1933, it developed bases for reliability beyond the power of the SA. Moreover, its smaller scope, limited potential and Himmler's concentration on the police power gave it relative freedom from powerful enemies, such as the *Reichswehr*, the party and the business world. Above all, Hitler and Göring did not need to fear Himmler, as they did fear Röhm not only as a rival but also as a blunderer who could upset the Nazi apple cart.

Both the SS and the SA doubled their membership between 30 January 1933 and May 1933, the SS going from 50,000 to over 100,000, the SA from 300,000 to about 500,000 before the addition of *Stahlhelm* units. However, where Röhm proceeded to incorporate a million more men from the *Stahlhelm* into his gigantic edifice, Himmler stopped all but a trickle of actual additions, to allow his processing procedures to catch up. The fifty *Standarten* were urged to develop three *Sturmbanne* (battalions), each of four *Stürme* (companies), and to fill these out to 100 each, but the formation of additional units was strictly forbidden. The temporary closing of SS membership, a technique already employed in October 1932, was borrowed from the party, which resorted to the same tactic in May. Thus, the SS not only strengthened its elite appearance but identified itself effectively with the party at a time when the SA seemed intent on accepting everybody and anybody.

Probably a more decisive factor in the long run, however, was the creation of specialised SS units at first within and later alongside the general membership. That this was not an exclusive SS procedure is shown by the formation of the separately garrisoned Auxiliary Police units of SA men as early as February and the parallel development of the so-called *Gruppenkommandos* z.b.V., Special Duty units for terror purposes attached to the SA-*Gruppe* headquarters. The SA-*Feldpolizei* is another case in point. Above all, the creation of the AW in July was a step toward the formation of an SA elite.

The first distinctive SS formation of 1933 was the *Sonderkommando* 'Berlin' (Special Detail for Berlin) begun by Sepp Dietrich in Berlin in March with 120 selected SS men as a *Stabswache* for Hitler's chancellery. From the beginning this unit was armed and designed as a self-contained combat force. It is referred to as a regiment (*Standarte* Adolf Hitler) as early as September 1933, with the feudal-sounding *Leibstandarte* (literally body-regiment, i.e. the personal regiment) added a few months later. Sepp Dietrich had made it his business to remain as a personal bodyguard of Hitler throughout 1932, thereby consolidating the prior claim of the SS to be the traditional *Führer* guard. The right to arm openly and to be detached from the main body of political soldiers created the basis for its participation in the purge of 30 June 1934, as well as its role thereafter as the nucleus of a future field SS (*Waffen*-SS). It is improbable that this latter development was the intention of Sepp Dietrich or Heinrich Himmler at the time, but the idea of protecting the *Führer* from an SA mutiny was certainly real enough. Hitler's choice of an armed SS unit for this protective purpose is also interesting: he did not choose a *Reichswehr* unit or a unit of Major Wecke's (Göring's) Prussian police. Thus, the SS came in handy again, as in 1925 and 1930–31.

Besides the *Leibstandarte* Adolf Hitler, the future *Waffen*-SS had other *Sonderkommandos* as indirect antecedents in 1933. These too had obvious SA parallels. Corresponding to the *Gruppenkommandos* z.b.V. (variously, *Gruppenstäbe* z.b.V.: special divisional staffs) of the SA, several of the SS *Gruppen* set up in the spring of 1933 garrisoned *Hundertschaften* or *Politische Bereitschaften* (political ready-reserves) as police reserves, who were not given regular police duties but trained for riot duty and used for terror raids. These units became the future Special Duty SS troops or *Verfügungstruppe*. Secondly, SS-*Sonderkommandos* were despatched by *Standarten* and *Abschnitte* to set up and operate concentration camps such as Papenburg and Dachau, much as SA-*Standarten* operated their own quasi-legal prison camps by means of detachments of unemployed SA men. The difference was that the SA never created a separate type of organisation for this purpose, while the SS *Wachverbände* (guard units) became the dreaded *Totenkopfstandarten* (Death's Head regiments), later a part of the *Waffen*-SS. Both *Politische Bereitschaften* and the guard units played a part in the purge of the SA in 1934 along with the *Leibstandarte*. These measures were not exclusively their province, however. Not only were the top regional SS commanders and their staffs vitally important in the preparation and execution of the coup, but the planning and leadership came from the oldest separate SS organisation, Heydrich's *Sicherheitsdienst*.

Consisting first of Heydrich and three assistants, the SD had grown in 1932 to between twenty and thirty paid agents scattered throughout the Reich and the Nazi apparatus by 30 January 1933. About 200 'volunteers' in the world of business, government and education supplemented Heydrich's information-gathering system. These persons were not synonymous with the I-C personnel of the SS, although some of the latter joined the SD later, even after 1934. Heydrich certainly did not break contact with his embryo apparatus when 'reassigned' to Himmler's personal staff on 27 January 1933, and sent to Geneva as an SS representative along with Friedrich Wilhelm Krüger for the SA. Heydrich's actions there (unauthorised display of a large swastika banner) seem almost extracurricular. Heydrich continued 'on special duty' when put in charge of the Political Police section of the Munich Police Presidium on and after 9 March. The twenty-nine-year-old, who could not even get in to see the self-important *Kommissar* z.b.V. (Commissar for Special Duties) Daluege in the Prussian Interior Ministry on 15 March, rapidly set about weaving a net of SD men in and around Prussia by commissioning often very young lawyers and academics to act in Himmler's interests within the newly formed Political Police of neighbouring states, such as Württemberg, Baden, Saxony and Thuringia, as well as in Hessen-Darmstadt, Lübeck, Hamburg, Bremen and Mecklenburg. Indeed, Heydrich opened an SD office in Berlin's West End (Eichen-Allee 2) in a small villa, where he installed twenty-six-year-old Hermann Behrends, one of his earliest admirers, as his personal representative.

During the next few years, Heydrich's major rival for influence with Heinrich Himmler was Richard Walter Darré, the chief of the SS-*Rassenamt* (Racial Office), soon to become, on 28 June 1933, Reich Minister of Food and Agriculture. With its name changed to fit its ever-widening duties (*Rasse und Siedlungs Amt* – Race and Settlement Office), his still-diminutive organisation began in 1933, a growth which carried it past the SD in size if not in influence. In 1935 it became, alongside the administrative headquarters of the SD and SS, one of three Main Offices (*Hauptämter*). The Racial Office assumed a significance out of proportion to its couple of desks in the Munich SS headquarters for two reasons: Darré supplied Himmler with a pseudo-scientific 'intellectual' rationale for his elite corps, and Darré proceeded to form a branch of the SS out of his own independent political apparatus, the network of agricultural advisors to the *Gau-* and *Kreisleiter* (County Leaders) of the NSDAP. This Farm Policy Apparatus, headed by the Office for Farm Policy, dated back to 1930 and played a decisive role in many Nazi election upsets in farm areas. It was composed of fairly well-educated middle- and upper-class farmers with a community following. Though like the SD it included a number of young men beginning their careers, it also attracted a good many older persons with political experience. Some of these younger men joined the SS in 1931 and 1932, copying Darré, while the majority merely joined the party at this time but the SS only in 1933 and 1934. The latter rarely came through the SA.

In 1932 the SS Racial Office had a staff or advisory function in connection with the approval of new engagements and marriages of SS members, the approval of new applicants for the SS – especially upper ranks – and in granting officers' commissions. It should be remembered that in the depression new engagements and marriages were few and far between, especially in the lower middle class, from which the SS drew its membership; nevertheless there is evidence that not all of these were formally approved in advance in 1932 and 1933. Rather, the approval of the SS man's superior, usually the company or battalion commander, was forwarded to the Munich SS headquarters, often after the fact. Photographs, locks of hair, very occasionally a medical 'bill of health' on doctors' stationery, appear for 1933. The role of the Racial Office seems to have been largely limited to correspondence, advising and admonishing the commanders regarding criteria.

Himmler's reminiscences before the *Wehrmacht* officers in 1937 of examining 150–200 photographs a year of SS candidates probably dated not from 1929–30 as he implied but from 1931–32. Since there is no evidence for the use of photographs at the earlier date, and since photographs were required for officer candidates in the later period, it appears likely that what he recalled was the last step in the processing of promotions to officer status or original acceptances of new SS personnel at officer rank. The Racial Office's part in these procedures consisted of drawing up the regulations to be promulgated by the Leadership Staff or the SS Administrative Office, a new examination report form for the SS physicians (MUL) and correspondence with commanders and physicians.

During the period of mass recruiting in 1932 and 1933, there were a number of changes in the physical specifications for SS membership, notably age and height, representing a gradual tightening up for which the Racial Office was probably responsible. However, even the MUL had few or no racial criteria as such to follow, and the Racial Office staff were utterly incapable of checking on the mass of new candidates' records, not to mention those which never reached Munich or reached the headquarters without the data filled in. Darré could have devoted only very little time to this office during the hectic campaigning of 1932 and the first half of 1933, when he carried on the fight against Hugenberg in the agricultural pressure groups. When he moved to Berlin as minister, the office was moved there as well, but he was busier than ever. Nonetheless, the new SS branch actually began life at this time.

The real architects of the Race and Settlement Office (renamed in 1933) were Dr Bruno K. Schultz and Dr Horst Rechenbach, respectively an academic anthropologist–publicist and an army teacher of veterinary medicine. Their collaboration with Darré dated back to 1930, but their direct part in the SS began only in late 1932; in fact their full-time activity did not begin until 1934. Nevertheless, these two provided Darré, and thus Himmler, with the concept of the racial examiner, the white-coated technician with calipers and measuring tape employing standardised and scientific-looking ruled worksheets and number-letter combinations as symbols of human worth. Like the lawyers and academicians of the SD, these chosen few of the Racial Office helped the SS to appear 'scientific', thus helping to distinguish the SS officers' corps from the SA by giving them a sense of being on the inside track, of being winners, of being correct.

The press to join the SS in 1933 gave the Race and Settlement Office a double opportunity. First of all, it acquired a chance to acquire medically or academically trained agents and collaborators in the *Standarten* and regional staffs among the numerous physicians, professors and lawyers who clamoured for the opportunity to join an 'exclusive' Nazi unit. Secondly, it could begin to enforce a genuine screening at the time of admission, since commanders could no longer claim the necessity of a broad acceptance policy. The *Rassereferent* (race expert) at regional headquarters and the *Musterung* (a kind of army 'physical') of new recruits by this expert date from around late 1933 and early 1934. An especially important aspect of this new SS branch was its educational function, symbolised by the formation of a training division and the naming of education officers in all units, responsible for the general indoctrination of the men but especially for their training in 'racial eugenics', particularly racial anti-Semitism.

The idea of combining the settlement of SS men on farms with their placement in suburban garden homes came from Darré himself. It was almost fully developed in his 1930 book, *New Aristocracy of Blood and Soil*, but nothing could be done to apply it to the SS until he was in power. With the formation of the Reich Food Estate (RNS) on 15 July 1933, Darré had the mechanism for controlling agricultural production and to some extent the transfer of farmland. The RNS was in fact the Farm Policy Apparatus invested with state powers. Although it is probably untrue, as alleged, that the Nazi *Erbhof* (hereditary estate) and production control laws were first written in the Munich and Berlin offices of the SS Race and Settlement unit, the authors were Werner Willikens, Herbert Backe, Hermann Reischle and Wilhelm Meinberg, all except

Willikens in the SS since 1932 (Willikens joined in May 1933). Reischle and Meinberg started the Settlement Office and joined Rechenbach and Schultz to become pillars of the SS Race and Settlement Office. While these gentlemen were far too busy in 1933 reorganising German agriculture to plan in detail for SS settlement, junior academicians and lawyers with time on their hands were not hard to find in the SS. Before long there were elaborate plans for SS suburban housing developments, no end of financing schemes for the purchase of homes and farms and training programmes for new farmers. The race experts became specialists on race and settlement. Above all, they were recruited increasingly from the County Farm Leaders and State Farm Leaders of the Food Estate, the old-line personnel of Darré's apparatus who were increasingly strategic individuals in the countryside.

Thus, by the autumn of 1933, there was in embryo the SS state-within-a-state. It was largely obscured by the whole revolutionary process and more especially by the visibility of the 'SA state'. Nonetheless, the major parts of Himmler's apparatus for the conquest of state power were in existence, like the miniature hands, feet, nose and ears of a human foetus. Still delicate and quite underdeveloped, each of the SS offices and the command structure, the special units and the General SS – with its corps and divisional staffs, technicians, and sponsoring auxiliary – all were ready to be strengthened, to expand and to operate. Many of the leading lights of the period 1934–39 and some of the 'brass' of 1940–45 were in place or at least approaching the starting mark.

5

THE BETRAYAL

WINTER 1933 – 30 JUNE 1934

The brownshirted Storm Troops were the hallmark of the National Revolution in 1933. The SS – the men in the black coats – were somehow different, but they were merely one of many Nazi variants for Germans and foreign observers that year. Only a few who were 'in the know' grasped their potential and their special threat.

As early as June and July 1933, perceptive and perhaps wishfully thinking observers thought they recognised signs of stabilisation in the Nazi revolution – even a counter-revolutionary tendency. In actuality the struggle was shifting in Germany away from the seizure of power from the Weimar executors to a struggle to control the institutions of national defence – the army, the police, the ministries and the bureaucracy. The need to gird Germany for battle, including the need to restore its productivity, was felt throughout the length and breadth of the land, without reference to Nazi affiliation. Only the methods were at issue – and also who might be allowed to lead or even participate in the reconstruction. Yet autumn and winter brought more disorder, and the radical elements not merely of the SA and SS, but also of the party and its affiliates like the Factory Cell Organisation and the Small Business Employees' Organisation (NS Hago) carried out attacks on chain stores, Jewish firms and unpopular employers. The conservative right also showed its teeth and even pressed for a restoration of the monarchy. Yet what was needed to signal the 'end of the revolution' simply could not be identified. Ultimately the bloodletting of 30 June 1934 required no civil war, no vast measures of repression, but only a resolute action by a small, reliable force. But neither the army nor the Storm Troop leaders could make up their minds to provide that intervention, though even Röhm and his deputies recognised the need for action. The army was not ready to destroy its potential allies on the political right; Röhm and his top colleagues were unwilling to destroy the revolutionary forces which had brought them into power. Both sought for a year to temporise, aided by Hitler's own indecision.

Röhm's method was to preach the permanent revolution while reorganising his leviathan SA into numerous specialised segments, with emphasis upon military tasks. In July he restructured the *Obergruppen* (SA corps) along the lines of the army's seven *Wehrkreise* (defence zones), re-emphasising liaison facilities with the *Reichswehr*. In August in Berlin and again in September at the Nuremberg Party Day, he marshalled vast brownshirt armies, decked out as much as possible like soldiers. He strove to integrate the ablest ex-officers and ex-NCOs of the former *Stahlhelm* with his own hand-picked SA front veterans in the five succeeding classes of the AW military training programme beginning in October. He set up recruiting and training units (*Hochschulämter*) at every university to skim off the cream of the nationalistic student corps. He encouraged his units to toughen themselves and vie with each other in sports and combat manoeuvres. By setting up press offices for every SA region, he saw to it that the local populace read what served SA interests. He expanded SA ranks once again to make promotions easier, and he awarded honorary SA rank to party bigwigs and business tycoons whom he despised, hoping to gain their support by appealing to the widespread love of martial splendour. He even wooed Heinrich Himmler with the privilege of being addressed as '*Mein Reichsführer*', instead of the less exclusive '*Herr Obergruppenführer*'. An enormous increase in the use of colour in SA uniforms gave SA gatherings the gaudy aura of a circus or a cage of tropical birds. Meanwhile Röhm made speech after speech warning the conservatives that the revolution was far from over, seeking thereby to keep alive the forces he hoped would thrust him (and Hitler) into the saddle still firmly occupied by the old German military and economic elites.

The army's method was to keep 'hands off' the Nazi movement, to encourage its nationalism and *élan*, to use its volunteers in the quasi-secret Border Defence (*Grenzschutz*), to resist all efforts to combine the SA with the *Reichswehr*, and to press Hitler for economic and political stabilisation and an end to revolutionary terror while insisting that he carry out his own house-cleaning. By refusing to participate directly in the restoration of law and order, army leaders thrust authority into the hands of Himmler and Heydrich. When on 30 June SS units were assembled and armed in *Reichswehr* barracks, the army was putting the stamp of approval on a measure which it neither initiated nor controlled.

For the time being Himmler avoided reorganising the SS regionally along military lines as the SA had done. While the masses of the *Stahlhelm* and even small groups of the *Reichsbanner* and the *Roter Frontkämpferbund* entered the SA, Himmler opened and closed the membership of the SS selectively, on a regional and an organisational basis. He also made revolutionary speeches supporting Röhm, and the SS vied with the SA in military precision at Berlin in August and at Nuremberg in September. But Himmler did not seek to penetrate into the AW training system. The differentiation and the separateness of the SS began to be emphasised. Indeed, the SA took issue with a newspaper article appearing that September in Hamburg which contrasted the SS as elite with the SA as mass. The SS began to compete with the SA for the students, the business leaders and professional people in a community, and above all for the party bigwigs. A race began in the summer and autumn to see which could attract more *Gauleiter*, Munich *Reichsleiter* (National Officers), and party heroes. *Gauleiters* who quarrelled with the SA – Goebbels and Mutschmann, to mention only two – favoured the SS and employed SS men as bodyguards and private detectives even when they resisted SS membership.

More important, however, was Himmler's and Heydrich's exploitation of the traditional SS police and intelligence function to seize the German police apparatus. Although the Storm Troops actually had a head start in their Auxiliary Police role and their control of all the largest urban police headquarters (as police presidents) outside Munich, their great disadvantage lay in the need to repress the excesses of their own members, only partially met by the *Feldpolizei*. In August Göring in Prussia and Frick outside Prussia had sought to tame the SA by abolishing the Auxiliary Police and resisting further SA encroachments on police prerogatives. The SA responded with the formation of armed and motorised Special Duty units and headquarters guards.

A defiance of the police in non-political crimes, SA complaints of police brutality and 'old-style' police bureaucracy, and court sentences for

SA men engaged in rioting and looting filled the press. Amazing cases of 'Wild-West' gunplay and private feuding among Nazi officials occurred that autumn. Naturally, the SS was not aloof from all this, nor was it much better disciplined. However, the SS had several advantages: (1) it had fewer members – the troublemakers therefore represented a smaller percentage of the total problem; (2) national-minded police officials were more willing to join the SS than the SA because the SS already had a superior social status due to its appeal to business and professional men in previous years; (3) Heydrich's SD provided a co-ordinative national network lacking in the SA, a device permitting plain clothes if not conspiratorial secrecy and party backing for claims to control at least the Political Police in a community.

With the assistance of Reich Interior Minister Frick, between October 1933 and January 1934 Himmler had himself made Political Police Commissar in all the German states except Prussia. The Political Police were already opened to Himmler through a few (usually younger) police-men who joined the SS (and/or SD) in 1932 or even as late as 1933 – or else I-C personnel from the local SS were hired by the police following the erection of a special local bureau in Himmler's name. There was amaz-ingly little bureaucratic opposition to this move, owing perhaps to the massive confusion of the times, dislike of the SA commissars, the youth of the SS and SD personnel making them seem 'harmless' or the assimilation of more trusted older Criminal Police (Kripo) officers into the SS and SD. The erection of an SD headquarters in Stuttgart is a good example. The young Hessian Nazi police official Werner Best made a name for himself there as both efficient and diplomatic. Naturally, the SA police officialdom recognised and resented Himmler's and Heyrich's tactics, but Röhm and the SA seem to have isolated themselves both from the local party head-quarters and police officialdom, so that they had no allies except in the streets – exactly the spirits which needed to be exorcised.

In Prussia Daluege held the key to SS police power. He fought for his independence from Himmler under Göring's aegis and with the aid of the Nazi criminal investigator Arthur Nebe. Probably due to a recogni-tion of his limitations and those of Gestapa chief Rudolf Diels regarding SA commander Karl Ernst and Reinhard Heydrich, Daluege as a Prussian *Landespolizei* general conspired first with the Berlin SA to 'get' Diels, and when unsuccessful turned to Heydrich. Heydrich's character-istically indirect methods are shown by Diels's appearance in September in the SS promotion lists as a *Standartenführer*. Diels represents the type of revolutionary conservative with whom the army should have been allied; however, as revealed in his memoirs, the generals continually underestimated their Nazi partners. Diels was a clever man, cleverer than Daluege although not a match for Heydrich. Allied with Göring, Diels was still a far more powerful man than was Heydrich allied with Himmler. Daluege had to separate Diels from Göring – in which he almost succeeded despite his clumsiness, due to Göring's lack of principle – but the rebellious SA were the wrong allies to use with Göring. In the autumn Daluege tried again, again clumsily and again failing; yet this time SS organisation succeeded in intimidating both Diels and Göring, so that a bridge of co-operation could be built between the SD and the Gestapo (*Geheime Staats-Polizei*, Secret State Political Police) while Daluege fell rapidly into line as a loyal SS officer.

In the course of the intrigue, Himmler relieved Daluege of the command over the relatively weak, ultra-critical SS-*Gruppe Ost* with its headquarters in Berlin. He replaced him with Sepp Dietrich, whose embryonic *Leibstandarte* had been installed by Göring in the *Lichterfelde* police barracks of Major Wecke's special police detachments – which Göring used as his personal paramilitary unit. Thus, Dietrich had ample resources for controlling SS-*Gruppe Ost*, an area rich in the traditions of the SA fronde since 1930. Even before Diels's final defeat in April 1934 when Himmler and Heydrich occupied the Gestapa at Prinz Albrechtstrasse 8, Daluege, Heydrich and Himmler had used Göring's fears of the SA to penetrate what had been one of the strongest conservative bastions, the Prussian police system. Far from resisting SS-SD penetration into the Prussian police, Göring actually encouraged it in the winter of 1933. Himmler and Heydrich aided the penetration by stressing their interest in law and order, the collection of incriminating evidence against SA terror, and absolute loyalty to Göring's master, Adolf Hitler.

During the Munich ceremonies on 8–9 November 1933, commemorating the triumphant tenth anniversary of the beer hall putsch, Himmler submitted the SS men gathered before the Feldherrnhalle to an oath to Adolf Hitler:

> We pledge to you, Adolf Hitler, loyalty and bravery. We swear obedience to you and the superiors appointed by you, even unto death, as God is our witness.

Foreshadowing, if not serving as a model for the momentous oath of the *Wehrmacht* of 2 August 1934, this personal SS pledge of loyalty came to hold far more significance than Röhm's earlier SA oath of October 1932. SS men were thus provided with a visible focus of loyalty modelled after the old army's loyalty to the sovereign. The SA failure to follow up and consolidate their lead in this respect was symptomatic: loyalty to Hitler was irrelevant to them. In this they were in error.

The award of a ministerial seat to Röhm, along with one to Hess on 1 December 1933, has seemed to many observers a mere 'plastering over the cracks' by Hitler preparatory to his breach with Röhm in good time. In view of his earlier treatment of Stennes, Hitler's move might well be taken as an effort to deceive and mollify Röhm. Without destroying this dimension of Hitler's tactics, it may still be possible that Hitler thus gave Röhm a new arena of activity, parallel with Hess, in which he hoped the former would develop his SA into a viable training institution, not merely for pre- and post-military exercises but also to train Germans in political struggle with Jews, Catholics, reactionaries, etc. Nor did Röhm leave his appointment in the realm of a gesture; he capitalised mightily on the potential of a state apparatus that he could wield in the power struggle. In the Ministerial Office, handling his cabinet duties and the Political Office, handling his relationships at state and local levels, Röhm was copying Schleicher's tactics and developing control facilities which were formidable powers to reckon with. For personnel he drew upon the Liaison Staff, a joint SA-SS-party Berlin installation of March 1933, which had already played a vital role in channelling and sifting information passing between the ministries and party agencies. The overlapping of the work and personnel of Röhm's new offices with the Liaison Staff in the early months of 1934 suggests that he was not as yet descending in power. SS officers sought positions in his new apparatus, and high-ranking SS men who met with his disfavour had to be consigned to limbo by Himmler. Röhm, not Himmler, recommended all SS appointments of field grade to Hitler, even and especially those of honorary ranks. Röhm was in a position to stifle the SS, and only his dogged determination to challenge Hitler and the *Reichswehr* delivered the Storm Troop leader and his mighty SA-State into Himmler and Heydrich's hands.

During the winter months of 1933–34, Himmler cautiously began the reorganisation of the SS structure, partially to bring it more in line with the SA reforms of the previous summer and autumn, partially to strengthen it for a possible struggle for power with the SA. It was at this time that the SS-*Oberabschnitte* (main sectors) made their appearance in place of the old *Gruppen*. The SS main sectors were organised, like the SA-*Obergruppen*, to conform to the army's seven *Wehrkreise*. Tactical military training was secretly ordered in January 1934 in rifle practice, extended order drill, light machine gun and patrols in preparation for training in AW-*Sportlager* (sport camps). A combat officers' school was announced to be opened later at Bad Tölz. SS membership rapidly doubled, going from 100,000 to more than 200,000, as tens of thousands who had applied during the closure of April to November 1933 were admitted under the new, stringent standards of the SS Administrative Office and the Racial Office. The number of *Standarten* rose from fifty to 100, with *Sturmbanne* in every town of consequence. Rapid promotions were the rule, and most of the men who had joined in 1930, 1931 and 1932 were given opportunities to try their hand at commanding. More systematic evaluation of each officer was now demanded, however, and also more careful methods of reporting unit strength. Both the field and headquarters structures of the SS in the spring of 1934 began to assume the form that they would keep until wartime. About 2,000 officers formed the basis for a future SS officers' corps which could grow and differentiate itself but would retain until 1939 its basic character.

The pioneers of 1930–32 who attained officer rank at this time were to form the backbone of the SS; the second wave of 'March casualties' (a term of not-so-good-humoured contempt for the opportunists of March 1933) formed the 'replacements', long regarded as second best, until the war began. In 1934 special emphasis was placed on the recruitment of personnel for the military support organisations, engineers, communications, motor and cavalry units. Standards were kept low for these recruits, who might otherwise go to the SA. In the case of the SS cavalry, there was a distinct snobbery involved as whole rural riding clubs were assimilated in a body. Here too there was a direct challenge to SA ambitions for an SA cavalry. The SS had very few paid positions to offer compared to the SA, which went on the Reich Interior Ministry payroll in October 1933, to the tune of 2.6 million marks per month. Yet quite a few of the new SS were unemployed lower middle class hopeful of winning state or private business positions through 'connections' with the large number of regularly employed civil servants and professional people being wooed by the SS for prestige, as well as penetration into their social milieus. Academics, for example, were sought after, first for the SS and then for the SD. Often secret 'supporting members' from the business and professional community revealed their interest after a little urging and joined the SS without joining the party. Thus, the atmosphere of being socially 'a little better' was reinforced after 1933. For example, the Berlin SS gave a 'spring concert', featuring a chorus of the *Leibstandarte* singing 'songs of the black hundreds of 1813 around the campfire'. It supplied honour guards for the wife of the Shah of Persia on tour in Germany and protested with feeling against 'roughneck' treatment of foreign guests by a minor rival, the Berlin Watch and Ward Society.

The winter of 1933–34 was harder on the SA than the previous one, which had been bad enough with its mutinies and desertions. To the simple SA man, Röhm's high politics meant little. Jobless, this man was supposed to content himself with party handouts from the Winter Help Campaign. If he had got a small position, often conferred on him by labour office officials and Nazi employers as a huge favour, he had to see his SA unit filled with better-heeled ex-*Stahlhelm*ers and with perhaps a few of his former foes, the '*Bananen*' (the Nazis called the *Reichsbanner* people 'bananas') and 'reds' who argued openly that the time was ripe to hold Hitler to his promises. The local SA leaders discharged some of the pent-up frustration in protest marches against exclusive social clubs, unfriendly factory managers and reactionary communal authorities. Much was made of decorations and awards for the Old Guard of SA, SS, *Bund Oberland* and *Reichskriegsflagge*. Plans for summer vacations for adults and camps for children were announced. Housing developments for SA and SS men were started. But Röhm was forced to take cognisance of chronic complainers who protested against the deluge of opportunists, increased deductions from their pay envelope, repetitious drill and derogating tone of the *Reichswehr* drillmasters, neglect of units by the commanders, etc. A secret order of SA-*Gruppe* 'Berlin-Brandenburg' warned against drunken battles with the police and with opponents in the taverns. Noisy talk about a 'second revolution' could be heard in SA circles by early spring. On the other hand, Röhm seems to have made serious efforts to rid the SA of its dead weight and its worst troublemakers.

While Röhm's foreign press conferences and meetings with the foreign diplomatic corps and military attaches do not quite deserve the suspicions Hitler lavished upon them – since they really seem designed to reassure other countries, especially France, about the non-aggressive character of the SA – the conduct of Röhm as Reich minister was, to say the least, aggressive. From January onward a definite polarisation between him and Hitler set in, which Göring and Himmler were quick to capitalise upon. Both set to work to collect as much information about SA excesses as possible. Yet mutual suspicions kept them working against each other as well. When Gisevius was forcibly taken to the *Lichterfelde* barracks in mid-February, Sepp Dietrich wanted information about Diels's Gestapo as well as Karl Ernst's SA. As late as March Diels descended on the new SS concentration camp on the Vulcan Wharf in Stettin and with Göring's support cleaned it out. This was the last straw, however; in the inevitable 'talking it out', Göring agreed to install Himmler as his 'deputy' in the Gestapo. Heydrich installed Werner Best, the young Hessian Nazi, as his deputy in the Bavarian Political Police and moved up to Berlin, where he split his time between Prinz Albrechtstrasse 8 and the new SD offices at Wilhelmstrasse 112 nearby. Diels's appointees were rusticated in the provinces, replaced by SD people from Munich, many of them old Munich Kripo (Criminal Police) officials like Heinrich Müller. On the other hand, the Berlin circle of Arthur Nebe went directly into the SS, though Nebe himself remained in the SA until 1936.

Himmler thus acquired the whole Prussian Political Police apparatus, while Daluege won control of the rest of the police throughout the Reich. The regional offices of the Gestapo had been rendered independent of the regular police channels on 14 March; now a systematic assignment or appointment of an SD official to each '*Stapostelle*' occurred in every Prussian *Regierungsbezirk* (section of a province). There were about 300 Gestapo officials throughout Prussia, and about 250 more in Berlin when Heydrich took over. Only a few of them were in the SS; most were nationalist police officers from before 1933. The Gestapo consisted of three main offices: (1) administration; (2) investigation and prevention; and (3) espionage and treason. Heydrich took personal charge of the second, placing Heinrich Müller, neither a Nazi nor an SS man but a hard-bitten Bavarian rightist from the Munich Criminal Police, in charge of 'fighting Marxism' and of all political arrests (so-called protective custody in concentration camps). Another Bavarian policeman named Reinhard Flesch, with an SS and Nazi past, was set to watch Müller for a time (he resigned in 1935), and Müller's friend Friedrich Panzinger was put in charge of the Berlin *Stapostelle* (he finally joined the

SS in 1939!). Franz Josef Huber, who had prosecuted Nazis in Bavaria before 1933, came to the Berlin Gestapa and joined the SD to fight 'reaction, the Church, and Austria'. Josef Meisinger, also from the Bavarian Political Police, was literally put in charge of investigations of the NSDAP, SA, SS and homosexuality! SS and SD membership for them came after the fact of their employment by Heydrich, either in Munich or Berlin. Exceptions with a Nazi and SS past included the Bavarian career policeman Hans Rattenhuber, who was charged with setting up Hitler's personal security guards; Anton Dunckern, who went to the Berlin *Stapostelle*; and Walter Potzelt, SS since 1930 and SD since 1932, who became chief-adjutant of the Gestapa. Heydrich brought his personal adjutant and factotum, SS-*Sturmführer* Alfred Naujocks, up from Munich. Holdovers from Diels's staff included the non-SS-*Oberregierungsrat* 'Bode', the local Berlin expert on Marxism and trade unions; Reinhold Heller, who did not join the SS until 1938; Günther Patchowsky, SD member from 1932 and now in charge of the main office for espionage; Karl Hasselbacher, specialist for Freemasons, sects and Jews (joined SS and SD December 1934); Ernst Damzog; Kurt Riedel; and Walter Kubitsky, who worked with Patchowsky in espionage.

Heydrich was a shrewd and effective organiser. He did not merge the SD with the Gestapo and only slowly brought the Secret State Police of the other *Länder* into line with the excellent Prussian apparatus that Diels had left him. The SD was to remain an SS installation par excellence, and in fact a Heydrich installation! At the *Sicherheitsamt* (SD headquarters), he set up five sections: administration, archives, Political Police, counter-intelligence-inland and counter-intelligence-foreign. Müller of the Gestapo he put in charge of all Political Police operations; to Best, still operating the Political Police for the time being in Munich, he gave the internal security section and the administration, retaining foreign intelligence for himself. The archives went to a capable thirty-one-year-old SS captain, a doctor of law. The SD recruited many young lawyers in the spring of 1934 as well as businessmen, judges, state councillors, mayors and police officials in the middle or lower ranks. Many of them seem to have functioned with the SD for months or even years before acquiring SS membership and rank. Some served in the SS without rank in 1934. Certainly the SD was too embryonic in June 1934 to be capable of running the whole German police, let alone the SS. At best it could serve as a transmission belt. Its potentialities in these directions were shown, however, by Hess's order of 9 June forbidding other party agencies to maintain intelligence nets. Unfortunately for the SA, it lacked a unified intelligence system to warn it of the impending denouement. Army intelligence even soaked up false reports about the SA planted by the SD.

Understandably, the *Reichswehr* had been loath to give up on the SA. Even in the autumn of 1933, confronted by hostility from high-ranking SA leaders like von Jagow in Stuttgart and von Obernitz in Frankfurt-am-Main and by 'strikes' and mutinies among companies assigned as border guards in Pomerania, Silesia Frankfurt-an-der-Oder and Saxony, the *Reichswehr* went ahead with AW training in SA field sport schools and on its own training grounds, putting five SA classes through one-month basic training until March. The fear that the eastern units of the SA would prove useless against a Polish invasion was less troubling after the signing of the non-aggression pact with Poland on 26 January 1934, but SA efforts to maintain control over *Reichswehr* weapons depots during the spring months helped to harden the resistance of the army. Army inability to dislodge F. W. Krüger by naming a regular army officer as AW executive officer in January also may have contributed to the army's decision to withdraw training officers from the SA in March. Actually the 13,000-man AW was the friendliest segment of the SA, and Krüger himself was disliked by many of the SA officers' corps and party leaders like Baldur von Schirach of the National Youth Leadership who suspected him of playing a double game and building up a personal following through control over the chief route to *Reichswehr* appoint-ment. Krüger, an ex-SS officer, seems to have tried to serve all his masters. His extensive plans for a great network of SA 'sport' schools were later realised when the AW no longer existed and he had returned to the SS. The army was disappointed, however, in the low military quality of the SA both as officers and as troops. Fritsch's ascendancy over Reichenau may also have helped prepare the *Reichswehr* leadership to believe the worst about the SA.

Whereas in mid-1933 Hitler and Röhm had been thinking of a 300,000-man militia with one-year service, utilising a smaller perma-nent corps of officers, NCOs, technicians and training personnel, by February Hitler had moved to a more professional soldier's view of universal conscription, under the influence of French intransigence toward any and all of Röhm's blandishments. Hitler now shifted to Ribbentrop's 'British' line, making rather amazing offers to reduce the

SA by two-thirds and to allow international inspections to verify the non-military character of the SA, and rejecting wholeheartedly Röhm's conception of a people's army headed by Röhm himself. He met Röhm's mid-February cabinet proposals that he should head a new Defence Ministry by forcing Röhm into an abortive agreement with the *Reichswehr* which he could not or would not keep.

As Röhm found himself blocked by Hitler and the *Reichswehr* from February on, he permitted himself numerous incautious outbursts and stressed to SA and non-SA alike that the SA was to remain the revolutionary mainspring of the movement. Through the spring he permitted his commanders to channel the unrest of their men into marching demonstrations, which were clearly unsafe for public order. He did nothing to prevent the arming of SA headquarters guard detachments, Border Defence units, and even work camps housing unemployed SA men, including refugees from Austria. Nevertheless, there is no evidence that he planned a putsch, though he kept up a steady system of contacts with his SA leaders, as well as with top SS officers and leading figures in German and international life. This system of contacts was doubtless his device for heading off surprises both from within the SA – for he must have been aware of the readiness of some of his highest-ranking officers to putsch – and also from Berlin, Munich, or abroad. Its failure to aid him implies that there was no clear and firm putsch plan either among his own officers or among his opponents at the time when the July SA furlough was announced – as early as April 1934. Even his 16 May Order to SA units to collect files on critics of the SA must have been largely intended as intimidation for noisy spokesmen of party and right-wing circles, for it was rather late to start intelligence operations in earnest and especially with a public announcement.

Röhm probably had to give his SA their long-promised furlough, and he may have welcomed their temporary removal from the social scene as a means of quieting down negative public sentiment. He doubtless reckoned on an autumn or winter crisis brought on either by continued unemployment and/or von Hindenburg's demise, at which time Hitler would be more willing to make concessions to the guarantors of the revolution. Nevertheless, Röhm must be held largely responsible for the easy destruction of his edifice by a tiny minority on 30 June; no more telling condemnation can be made of a military commander than that of total ignorance of an impending attack. Röhm's isolation from party leaders, military commanders and his own SA system in spite of his 'contacts' – perhaps involved in some way with his homosexuality – was a death blow to an organisation erected, after all, on charisma and *Führerprinzip* (the principle of authoritarian leadership). Röhm remained an amateur to the last: the amateur leader of an amateur army. Himmler also was an amateur, but many of his lieutenants were not. Indeed, he developed his professional side as a policeman (with their help) at this very time.

The army had begun to collect data on the arming of the SA *Stabswachen* (headquarters guards) and on arms transports in April; and Captain Patzig, head of the army *Abwehr* (intelligence), had his agents in the AW even earlier. Von Reichenau is alleged to have gone over to Himmler after a partnership with Röhm failed, but the evidence for this is slim (such contacts seem provable only in the last two critical weeks of June). May was a month of intensive staff meetings, tours of inspection and speeches. Not only was the army consulting but so also were the SA and the SS, the party and the reactionaries. Röhm and Himmler both were checking on their new regional structures; Hitler, Goebbels, Hess, Bormann and Buch feverishly harangued and intrigued to bring their enemies out in the open, while the monarchists and conservatives plotted and speculated on the death of von Hindenburg. There was much less anxiety in the SA camp than around Papen, in army, right-wing and party circles. A civil war seemed in the offing with two clear-cut sides, a strong radical protest in which the non-Nazi left might be expected to join along with a hard-bitten reactionary core of army, big business, the Catholic Church and royalty. The middle class and many Nazis saw themselves caught between the fronts. Uncertain even of Hitler's choice, they fed the atmosphere of deterioration which drove him to act. Characteristically, he struck at both fronts.

The earliest signs of an SS alert appeared in Munich at the outset of June. The Bavarian Political Police and the SD, under the command of Werner Best, received orders to prepare for suppressing a revolt. Theodor Eicke, commander of the special SS troops at the multi-purpose Dachau installation (a concentration camp with a quartermaster unit, an embryonic *Politische Bereitschaft* (Political Emergency unit) and an Austrian SS refugee camp) began practising seizure of positions in the Greater Munich area, including Bad Wiessee. The regular SS-*Standarten* in Munich received sealed mobilisation orders to be opened on the code signal, '*Versammlung*'. No comparable SS alerts for the other regions occurred until the last week in June.

Already noticeable since April, the atmosphere of crisis worsened in June. Hindenburg retired, seriously ill, to Neudeck in East Prussia; Röhm went publicly on sick leave; and everybody made speeches. Papen's speech of 17 June at Marburg was thus part of a general wave of criticism and counter-criticism. Hitler's choice of this time to pay a visit to Mussolini was classic 'Hitlerian' tactics: he withdrew from the battlefield, hoping perhaps to come back with a triumph; at least he might throw many people off the scent. (Hitler was probably aware of Austrian Nazi putsch plans at this time – if indeed he did not instigate them through Theo Habicht, the NSDAP *Landesleiter*.) His interview with Mussolini was inconsequential, but the opportunity to pay a visit to Hindenburg on 21 June to 'report' and check up on the old man's state of mind and health may have steeled Hitler's nerve to proceed with his coup. That the decision may have come about at the time of the Italian trip or right after the Papen speech is suggested by the fact that Himmler on 19 June broke a more than two-week delay when he forbade higher SS officers to go on a northern cruise with Röhm in August, after temporising since the 1 June invitations went out. On 20 August Himmler claimed to have been shot at by an SA ambush. By 23 August the rumours of a forthcoming putsch were widespread. The SD representative in Breslau conveyed to the local *Stapostelle* secret orders to collect data on fifteen SA leaders, including Heines. As early as 22 June, Himmler told the SS commander in Dresden that an SA putsch was expected and to alarm his units and contact the army *Wehrkreis* commander for aid. Heines the following day got wind of army preparations in Breslau and alarmed Göring with talk of a Fritsch-led army revolt, while on 24 June Fritsch notified von Kleist in Breslau to expect an SA putsch there! Von Reichenau and Himmler were definitely now in contact, discussing the sharing of weapons and the use of army barracks and transport vehicles.

A summons to congregate in Berlin on 25 June went out to all SS regional commanders, and for two days Himmler held conferences with them, giving them sealed orders to be opened on the above code word and ordering them to make lists of suspected persons for automatic arrest. They were convinced of the reality of an SA plot by Himmler's manner. He described Silesia as the hotbed of the revolt. The regional commanders were impressed with the need for absolute security; only

SS-*Abschnitt* commanders and the *Standarten* commanders in Silesia were to be informed ahead of time. In Berlin Daluege and Sepp Dietrich did their part to alarm high *Reichswehr* officials with what appear to have been faked SA documents, including execution lists. Again Heines intervened on 28 June, warning von Kleist that Himmler and Heydrich were pushing things to a head; von Kleist actually flew to Berlin, where von Reichenau told him that 'it was too late to turn back'. Hitler made a phone call to Röhm that evening to put him off guard, announcing his own presence at a previously scheduled SA staff conference at Bad Wiessee for the morning of 30 June. At this time Sepp Dietrich had completed plans to move two companies of the *Leibstandarte* (SS-*Wachbataillon*) by train and army truck to Bad Wiessee for the same morning, on Hitler's orders. Clearly, Berlin was being left for Göring's measures and his units. No general SA alarm occurred, but it was not surprising that with all the rumours flying around about a Munich putsch, the SA there became alarmed on the evening of 29 June. Heines arrived, having sent only half his armed personnel on leave; yet he failed to arouse Röhm to serious defensive measures. That evening noisy SA rallies were held on the Oberwiesenfeld, and some troop commanders did tell their men that Hitler had joined the *Reichswehr* against them; but lacking Röhm's support, no council of war was held, and by 1.00 a.m. Munich was quiet. Efforts to trace rumours reaching the SA, probably spread by *agents provocateurs*, led SA Lieutenant-Generals Schneidhuber and Schmid to visit *Gauleiter* Adolf Wagner that evening. Wagner was probably an accomplice of Himmler, for he reassured the two, only to arrest them a few hours later.

The purge operations were far from uniform. They were most intense in Munich, Berlin and Silesia. In most of the other areas, the SS operations did not extend beyond routine arrests of top SA leaders. In Pomerania, East Prussia and Saxony, SS leaders protected their SA comrades by refusing to send them to Berlin. Himmler and Heydrich stayed in Berlin, leaving Best and later Sepp Dietrich to carry out actions ordered by Hitler and *Gauleiter* Wagner. Hitler was accompanied to Wiessee by his oldest cronies, Christian Weber, Emil Maurice and Walter Buch. In Berlin Göring was in command, although he may have received proscription lists from the SS leaders. Arrests were carried out by all kinds of units, including plain-clothes SD personnel. In Breslau the alert came from the Berlin SD; and the regional SS commander, Udo von Woyrsch, personally supervised the roundup of SA and the attack on an armed SA work camp, which resisted briefly. Wild and irresponsible SS measures occurred in several parts of Silesia involving Jews. Most of the actual security measures in Munich and Berlin were carried out by *Reichswehr* and Prussian State Police. The secret SS orders, opened on an SD signal, sent the SS units to *Reichswehr* barracks to draw weapons and await orders. Most of them stood on guard duty in their communities, and many never left the barracks. On the other hand, the individual killings in Berlin and Munich were almost universally ascribed to the SS, especially since so many black uniforms were identified. Few if any of these murders were ever subjected to court investigation. At Wiessee Hitler's cronies did the first killings. In Munich the executions at Stadelheim prison were carried out by units of the *Leibstandarte* under Sepp Dietrich and units of Eicke's Dachau SS. Eicke and his aide, Michael Lippert, killed Röhm. In Berlin executions were carried out in the Lichterfelde barracks after a mixed court martial consisting at various times of Himmler, Daluege, Waldeck, Heydrich, Buch and Göring. The executioners appear to have been drawn from remaining units of the *Leibstandarte*. The *Feldjäger* and Major Wecke's *Landespolizeigruppe* General Göring were also closely involved. In Breslau the executions insisted upon by Heydrich were carried out by a small detail of regular SS after buck-passing because few wished to kill SA comrades. Here too *Feldjäger* and Prussian *Landespolizei* units participated in the arrests, if not the killings.

Of about 200 people who lost their lives during the terror of 30 June–3 July, over half were non-SA. SS men doubtless killed nearly all of them; the actual number of SS killers remains quite small, perhaps several dozen, and the number of SS officers who participated in the plot beforehand – even including those who seriously believed in a Röhm revolt – would not exceed fifty. SD network personnel might account for another fifty. The majority of the SS personnel employed on 30 June and thereafter knew little of what was happening and performed security functions no different from the army and police units alongside which they served. Nevertheless, Hitler chose to bestow and Himmler to accept massive credit for the purge. Though only a few were responsible, the willingness to kill and to take credit for the killings was to mark the Black Corps forever afterwards.

The peculiar service which Heydrich and Himmler rendered Hitler was the murder of persons whose killings Hitler did not wish to directly order. This certainly included Gregor Strasser, and probably several others. Heydrich's often-discussed regrets that he could not kill more highlight the prime fact that actually very few SA officers were killed. That the SA should have been so effectively maimed by the loss of these few regional commanders and staff officers indicates either their outstanding role in the organisation or the SA's general inefficacy, or a little of both. Lutze seems to have regretted his part in the betrayal of his comrades and voiced the view that even many of them had been killed 'unnecessarily'. Perhaps he had been led to believe that only Röhm and five or six others were to be eliminated. On the other hand, the intimidation of the rightist politicians was just as complete. The *Reichswehr* harboured a grudge against the SS for its brutality in the deaths of General and Mrs von Schleicher, and General von Bredow, but they still later conceded the SS a division's worth of armaments. The party gained new respect for the SS – largely out of fear – while a rivalry set in with the various branches of the police, who saw the SS as their major critics and possible replacements.

The independence that the SS gained from the SA by Hitler's order of 20 July 1934 did not require an immediate reorganisation. Rather, it was followed by a thorough house-cleaning, leading to the expulsion of as many as 60,000 of the newer members. The SA of course was thoroughly screened also, but its losses were proportionally no heavier than the SS. The AW continued on as an independent unit under Hitler through the autumn but was liquidated the following January. Krüger took many of the AW officers with him into the SS.

Himmler was to profit throughout the 1930s from many of Röhm's organisational innovations of 1933–34, above all from the structural 'co-ordination' with the *Reichswehr* districts but also from the idea of penetration into the university community, the development of an independent press agency and the emphasis on the sport achievements associated with the SA Sport Insignia; and finally from the notion of a military elite for the *Leibstandarte* Adolf Hitler and the *Verfügungstruppe* (Special Duty troops) which realised the ideal of the AW. Yet Himmler knew better than to let the SS proliferate visibly in the Third Reich. The contrast of 1934 between the noisy SA demonstrations and the quiet work of the SS was never entirely forgotten, even in the war years.

THE YEARS OF GROWTH

1934–39

Consolidation

In the aftermath of the Röhm purge, the position of the SS was far from a settled matter. An atmosphere of tension, mutual suspicion and open recrimination coloured the relations of the SS with the *Reichswehr,* and with state and party officialdom. In August, at the time of Hindenburg's death, an SS unit was employed to control access to his estate, much to the chagrin of *Reichswehr* and nationalist figures who had hoped to find an anti-Nazi will. On the other hand, the SS (and SA) sought in vain to worm information from the *Reichswehr* about its plans for expansion. Fritsch complained that SS personnel in the *Reichswehr* spied on their commanding officers. Tension reached its height in December 1934 with rumours of a showdown between two evenly matched adversaries of about 300,000 men each, the *Reichswehr* and SS, some favouring the idea of an SS putsch-initiative, others of a counter-revolutionary army manoeuvre. On 3 January 1935, Hitler held a meeting in the Kroll Opera for party and *Reichswehr* leaders, where he warned the party against encroachments on the army and called the *Reichswehr* 'the sole bearer of arms'. British papers at this time noted that the SS was to be reduced, but references were made to more heavily armed SS 'riot units' in the process of formation – the future *Verfügungstruppe*. Then at a conciliatory *Bierabend* (beer evening) sponsored by Blomberg, Himmler on 10 January had the bad taste to accuse Fritsch of meddling in party matters by inviting Professor Carl Schmitt to address select *Reichswehr* officers on the justice of putsches. At another *Bierabend* matters were apparently patched up enough for Himmler to be invited to address Hamburg *Reichswehr* officers in February about the need for his 'riot squads', one of which was in the process of formation in their district (SS-*Standarte 'Germania'*). Characteristically, Himmler dwelt on the 1918 experience, the 'stab-in-the-back' and the need to free the front soldiers of the worry and responsibility about the home front in time of war. Of course, the cause of this tension and jockeying was the imminent procla-mation of *Wehrhoheit* (Defence Sovereignty) and the part an armed SS might play as units in a new *Wehrmacht*. Although Hausser errs in claim-ing that Hitler announced to the *Reichstag* that an SS division would be included in the thirty-six proclaimed on 16 March, he reflects Himmler's expectation that the special, armed SS regiments being formed in Munich, Hamburg and Berlin would become a regular army division in time of war. Hitler does not seem ever to have made so clear-cut a promise.

One of the chief reasons for army leaders' resistance to SS ambition may have been their doubts about the discipline and counter-revolution-ary reliability of Himmler's units. This same doubt was rife among state authorities, both in late 1934 and well into 1935. One of the worst areas of SS offence was Silesia, where in August 1934 the regional SS commander, von Woyrsch, gave the provincial attorney general an ulti-matum to release SS personnel accused of illegal actions in the purges; and in September SS men accused of wanton murders on and after 30 June were given light sentences, while the Gestapo persecuted state officials who sought to bring them to justice. The regular police were distressed by SS officers who not only appeared in public in a drunken condition but also beat up people with whom they disagreed in public places and generally challenged the forces of law and order much as had the SA (and the SS) before 30 June. While Hitler and men like Göring, Goebbels and Himmler clearly desired to perpetuate ambiguities regard-ing the purpose of the purge for the purpose of intimidation, they also had to control the perception of lawlessness abroad in the land. Individual SS commanders could not be left free to determine whom they would frighten.

The manner in which Himmler mastered this problem, insofar as he did master it, by rationalisation and bureaucratisation deeply affected the kind of leadership corps ultimately evolved by the SS; but in a sense the direction had already been taken within the SA. The anti-bureaucratic tendencies of the free corps tradition, indeed of the freelance street fighter leadership, had already been subjected to an organisational strait-jacket even within the SA of Röhm and especially in Himmler's units. However, just as Röhm's SA had threatened toward the last to institu-tionalise dissent in its very bureaucracy (for example, Political Office, Training System), so ultimately the SS, having reined in its untamed rowdies and free spirits of the streets, was to pose a far greater threat to rival German institutions as the embodiment of political soldiering in the interests of permanent revolution. In the short term, however, the SS faced the problem of indiscipline left over from its SA heritage. Rapid growth and congruence with the SA structure had made its central administration, although modified repeatedly, disjointed and overlapping – while its regional structure was essentially a continuation of that of the party from the *Kampfjahre*, with the SS leaders embedded for better or worse in sticky conflicts or bosom friendships with old party comrades.

Austria, where the SS was embarrassingly involved in the putsch fiasco of 25 July 1934, less than a month after the supposed Röhm putsch, is a good illustration of Himmler's problem of SS reorganisation. The Austrian SS, *Abschnitt* VIII, was characterised by both its noisy vigour and its unruly character. One of the oldest *Abschnitte* – with strength in nearly all the Austrian *Länder* – the Austrian SS, like the Austrian Nazis as a whole, was little inclined to subordinate itself to Munich and even less to Berlin. The despatch by Himmler in 1932 of a commander in the form of a Berlin *Oberführer* and intelligence agent (Dr Walter Gräschke) had not helped matters at all. The tangled network of intrigue characteristic of the Dollfuss dictatorship enveloped the Austrian SA and SS in 1933, so that control became even harder for Himmler and Röhm than might have been expected from the international aspect. When Dollfuss drove the SA and SS underground in June 1933 due to the widespread partici-pation of their membership in overt violence, he began a process of split-ting the Austrian Nazis between those who remained to fight and those who fled to Germany. The SA and the SS who fled were to form the nucleus of a faction willing to subordinate themselves to the Nazi and Reich German purposes and timetable, while those who remained became increasingly restless and activist, anxious to use Hitler's Germany rather than be used by it. The former group were headquartered in

Munich, with many refugee camps – primarily of young men – located in Bavaria near the frontier. The latter group remaining in Austria were very loosely organised, with an estimated SS strength by January 1934 of about 5,000 (less than 1,000 of whom had been recognised by Munich) in five *Standarten*.

Utilising the cross connections of the Austrian Nazis with the fascist Styrian Home Defence and the nationalist *Heimwehr* (Home Army), Himmler appears to have conducted his own version of foreign policy in league with Theo Habicht. In October 1933 Himmler arranged for Schuschnigg to visit Hess secretly in Munich, probably as an agent for Dollfuss. In January 1934 Himmler sent Prince Waldeck-Pyrmont to Vienna to attempt a further rapprochement between the Austrian Nazi Party and the *Heimwehr*. When a leak developed and the home of the Austrian party chief was raided, the SS officer had to be recalled. A temporary wave of caution swept over Hitler and Himmler at this time, associated with the growing division of policy between Hitler and Röhm. Alfred Rosenberg warned Röhm in February 1934 that rumours of a putsch instigated by the SA from Bavaria were circulating in Vienna. In Bavaria both the SA and the SS were gathering young Austrian male refugees into military units on the frontier, known collectively as the Austrian Legion. Efforts to remove them from the immediate proximity of the border resulted in rioting. The tension between Austrian legionnaires and German SA broke out in clashes that April in Vilshofen, near Passau. SS units were even used as border guards to prevent raids across the frontier from the German side.

Meanwhile in Austria intrigues continued. Theo Habicht continued to seek accommodation both with the supporters of Dollfuss and with Starhemberg of the *Heimwehr*. Habicht worked with high Austrian SS and SA leaders, probably with Himmler's and Röhm's knowledge, but the rivalry between the two formations led to separate negotiations. Probably Hitler and some members of the German Foreign Office were informed, although incompletely, especially as the idea developed of a 'faked' putsch in which elements of the Austrian SA and SS were to capture Dollfuss and proclaim a new pro-German government with the co-operation of the Austrian police and army. The mutual suspicions, perhaps the underlying intent of the several groups involved to trick each other, led to serious leaks resulting on 25 July in the fiasco of the murder of Dollfuss, the isolation of the participating units of the 89th

SS-*Standarte* and the official repudiation by Hitler of the revolutionaries.

The failure of the Austrian SA to assist in the plot may be traced in part to the Röhm purge three weeks earlier in which SS elements of the Austrian Legion stationed at Dachau concentration camp had played a part. The Austrian SA was later accused of leaking critical information to the Austrian authorities in regard to the putsch plans, but there could have been other sources for these leaks. The Austrian episode suggests that the SS was not yet wholly a reliable instrument of Hitler, for Himmler was most certainly acquainted with the intentions of the plotters, though he may have been carried along by the enthusiasm and vigour of his Austrian subordinates and by Habicht's ill-informed optimism. It is not impossible that Hitler was kept partially informed and that he hoped to mask the Röhm purge by a cheap diplomatic victory in Austria, but the ineptitude of the entire plot and the dangers it involved are inconsistent with Hitler's careful preparation of the Röhm purge. It would seem more likely that both Hitler and Himmler were the victims of overconfident and uncontrolled subordinates.

The consequences for the SS were increased bitterness between it and the SA; renewed suspicion on the part of governmental and military figures among conservatives toward the SS as a reliable political tool; loss of its organisation in Austria through imprisonment, flight and withdrawals from activity (partially recouped after 1936); and a heritage of difficulty with the Austrian SS forever afterwards. On the other hand, individual Austrian SS men who fled to the Reich swelled the corps of competent SS officers, and the SS portion of the Austrian Legion became a battalion of the future *Verfügungstruppe* – 2nd battalion, *Standarte 'Deutschland'*. In 1938 a plaque was erected on the Austrian chancellery commemorating the seven men of the 89th SS-*Standarte* who were executed for their part in the putsch.

Although the autumn and winter of 1934–35 remained a period of ambiguity for the SA and even the SS as to size, structure, scope and purpose – marked by contradictory utterances and tendencies – both units showed a steady tightening up, the SS first, the SA more slowly. A distinction was made between special courts of honour and disciplinary powers within the SS and SA, and claims of both units to be independent of the state courts – the SA claim being disallowed. The SS finally set up its own system of disciplinary courts, separate from the SA and headed by Paul Scharfe, a sixty-year-old ex-police major directly subordinate to

Himmler. On the other hand, the authority of the *Feldjägerkorps* over SS personnel was reasserted. Persons who did not really intend to serve in SA or SS units because they were full-time civil servants, students, business people or were in the Voluntary Labour Service, were put in reserves or even forced to resign. Earlier regulations which had gone unenforced were taken up, such as requiring gun permits; collecting dues; getting marriage, health and ancestry certification; making sure all had taken the oath to the *Führer*; punishing clandestine clients of department stores, and Jewish merchants and professional men; forbidding attendance at church functions in uniform; and removal from the SS (on honourable terms) of all ministers of religion.

The process of differentiation within the SS according to specialities had been very irregular up to the time of the Röhm purge. Physicians, flyers, motorcyclists, cavalry, engineers and radiomen – both active and reserve – could either regard themselves as in special formations or not, depending on local conditions. Only the *Sicherheitsdienst* had really been cut off organisationally from the SS unit structure. However, by December 1934 a decisive distinction had developed between the so-called General SS (*Allgemeine* SS) – actually the bulk of the membership both paid and unpaid, both active and reserve – and certain special units. A secret order by Himmler does not mention the SD among these special units; it does mention: (1) *Verfügungstruppe* – the former *Politische Bereitschaften* including the *Leibstandarte* Adolf Hitler; and (2) *Wachverbände* – the former *Sonderkommandos*, organised in *Wachsturmbanne* and *Wachstürme*. In each case, the initiative had come from regional *Oberabschnittsführer* (regional SS commanders), who had created from their subordinate *Standarten aktive Hundertschaften* or *Sonderkommandos* (special riot or guard units) subordinate to themselves in 1933. As early as 4 July 1934, Himmler, probably on Hitler's suggestion, had made Theodor Eicke – since June 1933 Commander of the SS concentration camp at Dachau – Inspector of State Concentration Camps and Chief of the SS Guard Troops. These camps and the guard units in them were then systematically removed from local police authority as Himmler was both head of the regional Political Police and the SS superior of the regional SS commanders who had detailed the *Wachverbände* in the first place.

In November 1934 Himmler also appointed Lieutenant-General (retired) Paul Hausser to head up SS Officer Candidate Schools for the future *Verfügungstruppe*, but he did not create the parallel inspectorate of the *Verfügungstruppe* until October 1936. The date of 10 October 1934 may be taken, however, as the official beginning of the *Verfügungstruppe*, since it was selected later by the *Oberkommando der Wehrmacht* (Supreme Command of the German *Wehrmacht*, OKW) as the date for reckoning seniority in the *Verfügungstruppe*. Probably before this date the Political Emergency units had been solely financed by the SS-*Oberabschnitte*, while thereafter the Reich Ministry of the Interior or the *Länder* were at least partly responsible financially. In the case of the *Wachverbände*, the *Länder* became financially responsible in the latter part of 1934.

Thus after an initial stage where ordinary SS personnel were 'detailed' for special duty as Auxiliary Police on an individual basis or occasionally on a unit basis, the SS began to make the transition to quasi-state status for some of its formations. During 1933 and 1934 this relationship was somewhat irregular as symbolised by one-year contracts drawn up between individuals involved and their commanders. They 'enlisted' for one year. It is probable that for the most part neither they nor their commanders made a clear distinction between party service and state service. In July 1935, however, a regular enlistment procedure was worked out whereby the Reich Ministry of the Interior granted Himmler the power to administer oaths, which he then reassigned to the unit commanders of the *Verfügungstruppe*. Regular enlistment documents in the name of the Reich Ministry of the Interior were drawn up in 1935 but predated at some time in 1934 (some earlier than 10 October 1934). The *Oberabschnitte*, however, retained control over the *Verfügungstruppe* formations throughout 1935 and most of 1936. In the case of the *Wachverbände*, there was greater but not uncontested autonomy *vis-à-vis* the SS regional commanders in 1934 and 1935, probably due to the concentration camps' tie to the Gestapo. By 1936 Eicke was strong enough to earn the simpler title of Commander of the Death's Head Troops and complete independence of the regional authorities both of the state and the local SS. On the other hand, tendencies toward autonomy in the auxiliary units such as cavalry, motors, engineers and communications were sharply checked, first in 1934 by placing their commanders on the staffs of the regional chiefs of the General SS and later by reductions in size (1935) and the destruction of higher level staffs (1936). After having allowed these units to grow out of proportion to their usefulness in an effort to attract skilled personnel, it was obviously necessary to restrict them to the really competent. In spite of their

obvious relevance to the mobilisation potential of the SS, these units were
not made part of the state-paid troops. Nevertheless, by 1936 it became
necessary to create state-paid medical units outside the General SS
structure.

New Staff Offices

The first significantly new top-level structure in the SS after the Röhm
purge was the SS-*Hauptamt* (SS Main Office), created on 20 January 1935.
While Darré's Race and Settlement Office and Heydrich's Security
Police Office were both promoted to *Hauptamt* status as well at this
juncture, their autonomy was already of long standing. On the other
hand, the co-ordinative tasks of the new SS Main Office were more
than an extension of the duties of the old SS-*Amt* and less than the all-
encompassing conception of the defunct *Oberstab* of the years before
1933. Himmler had experimented in 1932 with Prince Waldeck-Pyrmont
as personal adjutant and simultaneous executive officer or *Stabsführer*; and
in 1933–34 with Siegfried Seidel-Dittmarsch, a former Prussian officer
who was a super liaison man called *Chef des Führungsstabs* (Chief of the
Leadership Staff), no longer Himmler's adjutant but also detached from
narrow administrative duties. When Seidel-Dittmarsch died, Himmler
abolished the Leadership Staff and turned to the idea of strengthening the
administrative prerogatives of the old SS Office, which had been overshadowed by the Leadership Staff. Himmler found for the position Curt
Wittje, another retired army officer with business connections, whose
energy as Main Sector commander in unfriendly Hamburg had recommended him. After a few months of familiarising himself with the role,
Himmler asked him to co-ordinate such SS tasks as the concentration
camps, the *Gruppenstab* z.b.V. (an SS liaison office at Berlin working with
the *Reichswehr*, Foreign Ministry, etc. – disbanded in July 1935) and the
garrisoned SS units under arms, as well as to supervise training, weapons,
inspections, personnel, judiciary, budget and maintenance, and medical
services. The SS Main Office under his charge was divided into *Ämter*
(offices), *Hauptabteilungen* (main sections) and *Abteilungen* (sections), the
heads of which met monthly as a group. Transfer of the SS-*Hauptamt* from
Munich to Berlin, a process which had been begun but not completed in
1933 and 1934 under the *Führungsstab*, took place in the first half of 1935,

delaying somewhat the centralisation process in the SS. In May 1935 Himmler suddenly removed the recently named Main Office chief because of charges of homosexuality during his army career (perhaps revealed to Himmler by the *Wehrmacht*), replacing him with August Heissmeier, a younger man with an academic background. In spite of ambition and vigour the latter never succeeded in mastering the drawbacks in his position, so that he left the SS Main Office in 1939 no stronger within the ramified SS system than it had been in 1935. He did, however, make an elaborate bureaucracy out of the rudimentary staff system on which his predecessor had only just begun to build.

Just as in 1932 and 1933 the staff positions in the old *Oberstab* had tended to become independent offices (*Sicherheitsamt* and *Rassenamt* – Security and Racial Offices), so ultimately several SS-*Hauptamt* offices also broke off and were set up independently. The Administrative Office even in 1932 tended to be a separate operation, with its own training, uniforms, promotions and procedures – based on the so-called treasurers in the units, who managed the sponsoring or supporting members of the SS (*Fördernde Mitglieder*) programme. Renamed *Verwaltungsführer*, they still retained a certain separateness. When Oswald Pohl, a dynamic ex-naval officer, took over the Administrative Section of the supposedly strengthened SS-*Amt* early in 1934, he worked steadily to become *Verwaltungschef* ('Chief of Administration') directly under Himmler, responsible for administration in the *Sicherheitsamt*, *Rassenamt*, *Verfügungstruppe* and concentration camps. By 1939 he was head of two overlapping main offices, the SS-Administrative and Economic Main Office (VWHA), and the Police Main Office for Budget and Construction. While the former was financed from the party funds controlled by F.X. Schwarz, the latter tapped the resources of the Reich for the future combat SS (*Waffen*-SS) and the concentration camps.

A similar process, complicated by many changes in the top personnel, occurred with the *Führungsamt* (Leadership Office). Its first chief had been an ex-*Reichswehr* major who had taken it over as the Munich *Führungsabteilung* (Leadership Section) when it was still overshadowed by the Berlin *Führungsstab*. He never succeeded in becoming more than an office manager; he was replaced temporarily in 1935 by Leo Petri, a fifty-eight-year-old ex-lieutenant-colonel of police with First World War occupation experience in Poland, China and Africa. When the latter was given a new post as head of a special Security Office to combat assassination of Nazi leaders, Himmler experimented with having the chief of the SS Main Office run the Leadership Office personally but soon gave it up. The Leadership Office then gravitated into the orbit of the future combat SS and was headed for a time in 1936 by Paul Hausser until he was named Inspector of the *Verfügungstruppe*; but it was largely run by Hermann Cummerow, also an ex-*Reichswehr* colonel.

An elaborate bureaucracy within the rest of the SS Main Office developed for much the same reasons. In 1935 sections for SS welfare, recruitment, security, population policy and the press were added along with a big chancellery. In 1936 three new inspectorates were added to that for the concentration camps (now changed to a regular command over the Death's Head troops as well): *Verfügungstruppe*, Border and Guard troops, and Officer Candidate Schools. But the press section soon had a press chief and in June 1937 had to give way to an independent agency known as the *Pressestelle* SS *und Polizei* (Press Office of the SS and Police), reflecting an amalgamation process of SS and Police which had produced the two overlapping Administrative Main Offices referred to earlier. 1937 did not reduce the number of departments in the Main Office, however, for with Himmler's approval its bureaucratic chief added offices for calisthenics, communications, archives and procurement. In 1938 Himmler split the recruitment office in two, to separate the record-keeping and statistical functions from the active, policy-forming operations. This fragmentation did nothing to strengthen the influence of the SS Main Office due to delays, as well as shifts in emphasis and personnel, even though a kind of bureaucratic imperialism within the agency had produced the office. Its ambitious members had to leave it to achieve power and prestige – led by Heissmeier, its chief who as early as 1936 began to diversify his interests by becoming Inspector of the National Political Training Schools (Napolas), not an SS operation. By 1939 Himmler was willing to create for him another Main Office, designated simply by his own name, so that Heissmeier could pursue his schoolmasterly interests with the prestige of the SS, but without laying full claim to the Napolas. Whatever advantages this interest of his gave Himmler and the SS in influencing German youth, it reduced proportionately Heissmeier's attention to the SS Main Office, which found itself bypassed time and again by the other Main Offices, by regional SS and police commanders, and especially by Himmler himself. Himmler's own lack of sustained interest in a unified staff system was a serious contributing factor, although not the only reason for the problem. Changing conditions and functions within the SS also created difficulties.

The year 1936 was in many ways the key one in the evolution of the SS system, for it was in mid-1936 that Himmler was able to achieve the unification of the German police under himself, thus creating the basis for the steady amalgamation of SS and police in the following years. In 1935 the SS was still picking up pieces from the period of topsy-turvy growth, the revolutionary upset and the Röhm purge. Expulsions, consolidation and differentiation were the main themes. A basic, long-overdue reorganisation in the ranks of the General SS took place in January 1936 to reduce the variety of special honorary ranks. Henceforth there were merely paid, full-time SS and unpaid, part-time 'honorary' ranks. After 1936 the SS appeared to have found its direction and stride – perhaps also its limits, although these would not remain permanent – so that a kind of watershed is formed by the acquisition by Himmler, on 17 June 1936, of the title of *Reichsführer* SS *und Chef der deutschen Polizei* (RFSSuChddPol!). This change is reflected indirectly in the revision of the relationship of the *Oberabschnittsführer* to the Main Offices by Himmler on 9 November 1936. Formerly these commanders had been subject only to Himmler and to the SS Main Office. Now they were also made subject to the Security Main Office and the Race and Settlement Main Office, and also in a sense to two additionally created Main Offices, Himmler's *Hauptamt Persönlicher Stab* (Personal Staff Main Office) and a Main Office designated simply with Daluege's name but identical to the Main Office *Ordnungspolizei* (Order Police). This basic change meant that the SS regional commanders received nominal influence over the police operations in their regions, as well as over the activities of the Race and Settlement System, which at this time included ideological SS training, SS family welfare, SS urban and rural settlement and housing, and liaison with the *Reichsnährstand* (Food Estate System) in agriculture.

Even at this point, however, it is necessary to note an ambiguity, for the creation of the three new inspectorates in 1936 – including *Verfügungstruppe*, Border and Guard troops, and Officer Candidate Schools – plus the independence of the concentration camps and Death's Head troops took away with the left hand at least part of what Himmler had given with the right. The regional SS commanders were not to receive orders from the inspectors or from Eicke; thus the special SS units were in turn cut off from regional influence, a step in the separation of a professional military SS from the ranks of the traditional political soldiers. As we have seen and shall see even more clearly, the effort to amalgamate the SS and the police was a quite separate process, slow and uneven, and never more than partially successful. Similarly, the complete isolation of the professional SS soldier was certainly not openly striven for and was even opposed by Himmler himself on occasion in favour of a three-way amalgamation of political soldier (*Allgemeine* SS), police and professional soldier. Some leading SS officers managed this synthesis, but by far the majority combined only two of these features in their career and outlook; many remained only political soldiers, police-men, or professional soldiers. Some of the latter rose to very high rank, as did SS officers who could better be characterised in other terms than any of these, such as technicians and professional men.

Personal Staff (Persönlicher Stab)

Perhaps due to Himmler's split personality, which encouraged the bureaucratisation of the SS-*Hauptamt* but then sought to circumvent his own bureaucracy, the new and powerful Main Office known as the *Persönlicher Stab, Reichsführer* SS (Personal Staff, RF-SS), began in 1936 to collect and create responsibilities growing out of adjutants' duties. Formerly known as the *Chef-Adjutantur*, it had been headed since 1934 by Karl Wolff, a shrewd 'operator' who succeeded as Himmler's first adjutant where two or three previous men had failed because he was cleverer, more flexible and imaginative, and willing to take Himmler's abuse. His reward was to remain in Himmler's close confidence and to manage all aspects of his relationships with SS, party, and state agencies and person-nel – a role for which the SS-*Hauptamt* seemed to have been originally designed.

The *Chef-Adjutantur* had moved up to Berlin with five or six low-ranking SS officers and NCOs in 1935 as still primarily a letter-answering service. Its membership was young, willing and eager to please not only Himmler but also all SS, party and state authorities. In return, SS officers and other officials were grateful for little services rendered them in gaining a hearing or recognition from the *Reichsführer* SS, so that soon a tone of mutual accommodation and even intimacy entered the correspondence of the office. By November 1936 when Himmler erected it into the equivalent of a Main Office, ensconced in the Prinz Albrechtstrasse, the Personal Staff had basically three functions: (1) liaison, (2) financial and (3) cultural. Out of the letter-answering function developed an extensive forwarding mechanism, so that personal letters to Himmler could be passed onto one of his many subordinate agencies. At the same time as more and more high-ranking persons inside and outside the SS sought to gain Himmler's ear outside regular channels, the Personal Staff became the focus of influence in the SS. Himmler increasingly employed it for delicate negotiations where 'channels' had to be avoided. Matters properly dealt with by the Personnel Office – uniforms, decorations, even promotions – became the stock-in-trade of junior officers in the Personal Staff office, while the most sought-after honorary SS position after 1936 was *Stab, Reichsführer* SS because it opened official channels to the centre of influence.

The second aspect of the Personal Staff was economic, for Himmler ultimately controlled the sources of financial perquisites. SS salaries were low, and it soon became apparent that it was dangerous for Himmler to allow his officers' corps to become dependent on state offices controlled by Göring, Frick, or Gürtner, or on positions in private industry. Special allowances for expenses, in addition to grants-in-aid to get out of debt and loans, became available by 1936, from funds obtained by Himmler by private negotiation with the Party Treasurer, as well as from the circle of industrialists (*Freundeskreis*) founded in 1932. These funds were placed in 'Special Account R' under the control of the Section *Wirtschaftliche Hilfe* ('Economic Aid'). The SS Chief of Administration, Pohl, transferred one of his better officers, Bruno Galke, to Himmler for this purpose in 1936. Furthermore, starting in November 1935 with one of his Basic Decrees, Himmler founded a kind of compulsory SS credit union to which all had to contribute 1 mark a month. The management of these funds rested with the Personal Staff, who might use them also for the support of SS widows and orphans. No interest was paid, however, and there was no real insurance principle for survivors. In other words, Himmler and his adjutants gained an additional lever to ensure 'enthusiasm' among the SS and their dependents. In fact these funds were largely invested in business enterprises in which the Personal Staff owned more than 50 per cent of the stock. The first of these was founded as early as December 1934 – the Nordland Verlag, a publishing house set up in Magdeburg to further Himmler's Nordic ideas. The second was the Allach Porcelain Works, privately founded at Himmler's request in 1933 and then taken over by the Personal Staff as an SS enterprise to manufacture Dresden-like figures and 'Nordic' cult objects such as birthday candle holders. Other business enterprises founded in the mid-1930s by the Personal Staff included a photographic firm, a bicycle reflector company, a mineral water bottling works and several urban estate agents to provide housing for SS officers in model suburban developments or in new villas in the best neighbourhoods.

In the later 1930s the Personal Staff expanded its economic activities to include support of non-SS inventors (some of them unsavoury characters who ended up in concentration camps after embezzling Reich and party funds), the development of raw material supplies for the SS in conjunction with Göring's Four Year Plan Office, the search for manpower for German agriculture, and the finding of jobs in industry for retiring full-time SS officers. Inevitably they came into conflict with Pohl's equally ambitious SS administrative branch and were forced to part with many of their enterprises and activities by 1939. The war soon brought them plenty of new opportunities for regrowth.

The third function of the Personal Staff was related to Himmler's cultural pretensions, already somewhat involved in the development of the porcelain works to 'purify' German *objets d'art*. Here too the involvement took the form of foundation, in 1935, of the research and teaching society, *Ahnenerbe* (Ancestral Heritage Foundation), and in 1936 of the Society for the Advancement and Preservation of German Cultural Monuments. In each case the societies were governed as sections of the Personal Staff with SS officers at their head. Funds were solicited and collected from interested German individuals and firms for excavations and restorations of real and supposed Germanic cultural relics – including medieval cathedrals. Expeditions were launched to South America and Tibet, and expensive publications were undertaken in the archaeological and artistic fields. Again the Personal Staff was able to acquire extensive contacts in the intellectual and scientific field, as well as in the highest circles of German philanthropy and finance. Many persons who might otherwise have had no reason to associate with Himmler or the SS became thereby involved and often even joined the ranks as honorary members. Through the Personal Staff Himmler acquired a very broad range of 'respectable' friends and supporters whom he could draw upon for assistance, financial and technical, both for the furtherance of the SS and to help it perform more and more functions for the Reich. However, the second- and third-rate minds of the 'scientists' which the Ancestral Heritage Foundation, for example, sponsored tended to make SS 'research' the laughing stock of the universities Himmler wished to penetrate. This did not of course prevent even scoffers from capitalising on Himmler's naiveté or the SD from recruiting the scoffers for intelligence work.

Race and Settlement Main Office of the SS (RuSHa)

Another SS Main Office which tended to grow out of shape and fragment as it expanded in connection with ever-increasing involvement in government, party and business activities was Darré's Race and Settlement Main Office. While its original line of development came from the power to grant or withhold approval for marriage among SS men, Darré's affiliation with the Food and Agriculture Ministry and the Food Estate inevitably carried RuSHa into extensive economic activity in competition or in co-operation with party, state and private interests. We have already noted that it was this same Main Office which received in 1933 the main educational responsibilities within the SS, enabling it to penetrate the local units organisationally. Thus, by the time it became a Main Office in January 1935, it had acquired four duties: (1) ideological training, (2) racial selection, (3) liaison with German agriculture and (4) family welfare within the SS. For each of these duties, there was a section or office staffed by one or two paid SS officers and headed by an 'honorary' chief who was usually one of Darré's officials in the Ministry and Food Estate. Furthermore, every Main Sector had a *Rassereferent* (race expert), who was really a salaried officer of RuSHa, and a *Bauernreferent* (farm advisor), who was usually the *Landesbauernführer* (state farm leader) in the Food Estate system and an honorary SS officer. At lower levels there was a training officer (or NCO) who was also part of RuSHa, all the way down to company level. The latter were unpaid. Attached to units at every level was also a regional farm leader (normally an actual farmer) of the Food Estate with RuSHa (SS) rank, also a part-time volunteer. It should be noted that these training officers or NCOs and farm advisors were still just being taken into the SS at the time (1934 and 1935) and were thus well known neither to RuSHa nor to the local units. Their party back-ground and professional competence were usually stressed.

While the sections of the Race and Settlement Main Office worked out policy in their respective fields of competence and passed upon doubtful cases (primarily having to do with admission and marriage), the advisors and training officers were the executives of policies within their units. They were to help SS commanders and their men carry out the routines ordered by RuSHa. For their instruction RuSHa held a number of short courses at a special school in the Grunewald suburb of Berlin, as well as other professional gatherings. They were to subscribe to the Food Estate's newspaper '*Deutsche Zeitung*', which 'expressed the views of the Race and Settlement Office'. In July 1935 this was replaced by the official monthly magazine of the Training Office (RuS-*Schulungsamt*), the '*SS-Leithefte*'. Nevertheless, it appears that the whole network of training officers and farm advisors was very slowly filled and often changed. An endless flow of forms to be completed by command-ers and their men originated with RuSHa as early as 1934, combined with extensive training materials. Unit RuS representatives could rarely have had the time, education, enthusiasm and unit support for so much routine activity. Thus it is not surprising that RuSHa seems gradually to have grown away from the units to become its own executive in many fields. As usual, the turning point is approximately 1936, when Darré appointed a kind of field representative to regain contact with the RuS 'branch units'.

Whereas the 1935 structure of the Main Office for Race and Settlement was based on the use of a large number of honorary SS offi-cers whose chief focus of attention lay in Darré's state and party appa-ratus, with a small number of low-ranking officers and NCOs to tend the shop, changes initiated in 1936 and continued in 1937 produced a professional Main Office which attracted former General SS commanders and staff personnel to Berlin. One of the most marked examples of this was the Settlement Office, which was transferred in 1936 from Herbert Backe of the Agriculture Ministry to Curt von Gottberg, a minor aristocrat from East Elbia cultivated by Darré. Von Gottberg dabbled in Agricultural Settlement Companies, a form of real estate speculation associated with the conversion of East Elbian estates to small farms. He brought to RuSHa the scheme of working through these companies to aid in the settlement of SS men on the soil (also in suburban units). Under his leadership an old company (*Deutsche Ansiedlungsgesellschaft*) was reorganised with an SS majority (private stock purchase) on the board of directors for purposes of rural development, and a new company (*Gemeinnützige Wohnungs- und Heimstätten G.m.b.H.*) was organised to build and operate SS suburban settlements. Von Gottberg forced the co-ordination of all SS housing projects by local and regional units under his control. He persuaded Darré and Himmler that he should have an architectural and planning section under him which could be consulted even by the German police in barracks construction. By 1939 he had built up his office to twenty paid employees; there were at least seven settlement areas in the Reich administered by his office and numerous 'SS Settlement Companies' in which Himmler had a controlling interest, through private stock purchases made by Backe and other SS officers working with him. There were difficulties ahead, however, because Oswald Pohl, the Chief of the SS Administration, sought increasingly to bring all economic activities of the SS under his control. Furthermore, in 1938 Darré was to quarrel with Himmler and thus remove some of the Settlement Office's backing, though not all.

The other RuSHa office which developed far beyond its original scope was that known as the *Sippenamt* (Office for Family Affairs, sometimes translated as Genealogical Office). Whereas the original Race Office continued to function after 1936 as a 'scientific' or policy advisory unit for Himmler and especially for liaison with state and party bureaus, the *Sippenamt* took over the approval of admissions and marriages, and in 1936 launched an ambitious programme of Family Welfare Offices in the SS units at regimental level. The background of this programme lies not so much in an ambitious SS officer, although one soon turned up, but in Himmler's own personal interest. In November 1935 the *Reichsführer* SS determined that the SS should care for its own – specifically that the well-known reluctance of men who had just come through the depression to marry and have children could only be overcome by a sort of guarantee that the SS as a kind of family community would care for widows and orphans. Thus, the basic decree concerning widows and orphans laid the foundation for a network of Family Welfare Offices, formally headed by the regimental commanders but actually staffed by one or more unit officers taken into the *Sippenamt* for this purpose. Their functions overlapped those of the training officers, who were often given this position. In 1937 RuSHa received state funds for the upkeep of these offices on the grounds that they served the racial and eugenics programme of the Reich. By 1939 there were between 200 and 300 paid employees in the *Sippenamt*, many of them attached to the SS units spread throughout Germany, although it is certain that some of the funds were employed to erect a sizeable processing staff in Berlin for the great backlog of genealogies and racial–eugenics investigations they accumulated in the admissions and marriage approval operation.

This was not all the *Sippenamt* accomplished, however, backed as it was by Himmler's strong enthusiasm. In December 1935 it founded one of the most publicised and controversial of SS installations, *Lebensborn*, e.V. (the Well of Life Society). With marriage such a risky economic matter, large numbers of SS members were found to be fathering children outside of marriage. While many of them were contributing to the support of these illegitimate children, some were getting into trouble for their efforts at abortion, which the Nazi regime was engaged in suppressing. Thus, Himmler conceived of an agency to aid unwed mothers to have their children in comfortable seclusion in a well-run hospital and sanatorium. The organisation was founded as a registered society (*eingeschriebener Verein*, e.V.) with the *Reichsführer* SS as chairman. Although the SS did not appear in its official title, the administration of *Lebensborn* was placed under the *Sippenamt* as 'Section IV'. Its business manager was the staff officer of the *Sippenamt*, Guntram Pflaum, a career SS officer in his thirties intent on making a name for himself. The medical aspects, and indeed the official leadership, Himmler gave to his family physician, Dr Gregor Ebner, an old SS associate and fraternity brother. In 1936 they set up the first maternity home not far from Munich and began urging SS men to join the society by arranging for monthly payroll deductions. It was not long before all the higher ranking full-time officers were compelled to contribute on a scale which taxed bachelors and rewarded men with large families. The demand for the services of the home was immediately high, and three more homes were planned in 1937 and opened in 1938 in Brandenburg, Pomerania and the Harz Mountains. The homes were available to SS wives and young women referred to the SS by party and state agencies. Arrangements were made to place the children for adoption with SS families if the mothers wished, but efforts were also made to smooth the way for marriage or at least force the father to provide child support. The liaison operations naturally fell to the Family Welfare Offices, while the administration was taken away from the *Sippenamt* and placed in the *Reichsführer* SS's Personal Staff early in 1938.

This move of Himmler's seems to have been the first sign of a decline in the fortunes of the Main Office for Race and Settlement, reflecting underlying disagreements with Darré. While Himmler's real reason for quarrelling with the Minister of Food and Agriculture may have been Darré's independent position – possibly even strengthened by ties with Göring's growing economic empire – the SS reasons had to do with SS training. Not only had there been considerable turnover in the leadership of the Training Office, with none of the office chiefs a decisive personality, but the influx of academically oriented persons into this branch of activity had produced a plethora of abstruse and fantastic training materials quite unusable by the training officers. At the same time that Himmler was himself indulging in the sponsorship of pseudo-scientific investigations outside of RuSHa, he demanded that it limit itself to practical matters. The result was Darré's refusal in February 1938 to carry on the training role assigned to RuSHa; Himmler transferred the Training Office to the SS Main Office, although he retained its chief, Dr Joachim Caesar – an SS colonel whom he had previously castigated for academic tendencies – and the office remained in the Hedemannstrasse complex with RuSHa. Clearly, Himmler's real object was to drive Darré out entirely, which he accomplished in the summer, while keeping that from the public. Günther Pancke, the new RuSHa chief, was a practical administrator, an SS-*Altkämpfer* and free corps veteran, most recently *Stabsführer* (business manager) of one of the SS Main Sectors. It was to be his melancholy duty to preside at the dismemberment and shelving of RuSHa, though not before one last flurry of activity by the Settlement Office.

Pressed by the SS Administrative Main Office to surrender his control over SS-sponsored settlements, the head of the Settlement Office looked for new worlds to conquer in Austria and Czechoslovakia. Thus, in the spring of 1938 while Himmler was forbidding the formation of 'wild-cat' SS settlements, Curt von Gottberg quietly arranged the formation of the Viennese version of his *Gemeinnützige Wohnungs- und Heimstätten* GmbH and entered into the Aryanisation proceedings conducted by the Gestapo against Jewish real estate, 'in the interests of the SS', although with private funds. His *Deutsche Ansiedlungsgesellschaft* also soon appeared in the Sudetenland as trustee for confiscated Czech farmland, administered by SS person-nel recruited by the *Siedlungsamt* from the *Standarten* of the General SS as early as August 1938. Von Gottberg's real coup was achieved when Himmler named him, on Heydrich's advice, as chief of the former *Bodenamt Prag* (Czech Land Registry). Here he was heading straight for a fall, although as was so often the case in Nazi power politics, the immediate source of his success was Himmler's refusal to take sides against him; actually Himmler and Heydrich were obviously not averse to letting von Gottberg show them the technique of outfoxing their new rival, the Reich Minister of Food and Agriculture.

The Settlement Office had submitted a proposal to the new chief of RuSHa – who sent it on to Heydrich – for a Reich Settlement Commission, possibly modelled on the Prussian Settlement Commission of 1886, to co-ordinate all German 'internal colonisation' and beginning with a plan to settle SS families in Bohemia and Moravia. The eviction of Czechs and Jews 'dangerous to state security' would provide a base for property acquisition. Speed was of the essence, however, for the Food and Agriculture Ministry was already active in the former Czech Land Registry attaching former German properties taken in the Czech land reform. In co-operation with Wilhelm Stuckart of the Interior Ministry, a Himmler confidante and SS-Brigadier-General (in the SD), von Gottberg was ensconced with a team of SS officials from the Settlement Office at Prague in June. They proceeded to grab properties so ruthlessly, without careful investigation of the consequences and in such a strange mixture of private and public looting, that it was only a matter of months before even Himmler was forced to suspend von Gottberg and several of his henchmen. The subsequent investigation led back into Austria with such devastating revelations of venality and improprieties that Himmler sent several SS officers to concentration camps, although Heydrich managed to aid von Gottberg's rehabilitation in the course of the war. The latter's forthright brutality appealed to Heydrich, although it does not appear that the perenially indebted nobleman actually took anything for himself. The direction of SS settlement, however, left his hands for good, and the RuSHa Settlement Office declined accordingly.

Police

Darré and Heydrich were both relative newcomers to the top hierarchy of the SS, while Daluege was one of the true Old Fighters. Although Heydrich outstripped both of them in the erection of a personal empire, Daluege turned out to be more effective than Darré in combining his state position with SS power. The very narrowness of Himmler's concerns prevented him from following Darré too far into the bypaths of settlement projects; he preferred his police role, which meant that Daluege, and of course Heydrich, would have the advantage in their fields of ambition. In June 1936 when the latter two were made formal equals by each receiving a police *Hauptamt* in the Ministry of Interior, Daluege was consolidating a position he already had in effect as co-ordinator of the State Police in Germany (now renamed *Ordnungspolizei*, Order Police or Orpo). Heydrich, on the other hand, was entering a new position created for him by Himmler against the wishes of Frick as the minister, Nebe as the chief of the Criminal Police, and countless other police officials in the SS. Each man accomplished much in bringing about a national integration of the police, but neither was entirely successful, losing interest in the course of the war and turning to the problem of assimilating the Protectorate of Bohemia-Moravia, where both ultimately were to lose their lives.

We may recall that Daluege entered police activity in the service of the Prussian state, moving from *Kommissar* z.b.V. in the Prussian Ministry of the Interior to a generalship in the Prussian *Landespolizei*. When the two interior ministries were combined on 1 November 1934, Daluege took over the police section (*Abteilung* III) of the united ministry. Thereafter he was often, though incorrectly, referred to as the Commander of the German Police. Technically the State Police of the *Länder* still existed with their own budgets, locally subordinate to the interior ministry of their state and thence to the Reich governor (*Reichsstatthalter*), and only subordinate to the Reich Ministry of the Interior for technical instructions. What Daluege had done in Prussia before November 1934, he now sought to do throughout the Reich: to 'clean out' the ranks of the police officers' corps by speeding up the retirement of so-called Marxists, liberals, and 'political Catholics' (former Centre Party). He, of course, also removed many commissarial SA personnel after 30 June 1934. Serious efforts to locate SS officers in non-Gestapo police positions began in the summer of 1935, from the SS Main Office rather than from Daluege, which was understandable. Police directorships and presidencies were too often assigned to active SS commanders, with the result that one or the other position was neglected and often a transfer required by one service was inimical to the other. An unsystematic pursuit of paying jobs in the police bureaucracy was continued in the SS, much as it had existed in the SA in 1933, until the basic co-ordination of the whole system began with the appointment of Himmler as *Reichsführer* SS *und Chef der Deutschen Polizei* (*Reichsführer* SS and Chief of the German Police) as of 17 June 1936.

The conception of a unified German police under the control of Frick went back to 1933 and appeared as late as the second-half of 1935 in the form of a draft decree and memorandum stressing the loss of the garrisoned *Landespolizei* to the *Wehrmacht* and the need for a national police in their place, the more so because only police were still allowed in the 'demilitarised' Rhineland. While its author is not known, the draft decree and the memorandum sound enough like Daluege to suggest that it was at least written to meet his approval. With the military occupation of the Rhineland in March 1936, the need to include the Rhineland police formations in some national police force disappeared or rather was met in a different way by the SS-*Verfügungstruppe*. We find therefore a modification in the proposal of the Reich and Prussian Ministry of the Interior – again not strictly identifiable with Daluege, though certainly in his interest. An Inspector of the German Police was to be named in the ministry, probably originally meant to be Daluege; in fact he was proposed as the permanent deputy of Himmler in this post. This proposal was rejected by Himmler through Heydrich, who represented him in the negotiations. Instead Himmler wanted to be appointed as *Reichsführer* SS and Chief of the German Police. This he achieved, although Frick attached the words 'in the Ministry of the Interior' to the title. Nothing was said in the decree about Daluege being his deputy, although a press notice of 18 June stated that he would represent Himmler in the latter's absence, a quite different matter. Daluege's actual post was created on 26 June by Himmler on his own authority along with Heydrich's. There had never been *Hauptämter* in the Ministry of Interior; the two police offices were obviously copied from Heydrich's SS-*Sicherheitshauptamt*, which soon came to be called the SD-*Hauptamt* to differentiate it from Heydrich's new police headquarters.

While Heydrich truly had two offices with largely (but not wholly) separate personnel, Daluege's SS-*Hauptamt* 'Daluege' was exactly the same as the *Hauptamt Ordnungspolizei*, unless we count a police major who served Himmler as an adjutant and signed the SS orders of the *Hauptamt* Daluege. Furthermore, Daluege also lost from his field of influence the Criminal Police. He had gained, of course, a vast apparatus of uniformed policemen, which was especially large in a Germany where not only fire departments but numerous regulatory bodies were part of the 'administrative police'. Yet not until 19 March 1937 did he gain, through Himmler, direct power of appointment and budget determination for the police of the *Länder*, and even then, until 28 March 1940, certain state administrative police organisations eluded him. Nevertheless, after 1937 Daluege had a solid enough base to deal with Himmler and Heydrich for advantages for 'his' police within the SS and to open up lower ranges of police activity to qualified SS applicants – motorised *gendarmerie* and Protective Police (*Schutzpolizei* or *Schupo*) in the cities. In 1938 *Schupo* were permitted to wear SS runes on their uniform – perhaps to enhance their authority – and many of the higher ranks in the Order Police were taken into the SS with equivalent SS rank and a minimum of questions asked. The creation of the post of Inspector of the Order Police as early as 1936, a position to be occupied by a police colonel in each province of Prussia and at each Reich governor's seat, formed the basis of SS and Police union, for eventually these positions had to be filled with SS officers of comparable rank. Few if any were to come from the old SS ranks; however; inducted into the SS for this purpose, these career policemen would form a cadre for the Superior SS and Police Leaders of the war years and for the general staff which Daluege was reforming in his Main Office, at once both an SS and a state agency. There too his 'General-Inspectors' were not taken into the SS until the 'peaceful' invasion of Austria in March 1938, when SS status had begun to include quasi-military privileges.

On the other hand, Heydrich was nibbling away at the middle ranks of Daluege's apparatus, the twenty-eight police directors and fifty-six police presidents, by placing some in the SD as early as 1936 and more after 1938. While a certain number of these persons were indeed the 'old reliable' SS fighters who had been placed in these positions in 1933, the great majority were not even in the SS but went directly into the SD. Thus, Heydrich, as well as Daluege, carried out a union of the SS and Police largely by naming new SS officers via Himmler, not always through the personnel office and often with small regard to the formal admission requirements of RuSHa. In the *Sicherheitsdienst*, however, Heydrich possessed a better apparatus for SS penetration into the police, for its top echelons were more SS-oriented than Daluege's right-wing higher police officers, and its intelligence function destroyed its opponents by turning in damaging information about them to superiors. A police director or police president would often join the SD in self-defence against some junior officer. All these persons held unpaid positions in the SD, attached to the field apparatus of the SD run by a small professional cadre.

In the 1935 pamphlet *Changes in our Struggle* (*Wandlungen unseres Kampfes*), Heydrich managed to verbalise what both Hitler and Himmler had been trying to express for so long – that political soldier-ing had to combine ideological defence with some kind of inner loyalty so strong that police operations, military operations and propaganda operations would all be merely varieties of one reality. The old SA free corps spirit was not enough, and the corpse-like obedience of the drill ground was insufficient; the ethos of a sworn elite had to be created and preserved. It was for this purpose the SD existed. Heydrich was a true believer, whose cynicism was reserved for the faint of heart and hand. Perhaps a disbeliever in this or that 'Himmlerian' dogma about race, runes and natural religion, Heydrich was a consistent practitioner of the strenuous life, the imaginative innovation and the thorough solution. In the professional SD he sought out the most ruthless, the most consis-tent, the most unprincipled. With relatively low ranks and small oppor-tunity of promotion and public visibility, he dissuaded the grandstander and the venal. Persons who liked to wield power without responsibility, to weigh and judge their superiors, to torture and to kill coldly at a distance – these were the men Heydrich gathered about himself in the *Sicherheitsamt* in the Wilhelmstrasse and in the professional SD field structure of 1935 and 1936. Some were SS-*Altkämpfer*; some were from the SA; many of them had been unpolitical. With a few prominent exceptions, they remained unheard of in 1945, providing deadly mecha-nisms for the use of the more colourful SS and Police Leaders from the ranks of the career SS, the free corps and the SA. The criminality of the latter was plain for all to see, while clerks of the SD remained largely anonymous.

When we said earlier that Heydrich – unlike Daluege – achieved two separate headquarters, we were merely continuing an observation made in a previous chapter, where it was remarked that Heydrich cleverly did not attempt to merge the state Gestapa and the SS-*Sicherheitsamt*. Serving as bridges between the two offices were Heydrich himself, Heinrich Müller, an epitome of ruthlessness from the Bavarian Political Police without SS loyalties but very much Himmler's man, and Werner Best, who came up from Munich on 1 January 1935. Best was less ruthless than Müller and possessed some of the intellectual's complexities of personality. With more loyalty to SS ideas and ideals than even the pragmatic Heydrich, he served as a link to the party, as well as the professional and academic world within and beyond the General SS. In the Gestapa on Prinz Albrechtstrasse, he served as Heydrich's executive officer (I-AO) in 1935–36 and then deputised for him as its chief until the total reorganisation of September 1939 placing the Gestapa under Müller within the larger structure of the so-called *Reichssicherheitshauptamt* (Reich Security Main Office or RSHA). It was Best's legal skill and ingenuity which threw the Gestapa into the breach in February 1936, when the absence of a Reich police just before the reoccupation of the Rhineland seemed to threaten loss of regional control in a national emergency. The Prussian Gestapa by the law of 2 February 1936 was transformed into a Reich agency for the Political Police, months before Daluege and Frick reached agreement with Heydrich and Himmler about the Order Police. The mechanism which made this possible was Best's control position in the SS-*Sicherheitsamt* (later *Sicherheitshauptamt*) at Wilhelmsstrasse 102. Its five sections he reduced to three offices in 1935 to parallel the Gestapa, taking over the first, Organisation and Administration, which included the appointment and promotion of both professional and unpaid ('honorary') SD personnel.

During 1935 and 1936 some more of the Political Police, both in the Prussian *Stapostellen* and in the *Länder*, were added to the SS and SD above and beyond the original spies and agents of Heydrich from before April 1934. Aside from a hard core of old SS men in this group taken into the SD essentially as administrative measure, many of these new SD people were young lawyers beginning careers as police officials. Through the SS and especially the SD, Best and Heydrich played on their ambitions and intellect, so that they became willing tools. Through the SD system the larger Gestapo, recruited from older career officials and often from the criminal-investigation forces, could be directed and controlled.

In the Gestapo fear of the SD and ambition for advancement, which might depend upon SD co-operation, were sufficient to gain compliance with Berlin directives no matter how unpalatable. In August and September 1936, the Prussian system of *Stapostellen* was extended to the entire Reich on a systematic basis under the direct control of the Berlin Gestapa sections. Needless to say, Best had seen to it that the key personnel of the Gestapa were primarily loyal to Himmler rather than to Göring or Frick, with the result that a considerable shuffling had occurred and continued to occur with the headquarters and between it and the provinces. Since those loyal to Himmler were either SS officers already or were placed in the SS and SD, the result of this shuffling was the rapid promotion of this segment of the SS officers' corps to catch up with the General SS (and later the Order Police), so that by 1938–39 the SS-*Dienstalterslisten* (officers' lists by rank and seniority) had a markedly different complexion from those of 1934–36.

With the formation of the *Hauptamt Sicherheitspolizei* on 26 June 1936, the Gestapa was joined (on paper) to the former Prussian Criminal Police headquarters under Arthur Nebe – which now in turn was erected into a Reich police office in charge of a network of '*Kripostellen*' in the major cities. Increasingly the younger officials and later even the older ones in these offices succumbed to the advantages of SS and SD membership. Nebe, its opportunistic chief, who was well aware of the risks involved, himself finally joined the SS as a major on 2 December 1936, perhaps partly as a 'cover' for his rather modest oppositional role. Heydrich's control over the criminal branch of the Security Police (Sipo) was initially scarcely more effective than his influence via the SD over the police directors and police presidents of the Order Police, although the official lines of his command were extended even down to the criminal investigators at county and town police headquarters. It required his SD structure and the concept of SS membership to weld enough of this ramified apparatus into a responsive whole by 1939 so that a series of extra-legal orders and assignments could be silently accepted and carried out by middle-class German officials. The institution of Inspectors of the Security Police, parallel to the Inspectors of the Order Police but with fewer ties to the regional police apparatus, also provided tighter central control, since these posts were normally filled with the cream of the professional SD. However, the regional SD chiefs who held this position were not permitted to use the title publicly until 1939.

It was not until 1936 that the Berlin SD headquarters (SS-*Sicherheitshauptamt*) began its expansion into a true intelligence clearing house, with the SD field network increasingly devoted to depth reporting and special studies rather than the pursuit of specific enemies of the state. Its three-fold organisation was to survive its assimilation along with the Gestapa into the *Reichssicherheitshauptamt* (RSHA) at the outbreak of war. Indeed, many of its NCOs and junior officers of these mid-1930s were to become commanders of the death squads in Russia and managers of the Jewish Holocaust. Otto Ohlendorf, head of *Einsatzgruppe* D, which in 1941 killed Jews and communists in the South Ukraine, began here as a minor sub-section leader; and Eichmann started out as an assistant in the sub-section on Freemasons. On the other hand, some of its chief officials of the 1930s were to sink into oblivion or withdraw or be sent away from the centres of power. Its chancellery, for instance, was headed from 1935 to 1937 by an old Berlin SS comrade of Daluege, Siegfried Taubert, who had become the chief staff officer of Sepp Dietrich as regional commander of the SS eastern region. 'Opi' ('Grandpa') was in his later fifties and a favourite of Heydrich 'because he could play the piano', having once been a piano salesman. His connections were obviously of value in the transition years, but in 1938 he was 'promoted' to being in charge of the SS castle-school of Wewelsburg, near Paderborn. His departure signalled the end of the need for amateurs in the top SD leadership.

While Best had been originally designated to head the 'inland service', Heydrich soon discovered that the cloak-and-dagger fame of the composer of the Boxheim documents was perhaps exaggerated. Heydrich also preferred him as a bureaucrat, in charge of administration. He was assisted by Dr Herbert Mehlhorn, an early SD member who had helped subordinate the Saxon Political Police to the control of Himmler and Heydrich, and by Walter Schellenberg, who replaced Taubert at the chancellery. Heydrich did ultimately make Best his second in command in the *Sicherheitshauptamt*, and Wilhelm Albert replaced Best as head of *Amt* I, Administration. Albert had operated the SD Main Sector 'West' in Frankfurt and was also an early SD man.

Amt Inland (*Amt* II) went to Hermann Behrends, Heydrich's 'agent' in Berlin since late 1933. This was the basic information gathering and evaluating branch, with small teams of 'experts' on Marxism, Catholicism, the Protestant churches and sects, Freemasonry, the Jews, the business and academic world, the press, radio, film, and the arts. Elaborately sub-divided into sub-sub-divisions in Kafkaesque style, the *Judenreferat* (Jewish Desk) was II/112 – with II/1121 for assimilated Jews, II/1122 for Orthodox, and II/1123 for Zionists! These sub-departments and even sub-sub-departments were run by very junior SS NCOs and junior offi-cers with modest educations. Thus, better-educated men like Franz Alfred Six, Reinhard Höhn and Otto Ohlendorf were able by 1936 to insert themselves at higher rungs in the maze, and to climb through the professional policemen and political soldiers of the General SS to posi-tions of policy and prominence. Six and Ohlendorf were to overtake Behrends, who ultimately came to specialise in ethnic German intelli-gence affairs, Six managing the co-ordination of the numerous depart-ments of *Amt Inland* while Ohlendorf became its head and policy maker. Höhn invented the idea of running a permanent opinion-gathering system within the sectors of ordinary life in German society, which produced confidential reports on German political, economic and cultural opinion by 1936.

Amt Ausland (*Amt* III) was nominally run by Heinz Jost, the slippery, unsavoury chief of the former SD-*Rollkommando* (hit squad). In actuality Heydrich himself meddled in the operation of the division. For instance, Wilhelm Albert, mentioned above, functioned in collaboration with Heydrich as a specialist on counterespionage toward France both while in Frankfurt and later while officially in *Amt* I. *Amt* III maintained liaison with and surveillance over the *Wehrmacht* and developed the technical services necessary for espionage and counterespionage. Several of the most colourful adventurers in SS uniform served in this branch. Owing partly to the necessity for caution *vis-à-vis* the military, both the formal and the true head of this bureau did not fully emerge from their obscu-rity in the 1930s, and Walter Schellenberg, the future chief of this branch whose whole career and advanced education had taken place in the Nazi era, began not here but as an assistant to Best – first replacing Taubert, the old SS officer, and later Best himself as Heydrich's main advisor. Much like Darré, Best proved to be too impractical as an executive. Vain and sensitive, he came to detest Heydrich, the cutter of Gordian knots.

The process of forming more specialised varieties of political soldiers as illustrated in the SD and in the police generally, whereby new talent was added to a leavening of 'old fighters', contributed to the downgrad-ing of the regional SS structure in favour of the various specialised central headquarters. Thus, whereas the SD field system went on being organised in the same Main Sectors and Sectors (*Oberabschnitte, Unterabschnitte*) as the General SS – the regional SD chief even called 'SD-Chef in *Oberabschnitt*…' – between 1936 and 1939 the reality of the specialisation process made it increasingly unlikely that an SD chief or his professional staff would be recruited from the SS region, which was still occasionally the case as late as 1936 in spite of Heydrich's interest in separating his SD system from the General SS. The parallel structure of SD and General SS, which survived until the reorganisation of September 1939, made it easy to treat the lower units of the General SS as recruiting grounds for the unpaid SD (SD *des Reichsführers* SS) – occasionally even for new professionals though in declining numbers – and also as 'cold storage' for less able persons who had been tried and found wanting. Many of the latter, including many old fighters with intellectual and character defects, could be placed in the 'retired units' originally designed for those over forty-five, a kind of inactive reserve in contrast to the active SS reserve units for those between thirty-five and forty-five abandoned in 1936. Thereafter only persons under forty-five and active in the SS (though not necessarily in paid posts) were considered as a 'ready reserve' to be heavily drawn upon in emergencies, such as mobilisation. Naturally, persons over forty-five in paid positions were not in retired units. After 1936 the General SS at *Standarte* level and below tended to grow out of touch with the daily problems of the police and questions of military mobilisation, and to become the pool of less specialised, less able, less mobile and even less committed SS members at both officer and enlisted ranks. To remedy this and to enhance the ties between this 'ready reserve' and police and *Verfügungstruppe*, the institution of the regional Superior SS and Police Leaders was initiated in 1936.

Two steps in the conversion of the SS regional commanders into the Superior SS and Police Leaders (HSSPFs) have already been noted. Himmler's Order A 2/36 of 9 November 1936, placing the SS-*Oberabschnittsführer* under RuSHa and the Security Main Office gave them nominal authority over the SD chief in their Main Sector. The creation of both Order Police and Security Police Inspectors in the cities where regional SS commands were located brought police officials into parallel with the SS system. Since this move might seem to reassert the primacy of the police channels, and in fact did often result in bypassing the SS regional commanders, Himmler began in 1937 to have draft schemes drawn up for institutional unification at regional levels of the SS and police. Yet Himmler had to proceed with great caution and some camouflage, for not only did he still have to reckon with resistance from the State Police bureaucracy, but also party circles were less than enthusiastic about SS capture of so vital a regional citadel. Moreover, the SS and the SD were afraid of being absorbed into the state system. That the successful plans were drawn up by an Order Police colonel (von Bomhard) who was not even in the SS until March 1938 suggests Himmler's skill in balancing forces within his own field of competence. He did not let either the General SS leadership or Heydrich's minions have the prestige and advantages of authorship. Daluege's Order Police was successfully 'hooked' by involvement in the design for a wartime system of home-front controls. It was hardly accidental that the first formulation of the concept of this office of Superior SS and Police Leader placed it within the concept of war mobilisation: the need for a common leader for planning and execution of joint actions by Order Police, Security Police and SS-*Verbände* (a term referring specifically to concentration camp guards and *Verfügungstruppe*) within each army corps area. There is little doubt that the initial removal of the wraps around the new SS and Police structure, revealing parallelism with the army corps area system rather than the *Gau* and *Land* system of party and state bureaucracy, underlined the preoccupation of Himmler with 'battle theatre inner Germany' – the suppression of a future stab in the back in wartime. The move could have been known only to the initiated, for it was in an unpublished decree of the Interior Ministry, and its implementation was delayed and spasmodic enough to allow for considerable ambiguity and uncertainty in military and party circles. The HSSPFs were not announced publicly until mid-1938 and then not all at the same time; Daluege ordered them to issue a generalised press release saying nothing about the army corps area connection; ceremonial measures and the security of party and state personages were pushed into the foreground while the actual command over both Order Police and Security Police in the event of an emergency was concealed in all public documents. On the other hand, the subordination of the HSSPFs to the *Reichstatthalter* (viceroys of the realm) was stressed – a matter of great importance to the *Gauleiter* who held this position. Precisely this relationship was abandoned at the outset of the war.

1 *Right:* The official ceremony in 1942 to mark twenty years since the SA, under the leadership of Hitler, 'broke the Red Terror in Coburg'. The 1922 march was commemorated annually and on the tenth anniversary the NSDAP instituted an award for those who had taken part – its image can be seen in front of the large drape on the right of the photograph.

2 *Below:* The newly formed *Stosstrup Hitler* in 1923.

3 The *Deutscher Tag* in Nuremberg, 1923, precursor of the later 'Party Days' in the historic town.

4 *Freikorps Oberland* staging a street march.

5 Right-wing combatants in the 1923 putsch with street barricades. Heinrich Himmler carries the Imperial War Flag.

6 *Right:* Hitler in Landsberg Prison after the failed 1923 putsch.

7 *Below:* An early photograph of SS men in their black uniforms.

8 *Above:* Behind Hitler, from left to right, are Adolf Huehnlein, *Korpsführer* of the NSKK; Viktor Lutze, *Stabschef* of the SA; and *Reichsführer*-SS Heinrich Himmler.

9 *Opposite below left:* Adolf Hitler (right), with the *Blutfahne* of November 1923. Jakob Grimminger, holding the flag, was responsible for its safe-keeping and for carrying it on all official occasions.

10 *Opposite below right:* A demonstration of the NSDAP's fervour for ritual and relics, these early flags from the 1923 era are paraded here in 1933.

11 *This page from top:* The third Nuremberg Party Day, 1929. Standing on the running board of the Mercedes alongside Hitler is Franz Pfeffer von Salomon.

12 *Reichsführer*-SS Heinrich Himmler (front row, third from right) with other officers of the SS, including Kurt Daluege (front row, third from left) and Sepp Dietrich (front row, extreme right).

13 Hitler studies a road map. Behind him are Julius Schaub (left) and Sepp Dietrich (centre), who was in charge of Hitler's personal security.

ARBEITER

WÄHLT DEN FRONTSOLDATEN

HITLER!

14 *Top left:* Braunschweig, 1931. Hitler rallies his public, with protection from SS and SA personnel.

15 *Top right:* 'Workers – Vote for the front-line soldier – Hitler!' A poster from 1932 demonstrating the Nazis' appeal to the masses.

16 and 17 *Bottom left and right:* These private photographs, found in an SS barracks at the end of the war in Europe, show pre-war General SS men burning Communist banners.

18 *Top left:* Heinrich Himmler, photographed while watching Storm Troop manoeuvres with Hitler.

19 *Top right:* 5 March 1933 – early cooperation between the police and the Nazi auxiliaries.

20 *Above:* Nazi leaders in their first hour of triumph on 5 March 1933. From left: Röhm, Himmler and Daluege.

21 The Nuremberg rally of 1933, a powerful show of force by the paramilitary wings of the Nazi party.

22 Massed ranks of General SS at a Nuremberg rally.

23 Young drummers of the *Hitlerjugend*, which from 1933 incorporated the right-wing *Jungstahlhelm*.

24 The *Leibstandarte Adolf Hitler*, which acted as Hitler's personal bodyguard.

25 Sepp Dietrich (left) with Wilhelm Brückner, Hitler's personal adjutant.

26 General SS troops salute Adolf Hitler and General Karl Litzmann on the occasion of the latter's eighty-fifth birthday. With their pledge of personal loyalty, the SS enjoyed at least the appearance of closeness to the *Führer*.

27 *Top left:* Ernst Röhm, SA Chief of Staff, from Streicher's book commemorating the 1933 Nuremberg rally.

28 *Top middle:* Rank upon rank of the SS and SA at Nuremberg, giving some idea of the expansion they carried out in the 1930s.

29 *Top right:* SS-*Obergruppenführer* Eicke, who killed Ernst Röhm in 1934.

30 *Above:* Participants in and survivors of the June–July purge, pictured at Nuremberg in November 1934. Left to right: Göring (behind), Lutze, Hitler, Hess and Himmler.

31 *Top:* An early photograph of the new *Verfügungstruppe*, which gradually became organisationally distinct from the General SS.

32 *Above left:* SS officer Reinhard Heydrich in full uniform and loyal Nazi pose.

33 *Above middle:* Dressed here in SS uniform, Alfred Naujocks was in fact part of the Gestapo's far-reaching system. He is famous for commanding the covert operation which saw German troops dressed as Poles attack the radio station at Gleiwitz, on the German-Polish border. Giving Hitler his excuse for invading Poland, this was arguably the first act of the Second World War.

34 *Above right:* An early photograph of the Adolf Hitler regiment, with the Death's Head prominent on their banners.

35 *Top:* Himmler addressing SS officers in Norway. Scandinavians were among the first non-German peoples to be brought into the SS structure, partly because their Nordic background could be held to satisfy the criteria of the Race and Settlement Main Office.

36 *Above:* An example of the use of the General SS in domestic police duties – here performing crowd control during the celebration of Hitler's birthday.

37 *Top left:* Advancing *Waffen*-SS troops on the Eastern Front.

38 *Top right:* A pre-war scene at Oranienberg concentration camp, at this early point populated by German political prisoners and run by the SA.

39 *Above:* A wagonload of corpses epitomises the cold, business-like efficiency that came to characterise the SS concentration camps, in which human beings were viewed as an exploitable resource.

40 *Top left: Waffen*-SS on the Eastern Front. With the *Waffen*-SS part of the Russian military campaign, and the SS and Police system crucial in governing occupied territory, the SS was involved at every stage of the German expansion eastward.

41 *Top right: Waffen*-SS 'boys' on the Eastern Front, members of an SS *Panzergrenadier* unit.

42 *Above:* A *Waffen*-SS NCO with Russian prisoners.

43 The Commander of the Finnish Volunteer Battalion of the *Waffen*-SS (right), with Colonel Horn, Finnish Military Attaché to Berlin.

44 *Waffen*-SS officers pose with rifles. On the right is *Sturmbannführer* Dorr, of the *Wiking* division.

45 An SS NCO with volunteers about to leave Belgium to train as members of the *Freiwilligen Legion Flandern* (Flemish National Legion).

46 *Top left:* Troops of the *Légion Volontaires Français contre le Bolchévisme*, one of many European groups which collaborated with the SS.

47 *Top right:* The pan-European struggle against Bolshevism was a crucial ideological element in the cooperation of the various national legions which formed a parallel structure to the formal SS.

48 *Above: Waffen-*SS infantry with an anti-tank gun.

Concentration Camps

Next to the SD, the SS institution which earlier obtained its autonomy from party and state, and indeed in part from other branches of the SS, was the concentration camp system. Like the SA concentration camps, those of the SS had begun as 'wild camps' outside the authority of the state, sometimes in close co-operation with party leaders and sometimes not. The SS camp at Papenburg, which gave so much trouble to Diels and Göring in 1933, was such a local camp with purely SS connections – while the Stettin camp had been operated by the SS in collaboration with the local *Gauleiter*. Dachau, near Munich, and Columbia-Haus in Berlin-Tempelhof were early SS concentration camps affiliated with the SS-*Gruppen* (later *Oberabschnitte*) South and East. Theoretically, during 1933 and early 1934 each SS region (and SA region) had a camp at its disposal, staffed by regional personnel on detached service. Such personnel was often of poor quality by SS standards, and there are indications that even at this early date assignment to this service was regarded as a chance to prove oneself after failure of one kind or another. On the other hand, at first the camps were also used to carry out service punishments, and extensive numbers of uniformed SS and SA personnel turned up in camps in the spring of 1934. Right-wing Nazi efforts to regularise the punitive measures of the new regime in the winter of 1933–34 gradually led to the closure of many small camps, the transfer of others to state authority, and after the Röhm purge replacement of SA by SS guards, as well as subordination of all camps to Gestapa control, specifically Gestapa section II-D. SS concentration camp personnel played an important part in the SA purge (notably from Dachau and Columbia-Haus); and the newly acquired concentration camp at Lichtenburg, near Torgau, served the SS as a sorting centre for arrested SA personnel. Air Force General Erhard Milch was shown SA personnel in Dachau from the purge in the spring of 1935.

Even before the purge, but definitely after it, SS troops guarding concentration camps were enlisted for terms of one, four, and later, twelve years as state officials or employees. With the transfer of a camp to state authority, the pay for the SS guards came from the interior or police budget of the state in which the camp was located, but Gestapa regulation effectively removed the control from local *Gauleiter*. Moreover, Dachau remained a purely SS installation of several interlocking parts: the concentration camp, the General SS *Übungslager* (training camp), the *Ausrüstungslager* (supply camp), the headquarters of the Political Emergency unit for the Munich area and lastly an 'assembly point' (*Sammelstelle*) for male Austrian refugees (Austrian Legion). The battalion-strength guard unit at Dachau was separately distinguished from other detached personnel of the Main Sector as early as March 1934, as was the *Sonderkommando Sachsen* (Saxon unit). The generic term '*Wachverbände*' first appears in November 1934, a month before Eicke was named as Inspector of Concentration Camps, though his position as commander of all *Wachverbände* was uncertain until 1936. Technically the commander of the guard unit in each camp was still subordinate to the regional SS commander. However, Eicke is referred to as Inspector of Concentration Camps and Guard Units in a memorandum of September 1935 setting up a unified finance administration for both concentration camps and guard troops. From November 1935 onwards SS guard personnel are officially listed as assigned to the *Inspekteur der Wachverbände* rather than *Inspekteur der Konzentrationslager*. During 1935 five *Wachverbände*, each with five companies, make their appearance – first as *Wachtruppen*, then *Wachsturmbanne*, and last as *Wachverbände*: Oberbayern (Dachau), Sachsen (Sachsenburg), Elbe (Lichtenburg), Ostfriesland (Esterwegen) and Brandenburg (Columbia-Oranienburg-Sachsenhausen)

During 1935 a distinction begins between the SS administrative personnel of the camp proper, responsible for handling the prisoners, and the guard units stationed in the watch towers and in control of work details. The latter were recruited from the very young volunteers while the former were more often the old SS veterans. Separate commands for the two groups, separate barracks, and separate regulations established a foundation for the formation of the Death's Head units of 1936, no longer so much prison guards as a special police force capable of quelling both prison riots and civilian disorder by the same ruthless measures. In April 1936 Eicke received the designation of Commander of the Death's Head Troops, whereupon the small number of personnel under his command increased from 2,876 to 3,222. The newly designated units were given a place in the Reich budget and the right to recruit directly from the Hitler Youth instead of depending on what personnel the regional SS commanders allowed them. Although Himmler became Chief of the German Police in June 1936, the concentration camps and the Death's Head troops did not become a part of the German police system, but they were now also under the Ministry of the Interior. Eicke's post remained where it had been placed in 1934 – under the SS Main Office. Gestapa control in the camps continued to be exercised in a small delegation of Security Police Main Office officials known as the 'Political Section', whose authority extended over the prisoners rather than the camp proper but who also might 'watch the watchers' to prevent corruption and collusion, an ever-present danger. At this time the term 'concentration camp' was rigorously limited to a half-dozen official camps; and plans were made to abandon some of these (e.g. Columbia-Haus) and build newer, more economically advantageous installations, notably at Buchenwald, near Weimar.

A large reshuffling of commanders and personnel also took place in 1936 after a renewal of conflicts and complaints involving regional SS commanders, all branches of the police, and the Ministry of Justice. The core of the problem was the continued irresponsibility of the camp personnel, made up as it was of 'deserving' old SS men with very low SS numbers lacking most of the skills necessary to succeed in other SS enterprises and of rural youths in their late teens totally lacking insight even into National Socialist principles. An ideological training officer was assigned to them from RuSHa for the first time in May 1936, but there is little evidence of extensive RuSHA penetration into the Death's Head units. Ideological training seems to have been intensified largely in Eicke's own hands, whose simplified charismatic preachments did not place any intellectual strain on his charges and often stressed the apartness of his units and their task. Intense rather than measured punishment for offences against discipline became the fashion in the guard units, along with increased military training for the new recruits. A system of three-week basic training followed by one week of guard duty was instituted, concentrating contact with inmates upon whom the guards could wreak vengeance for the previous three weeks' indignities. If anything, the reforms of 1936 made the lot of concentration camp prisoners worse by removing some of the corruption and laxity of their keepers. No basic change in administrative personnel in the camps occurred. Indeed, most of the infamous commanders of the new camps in the war years came up through the ranks of administration in Dachau, Lichtenburg, Sachsenhausen (opened in 1936), Esterwegen (transferred back to the SA for the second time in 1937) and Sachsenburg (closed in 1937).

On the other hand, a top-level administrative hierarchy began to develop at Oranienburg with the formation of a two-fold staff, one for the camps' economy and the other for the Death's Head troops. The former were really part of the ever-increasing administrative empire of Oswald Pohl, the SS Chief of Administration, while the latter were successful unit commanders from the General SS and the ranks of the *Verfügungstruppe*, from the Officer Candidate Schools, and from the Death's Head units themselves. While SS experience in the *Kampfjahre* still predominated in this new hierarchy, the men in it were neither the misfits who preponderated in the concentration camps themselves nor the driving fighters and ideologues who rose as regional SS commanders to become the wartime Superior SS and Police Leaders. As a managerial bureaucracy, they were ruthless enough where the interests of the inmates were concerned but tended to be the colourless counterparts of the organisation men in the SD system.

None of the Nazis' complaints really concerned humanity or justice anyway – the issue was control, predictability and the meshing of the concentration camp system with other aspects of the SS and Nazi empire. Himmler was by no means interested in completely subordinating the camps to anyone's supervision except his own, resisting their takeover even by Heydrich as late as 1942. Thus, the system evolved autonomously by somewhat reducing friction with other agencies of the SS and Police (even here only in part) and by becoming more rational, not in terms of punishment or reeducation, but in terms of economic exploitation of the inmates.

From the outset at Dachau, and soon introduced into other camps, there had been an interlocking system of workshops to aid the equipment of the *Verfügungstruppe*. Pohl, the head of the SS Administrative Office, had been hired in late 1933 to help with the equipping of an SS military force; and well before 1936 concentration camp inmates had been employed on construction details on behalf of housing the *Verfügungstruppe*. With the intensification of military–economic planning in Germany associated with Göring's appointment as head of the Four Year Plan (October 1936), the concentration camp system focused more systematically on economic goals. After the Olympic Games of 1936, roundups of potential slave labour for camp workshops began among the so-called 'work-shy', 'asocial elements', professional criminals, and pacifists and religious sectarians. At this same time Himmler announced to the *Wehrmacht* that he planned to expand his 3,500-strong Death's Head battalions to 25,000 in thirty units built on cadre formed by the twenty-five *Hundertschaften* (guard companies). While the army was reassured that these forces were there to relieve them of concern for the home front in time of war, the increased military training of the Death's Head units, the exchange of personnel with the *Verfügungstruppe*, and the evolution of a common supply system based on the concentration camp workshops foreshadowed by 1937 the wartime striving of the *Waffen*-SS for equal rights with the *Wehrmacht*. Only the diminutive size of the two units combined (18,000 in January 1938) was reassuring. With the construction of the 'modern concentration camp' at Buchenwald in the summer of 1937, Eicke realigned the Death's Head troops into three regiments exactly like the *Verfügungstruppe*, each at its own *Standort* (headquarters): Oberbayern at Dachau, Brandenburg at Sachsenhausen and Thüringen at Buchenwald. In May 1937 Himmler had begun a programme of training 1,250 recruits for six months in special companies within each battalion, preliminary to the setting up of regular Death's Head Reinforcement battalions.

Verfügungstruppe (Special Duty Troops)

The parallelism of 1937 between the Death's Head formations and the *Verfügungstruppe* is expressed not only in numerous orders in which they are lumped together (VT *und* TV i.e., *Verfügungstruppe und Totenkopfverbände*) but also in a common term, *Sicherungsverbände* (security formations). This parallelism may be said to have its roots in the tentative separation in 1933 of armed or garrisoned units (*bewaffnete* SS, *kasernierte* SS) for special purposes, made definite after the Röhm purge by the contrary category of *Allgemeine* SS (General SS) and completed in January 1940 by the common term *Waffen*-SS (Armed SS). The line of development is, nevertheless, not so direct. While there is an initial period of least differentiation in 1933, when for example *Sonderkommando* 'Sachsen' probably served as both concentration camp guards and an armed reserve to suppress an insurrection in 'Red Saxony', the creation of *Wachtruppen* at the concentration camps quite separate from the Political Emergency units – and unlike them included in the category of General SS (still true as late as 1937) – meant that the *Verfügungstruppe*, as it was known after December 1934, appeared to be a unique military unit without parallel in Germany. Indeed, Sepp Dietrich on 12 October 1933 described the *Standarte* Adolf Hitler as 'solely and uniquely a special unit alongside the Army'. The future *Leibstandarte* was unique in that its commander was at the same time the General SS Main Sector Commander (*Oberabschnittsführer*), and it was formed in two battalions or six companies. However, the new garrisoned *Hundertschaften* were set up like the garrison police (*grüne Polizei*), of the Weimar Republic (still in existence as *Landespolizei* and shortly to be absorbed by the new *Wehrmacht*) in smaller units known as 'hundreds' to form a Political Emergency unit commanded by an SS major or lieutenant-colonel who was responsible to the SS Main Sector Commander, an SS General. Furthermore, while Prussia paid for the *Leibstandarte* out of its police budget (1934–36) and Württemberg, Bavaria, Saxony and Hamburg did the same for their garrisoned SS hundreds, the Reich Ministry of the Interior compensated only Prussia. Already before the Röhm purge, however, the SS-*Amt* on 5 May 1934 ordered markings for the Political Emergency units, which though distinct from the *Leibstandarte* now provided for three *Standarten* numbered 1–3 and assigned to the Main Sectors 'South', 'West' and 'Centre' – each consisting of three *Sturmbanne* of four *Stürme* each. In June 1934 Himmler ordered the *Leibstandarte* to abandon its too-military-sounding *Kompanien und Batallione* for the *Sturmbanne und Stürme* of political soldiering. On the other hand, the concentration camp guards retained the hundreds system until 1937.

Of the Political Emergency units, only the first of the three *Standarten* listed in the May 1934 order developed as planned, and that only in part by December 1934 when the *Verfügungstruppe* was announced. The Political Emergency unit at Munich had been formed from volunteers out of the 1st and 34th General SS regiments along with the initial *Streifendienst*. A second battalion was formed by December 1934 from the Austrian legionnaires at the so-called Dachau Collecting Point attached to the *Hilfswerklager* (Refugee Aid Camp) Dachau. At first it was unclear whether the Austrians should be regarded as part of the *Verfügungstruppe*, and for many years they were treated by the other units as undependable foreigners. This SS-*Standarte* 1 (as distinguished from 1 SS-*Standarte* of the General SS) was headquartered at the same location as the notorious Dachau concentration camp, for a time sharing facilities and personnel with the *Wachtruppe* which was to become the Death's Head unit 1 – Upper Bavaria.

The Württemberg Political Emergency unit had been intended for *Standarte* 2 and was so designated briefly; but the interruption of the purge and the limitations on an armed SS imposed by a jealous *Reichswehr* and a cautious Hitler led to the reduction of the Ellwangen contingent to less than a battalion, which was carried as the third battalion of SS 1. The balance of III/SS 1 was made up of additional Austrians at the Sammelstelle Dachau. Numerous young Württembergers who volunteered for the SS, as well as Hanoverians who enlisted for the still-born SS 3 ('Centre') were assigned as concentration camp guards instead, where they distinguished themselves by their human decency even to the point of being put behind barbed wire for it (perhaps out of pique at not becoming soldiers). Instead of the planned second and third regiments, three separate battalions were set up as *Standarte* 2: battalion one at Hamburg-Veddel; battalion two at Arolsen, Waldeck; and battalion three at Wolterdingen, near Soltau in Hanover. Judging by the dates when company and battalion commanders were appointed in both *Standarten* (spring 1935), the units were a long time in 'shaking down', probably with little if any professional military leadership and inadequate weapons. On the other hand, the *Leibstandarte* enjoyed extensive military training at army camps before the Röhm purge, and a secret order of March 1935 provided for training SS personnel by army units. Yet in July 1935 VT training regulations written by Himmler were still only promised for September. *Verfügungstruppe* officers and NCOs were provided specialised training beginning in September 1935 at Döberitz, Wunsdorf and Halle (Army Communications School).

We may recall that Paul Hausser had been signed up in the SS in November 1934 to supervise the erection of Officer Candidate Schools, for it was Himmler's intention to make himself as independent as possible of army training. The model for the schools, however, was the pre-1914 *Kadettenanstalt* (Teenage Cadet School). Actually the first Officer Candidate School at Bad Tölz (Bavaria) was begun with cadre recruited from various General SS regiments in Upper Bavaria starting in April 1934, along with preparations for the General SS training camp at Dachau. Its first commander, Paul Lettow, was a professional soldier who returned to the army in 1935. The first class at Tölz was conducted under the former commander and in early 1935 was under observation by the cadre of the second Officer Candidate School assembled by Hausser (Braunschweig). The first sixty graduates of Tölz became second lieutenants on 20 April 1935, two of them remaining as cadre at Tölz and three going to Braunschweig. Eighteen went to *Standarte* 1, sixteen to *Standarte* 2 and four to *Leibstandarte*; however, a year later SS 1 had retained only nine, SS 2 only eight and the *Leibstandarte* one. The biggest magnet for the young officers was the SD Main Office (thirteen), with another seven going to RuSHa and seven to the staff of the *Reichsführer* SS. Two went to the Death's Head *Standarte* '*Oberbayen*'. Twenty-seven of the sixty were already first lieutenants by November 1936. A second class was conducted at each school, sixty-two graduating from Bad Tölz and 142 from Braunschweig in April 1936. Thereafter there were annual classes until wartime. An increasing participation in the Officer Candidate Schools from the Death's Head units may be noted, with a continued heavy withdrawal of young officers for the Berlin Main Offices (more than half). Indeed, the *Verfügungstruppe* could have received only about 200 junior officers from the two Officer Candidate Schools by the outbreak of war; theoretically the whole output of more than 600 by April 1939 was available as reserves. Himmler conceived the idea in 1937 of assigning the graduates to successive two-year tours of duty with General SS, *Sicherheitspolizei*, and Special Duty or Death's Head troops. Although he did not repeat the experiment with further classes, the bulk of the 1937 personnel only returned to the combat units in wartime.

After first being appointed as commander of the Braunschweig Officer Candidate School, Hausser exercised direct control over the Officer Candidate Schools as Inspector of SS Officer Candidate Schools from August 1935 until his appointment as Inspector of the Special Duty Troops on 1 October 1936. During the period when Hausser also functioned as chief of the SS Leadership Office in the SS Main Office (May 1936–37), the commanders of the schools were subordinate to that office. Tölz was commanded by a retired police colonel for three years and then until the outbreak of the war by a temporarily 'retired' *Wehrmacht* colonel. Braunschweig was also turned over to a sixty-five-year-old *Reichswehr* colonel who had retired in 1924. In 1937 Himmler turned the inspectorate of the Officer Candidate Schools (redesignated as *Junkerschulen*) over to Walter Schmitt, the head of the SS Personnel Office who also had in his charge the General SS Officer School (the former training camp at Dachau) as well as Driver and Cavalry Schools for both General and *Waffen*-SS. This was no doubt an effort on Himmler's part to further the integration of the SS officers' corps as a whole. Another reason may have been a considerable turnover in the large training cadre of the schools. Both the schools and their products tended to give rise to complaints until well into the war years.

When *Standarte* 2 reached the approximate strength of *Leibstandarte* and *Standarte* 1 (2,500) in the autumn of 1935, the three units were held there for a full year. An exchange of officers also occurred between the regiments, even with a reduction in their absolute number as some went into the army or were sent to the General SS. A *Standarte* had to get along with less than 100 officers, less than half of whom had had front experience, although the majority were seasoned *Altkämpfer* who had joined the SS before 1933. The NCOs, who were usually also men with very low SS numbers, played a heavy part in the training and command structure. On the other hand, the recruits were largely new SS, not from the General SS at all but young men of between seventeen and twenty-three often without even a Hitler Youth background. In a period of continued wide unemployment, a four-year enlistment in what promised to be an elite troop with possibilities of promotion well beyond the tradi-tional limits of the German army was not a serious barrier. Selection commissions stressed size and brawn rather than education and ideology. Training programmes dwelt heavily on basic training of the soldier with rifle and bayonet, much like the AW training of 1933–34, which the offi-cers and NCOs knew by heart and which in fact their new battalion and regimental commanders had themselves conducted in *Reichswehr* and SA. Indeed, the majority of the *Verfügungstruppe* commanders came out of the most suspect circles of SA and *Reichswehr*, those who had believed all along in the possibility of a 'new model army' and who rejected the idealisation of the old German army yet also rejected party hegemony over military matters.

In 1936, during which elements of the new *Wehrmacht* entered the demilitarised zone without French retaliation and Himmler tightened his hold on the defences of 'battlefield inner-Germany', *Verfügungstruppe* and the new Death's Head battalions could be referred to together in SS orders as markedly different from the General SS. Plans for their increase might still arouse concern in the more jealous and conservative military quarters; but by now it was clear that, like the SA before it, the General SS was rapidly losing any claim to combat preparedness. The *Wehrmacht* seemed to be master in its own house as never before, and armed SS units with machine guns and mortars but without armour and artillery could be safely expanded to relieve *Wehrkreis* commanders of the need for holding army troops in their areas for security in wartime. The restructuring of the *Wehrkreis* and army corps area system following the inclusion of the Rhineland in the defence network led to modifications in the General SS Main Sectors, the SD Main Sectors, and the relocation and expansion of *Verfügungstruppe* installations. The SS Main Sectors were thus in the process of becoming the replacement districts of the *Verfügungstruppe* and Death's Head battalions and their commanders – the future Superior SS and Police Leaders – co-ordinators of security and emergency measures in their district. Step by step against weakening *Wehrmacht* resistance, *Verfügungstruppe* and to a lesser extent Death's Head battalions in 1937 won rights comparable to those of the *Wehrmacht* – reduced travel rates, postal privileges, pensions and emergency weapon use. But the pensions took years to be implemented; the right to employ weapons in home front emergencies was still subject theoretically to conventional German court adjudication until the war years.

The *Verfügungstruppen* of the mid-1930s were organised in a modified three-fold system of three regiments of three battalions, with four companies each, but there are signs that a four-fold system was contemplated. For example, SS 1, renamed SS-*Standarte* '*Deutschland*', acquired a fourth battalion at Ellwangen in 1937; and a fourth regiment, formed from elements of the battalion known as 'N' (for Nuremberg, though actually at Dachau) existed in 1936. Although there is a 1938 reference to 'SS VT Nürnberg,' the fourth regiment seems to have been postponed until the *Anschluss* and the forming of SS-*Standarte* '*Der Führer*' in Austria. Supporting units for a division in the form of a signal battalion stationed first at Berlin-Adlershof and after 1937 at Unna in Westphalia, an engineers' battalion at Leisnig and after 1937 at Dresden, and *Staffen* (medical teams) at battalion-level freed the *Verfügungstruppe* both from the General SS organisations with the same functions and from the corresponding army branches. An Officer Candidate School for medical officers for both *Verfügungstruppe* and Death's Head troops was begun in October 1936.

Above all, a co-ordinating system for the *Verfügungstruppe* was begun in 1936, first in the spring with the formation of the *Führungsstab der* SS *Verfügungstruppen*, constructed significantly of the same administrative personnel who were managing the concentration camps' economy, and secondarily in October with the development of a kind of general staff of the Inspector of the Special Duty Troops, soon replacing the *Führungsstab*. After a few years in the administrative branch of the inspector's staff, the former group gravitated back toward the concentration camp orbit in the war years, while the more strictly military figures from the SS Main Office and the office of inspector formed the nucleus of the *Führungshauptamt* of the *Waffen*-SS. Technically, all personnel and Hausser himself, as Chief of the Leadership Office, were still part of the SS Main Office; but instead of a gain in centralised control (which may have been intended), the failure of the SS Main Office head (August Heissmeier) to comprehend the military side of SS operations any better than he had the administrative empire of the SS Chief of Administration led to the disintegration of the SS-*Hauptamt* already noted above. When in October 1937 Hausser gave up the post of Leadership Office chief to a purely General SS veteran, the position reduced itself to housekeeping responsibilities for the General SS. By this time the Office of Inspector of Special Duty Troops amounted to more than fifty officers, the nucleus of a general staff. In 1938 with the restructuring of the Recruitment Office of the SS Main Office under Gottlob Berger, one of the most competent and ruthless of the old AW personnel fated to become one of Himmler's leading wartime lieutenants, another quasi-independent staff agency was formed which would aid the future *Waffen*-SS. Thus, little by little and camouflaged against a General SS and police background, an armed SS 'crystallised out' as a separate entity. Aided by its small size (12,000 in January 1938) and its divided nature – successfully bridged in the person of Heinrich Himmler – the combat branch of the SS was soon capable of effective employment in whole or in part and, above all, of massive growth in the interests of SS aggrandisement when Hitler's imperial designs had ripened.

Austria

The SS played an important part in the preparation and execution of every German conquest, and Austria was no exception. In fact, Himmler's Austrian SS played a decisive role in carrying out the pressure tactics of Hitler and even initiated a few parts of the scheme. The SS had been prominent in July 1934 also, we may recall; however, at that time serious doubts existed about whether it was truly carrying out Hitler's orders. Nor was the Austrian SS immune to the disarray in National Socialist ranks after the failure of the putsch . Many prominent SS leaders there were arrested and sentenced to long prison terms or fled to

Germany in 1935. However, the tightening discipline of the German SS, the close tie between SS and SD, Himmler's early foothold in the Bavarian Secret Police with old ties to Austria, and Himmler's control over the German–Austrian frontier not only through the Auxiliary Border Employees (HIGA) but also through the *Grenzpolizei* (Border Police) all combined to thrust the few loyal SS officers in each Austrian state into the centre of the inevitable Nazi conspiracy.

While Hitler disavowed connection with the Austrian Nazis and genuinely disapproved of continued insurgent tactics, he heartily approved of the 'iceberg' approach developed in Carinthia whereby an official group of moderate Nazis sought accommodation with the authoritarian Schuschnigg regime while an illegal network was perpetuated under the strictest discipline, primarily for communications purposes. Respectable, middle-class persons could be won for SD work, first in Carinthia and later in Vienna and elsewhere, while some of the most adventurous Carinthians and Styrians of free corps days were drawn to the SS, if they were not there already. Quite a few transferred from the SA, which in these regions unlike in Vienna and Linz had exposed itself in the putsch. By 1936 Himmler had enough control over the Austrian SS to guarantee that its members would not act up disobediently, a perennial problem with the Austrian party leaders. The agreement with Schuschnigg of 11 July 1936 not only created a dual system of financial aids – legal and illegal – for hard-pressed Austrian Nazis; it also set up a mixed commission under the chairmanship of Wilhelm Keppler, a businessman who was Göring's chief liaison with Himmler and now also became Hitler's secret mouthpiece to the Austrian Nazis. Since the control of funds for Austria rested to a considerable extent with SS personnel, either in the relief *Hilfswerk* system or through Keppler – who ranked as an SS General – the disobedient party faction could be brought to heel, not at once but in a matter of months. With the communications system between the Nazis and the Reich in SS-SD hands, it was also impossible for the dissident group to get a hearing from Hitler or Göring. On the other hand, the idea of bringing Schuschnigg to Berchtesgaden to be intimidated, the ferreting out of his plebiscite plans in time to intervene against them, and even the initiative in capturing power on the night of 11 March in Vienna and the state capitals can be traced to the SS. In fact, these can be traced to a single venturesome SS man, Odilo Globocnik, on whom Himmler bestowed a colonelcy the next day.

While it is certainly true that Hitler had no blueprint for the annexa-
tion of Austria and lacked even conventional military plans for an occupation, the SS provided him with a precision instrument of subversion
under the cover of legality, if it did not actually show him the way and
lead him step by step to success. Göring and Himmler, working through
Heydrich, had collaborated closely on the 'framing' of Blomberg and
Fritsch at the outset of 1938, meeting Hitler's desires as they had in June
1934. The Austrian *Anschluss* originated with them too, capturing opportunities presented by Hitler's search for a 'cover' for his purge of the
Wehrmacht and the Foreign Office and Schuschnigg's desperately staged
appeal to the victors of 1918 to defend their own creation. The smooth-
ness with which the Germans improvised the integration of army units,
the motorised *Leibstandarte*, 40,000 Order Police, the Death's Head regiment '*Oberbayen*', and elements of both '*Deutschland*' and '*Germania*'
regiments between 7 and 15 March all belie the notion that the very real
inter-service rivalries were strong enough to disturb co-operation in a
real emergency. Indeed, staff work and drills of some kind must have
preceded the first real test, even though no large-scale practice alert or
mobilisation scheme seems to have existed. Himmler may have been
surprised by Hitler's exact decision to intervene urged on by Göring, but
he was well prepared for the intervention, and his intelligence provided
the circumstances for it. Within Austria some 7,200 SS (called NS-*Dienst*)
members under the command of Ernst Kaltenbrunner – a ruthless
lawyer with a low SS number – went into action about 9 p.m. on 11
March to seize public buildings in the various state capitals along with
even larger SA contingents (NS-*Mannschaft*) already – though still illegally – designated as Auxiliary Police. By midnight Kaltenbrunner had
become Police Minister, and at 2 a.m. when Himmler arrived and
removed the non-Nazi Minister of State Security, this future Superior SS
and Police Leader of Austria (later 'Danube') had become the first of the
many SS proconsuls of a Nazi empire.

After a very brief transition as a single SS main district, the Ostmark or
Eastern March, was split into two Main Sectors, corresponding to the
Gaue, themselves following the old state boundaries. The *Gauleiter*
uniformly became high SS officers, by no means a regular procedure in
the past but here indicating the increased importance of remaining
within negotiating range of the *Reichsführer* SS. Indeed, Globocnik – the
new SS colonel who had done so much to assist the *Anschluss* – became

for a while the *Gauleiter* of the Vienna region until his involvement in flagrant 'Aryanisation' abuses along with hundreds of other Austrian SS officers forced his removal. The SS had to suffer a minor setback in the course of 1938 in Austria as Hitler placed control in the hands of a German Reich Commissar for Reunification, Josef Bürckel, who was a party stalwart and former *Gauleiter*. Although since November 1937 he had accepted the rank of SS General, this party man quickly disassociated himself from the SS and Police system, intimately associated as it was with the apparatus of the local Austrian Nazi leadership; and he quarrelled with Keppler, the other SS general who was Göring's (and Hitler's) emissary. After he had managed to embarrass quite a number of SS higher-ups in shady dealings with Jews and receivers of Jewish property, Bürckel himself was ultimately deposed, having made some serious foreign policy mistakes during the Czechoslovak crisis. In this way the SS could re-emerge in Austria in 1940 virtually unscathed, in fact much strengthened. Instead of three General SS–*Standarten*, Austria could boast of seven *Standarten* with 17,000 men. More important, Himmler had set about immediately in April 1938 to form a three-battalion *Verfügungstruppe* ('*Der Führer*') with elements in every state out of cadre from units sent in for the parade and occupation. A third Officer Candidate School was opened at Klagenfurt. Furthermore, a fourth Death's Head regiment (Ostmark) was also formed at the former Austrian concentration camp Mauthausen, near Linz, soon to become one of the deadliest of its kind. After a flurry of conflict over the relative powers of the new offices of Inspectors of Order Police and Security Police *vis-à-vis* the Superior SS and Police Leader, the system of treating the former as the very highest subordinates of the latter worked its way into practice, so that Austria almost never enjoyed the luxury of Nazi cross-purposes in police matters. The Austrian police were often Nazis of long standing, especially in Vienna and Graz; many of these quickly became SS colonels and even generals. No very extensive housecleaning of the police was necessary in Austria, and the SS assimilation of the police officers' corps in the Reich proceeded without marked exception in the former Austrian *Gaue*.

Well before the seizure of Austria, the *Sicherheitshauptamt* had made extensive studies of Austrian Jewry, since it was well known that Hitler's own anti-Semitism had arisen there. Thus, it was not really surprising that Adolf Eichmann should be sent to Vienna to pursue his specialised studies of how best to eliminate Jews from the German *Lebensraum*. What was notable of course was Eichmann's transition to executive powers in the Central Office for Jewish Emigration which he set up in Vienna on 26 August 1938, on specific orders of the Reich Commissar for Reunification. Eichmann was clearly not acting on his own initiative, nor was he carrying out a specifically SS policy, for the same Reich Commissar was making things difficult for the SS due to the latter's Aryanisation proceedings against the same Jews. When Göring (not Himmler) ordered the formation of a Reich Central Office for Jewish Emigration on 24 January 1939, as a multi-ministry agency, however, it was entrusted to Heydrich – who delegated his powers to Heinrich Müller, head of the Gestapa. Eichmann's Austrian bureau then became merely a branch office, although again a co-operative effort by bureaucrats of numerous agencies. The Gestapo chairmanship in this arrangement was to become the accepted form for other wartime state bureaus of immigration and deportation in which worked many officials both in and out of SS uniform.

Czechoslovakia

Because the public appearance of the SS alongside the police and the *Wehrmacht* in Austria had given rise to considerable speculation about the future role of the SS, especially in wartime, Hitler signed on 17 August 1938 what was intended to be the decisive ruling about the relations between it, police and *Wehrmacht*. The fact that it did not represent anything final at all, merely pointing in the direction in which Hitler wished the SS to develop, does not reduce its importance. Although its authorship is uncertain, we know that Himmler saw it and made some changes before Hitler signed it. The draft was drawn up as early as 3 June and was seen by the SS-*Hauptamt* in July prior to Hitler's signing it. The document was marked *Geheime Kommandosache* ('Top Secret') and certainly was not widely known, though referred to officially. After a brief introduction discussing the close connection between the SS and Police created by the 17 June 1936 decree, the order divides itself into four parts of unequal length: (1) General (one page), (2) The Armed Units of the SS (more than seven pages), (3) The General SS (one page), (4) Executive regulations (one page). The SS in its entirety is described as a political organisation of the party and without need of arms; however, for special internal tasks of the *Reichsführer* SS and Chief of the German Police and for mobile use with the army in wartime, certain enumerated SS units were excepted from that characterisation. These units were the *Verfügungstruppe*, the Officer Candidate Schools, the Death's Head units and the Police Reinforcements of the latter (not yet in existence). In peacetime Himmler had the sole authority over them, although he had to purchase his military equipment from the *Wehrmacht*. Of the *Verfügungstruppe*, it was written that it formed a part neither of the *Wehrmacht* nor the police but was part of the NSDAP for Hitler's exclusive use. It was budgeted in the Interior Ministry subject to approval of the *Oberkommando der Wehrmacht* (OKW). An enumeration of the elements followed, with Himmler's handwritten additions on the original decree, showing that he wanted to maximise motorisation. Certain special units were to be added for internal employment (e.g. an armoured car platoon), and in wartime the whole *Verfügungstruppe* was to be organised as a *Wehrmacht* division. In case of mobilisation, replacement units used in peacetime for training the so-called Police Reinforcements of the Death's Head units would produce replacements for the *Verfügungstruppe* division. In case of mobilisation, Hitler would determine when and how to turn the *Verfügungstruppe* over to the army (in which case he stipulated that they would still remain party troops) or he could still assign them to Himmler for internal emergencies. The only distinction Hitler made in the description of the Death's Head units was a lack of reference to their being solely for his personal use. They too are characterised as an element of the party, neither of the police nor of the *Wehrmacht*. Their purpose is said to be the solution of special problems of a police nature assigned by him. Duty with them did not fulfil military service requirements. After mobilisation they would form the cadre of the Police Reinforcements to be trained beforehand in the new replacement units with funds obtained by the Interior Ministry from the OKW. The concentration camp guard duty would then be performed not by the Police Reinforcements (who were intended for occupation purposes) but by members of the General SS over the age of thirty-five. The Police Reinforcements were to be counted as police troops. In wartime members of the General SS were 'mobilisable' in the armed services just like anyone else, except that the Main Office staffs as well as the Main Sector and Sector staffs were to be deferred 'for duties of a police character'. Executive regulations for police matters and internal commitment could be issued by Himmler, while the OKW was to issue such orders for all other mobilisation conditions affecting *Verfügungstruppe* and Death's Head units.

While SS expansion along purely military lines had seemingly been quite firmly limited again by Hitler in this order, Himmler had been developing a quite different alternative for increasing SS power and influence in the Germanic empire of the future. Taking advantage of Ribbentrop's need for a collaborative relation with the SS to advance his bureau in the aristocratic Foreign Ministry, Himmler had managed to appoint quite a few of Ribbentrop's personnel to SS rank and to have Werner Lorenz, an old SS fighter, made their formal superior for SS purposes. Lorenz was possessed of an East Elbian background, education in a *Kadettenanstalt* (cadet school) and an *entrée* into international society that made him seem suitable for appointment in January 1937 both by Hess for the party and by Ribbentrop for his Foreign Ministry bureau as head of the so-called *Volksdeutsche Mittelstelle* – the Liaison Office for Ethnic Germans. This was a typical 'iceberg' operation with nominal power to manage inter-state friendship associations and actual funds to aid German-speaking citizens of other nations to maintain their 'Germanness', to support German schools and in effect to influence so-called ethnic German groups to support Nazi ideals. Furthermore, from the start VoMi – as Lorenz's organisation soon came to be called – became a vehicle for SD penetration into German folk groups abroad, and indeed it was not long before the second in command at VoMi was Hermann Behrends of the SD. At no time was VoMi actually a branch of the SS, although later many, though not all, of its officials wore SS and police uniforms. Its chief advantage to Himmler was to provide him with a substitute for what he had had naturally in the Austrian SS and police – access to a controllable German apparatus. Himmler and the SS actually rode into influence and power in Czechoslovakia, Poland and the Balkans on the backs of agents of the party and the Foreign Ministry, assisted of course by the clever assignment of SD personnel as soon as possible. While there was no official SS connection with VoMi until the naming of Himmler as Reich Commissar for the Strengthening of Germandom in October 1939, to perform the task of resettling ethnic Germans originally given by Hitler to VoMi, in plain truth Himmler sought from the very beginning of 1937 to penetrate the east European ethnic German groups via SS recruiters in order to expand SS influence into what he already regarded as settlement territory.

Next to the Austrians, the easiest folk group for the Nazis to penetrate were the Sudeten Germans. While Hitler was to go to war ostensibly in the interests of the ethnic Germans of Poland, the party and the SS did not do half so well there before 1939 as they did in the second home of National Socialism – Czechoslovakia. A German National Socialist Workers' Party was founded there on 15 November 1918. As in Austria, the homegrown variety of Sudeten Nazi was hard to control from Berlin. However, in comparison with the ethnic Germans of Poland, divided in their traditions by the Polish partition, by religion and more recently by numerous party rivalries, the Sudeten Germans were a powerful, united front against Prague and Czechdom, eminently worth subverting to Hitler's cause. SD and *Abwehr* activity in the Sudetenland preceded 30 January 1933, as did Reich-Nazi activity in the form of a secret *Bereitschaft* (Alarm Squad) within an Austro-Fascist *Kamerad-schaftsbund*. The rise of Konrad Henlein's *Sudetendeutsche Heimatfront* was aided with funds from the Nazi-dominated League for Germandom Abroad (VDA) before VoMi took over in 1937. By that time SD influence in Henlein's immediate circle provided Heydrich and Himmler with information and control – if not over Henlein himself, over his deputy, Karl Hermann Frank, the future Superior SS and Police Leader in Prague. There was both an illegal SA and an illegal SS, the former masked as a sport or gymnastic society, the latter in various student associations. There can be little doubt that Henlein, who exercised a tight control over the vast majority of ethnic Germans in Czechoslovakia through a network of organisations besides his Sudeten German Party, was taking orders from VoMi by November 1937.

When Hitler decided to turn the heat on Czechoslovakia immediately after the *Anschluss*, VoMi was in on the conspiracy at every step. A *Sudetendeutscher Schutzdienst* (protective service) was formed openly from the secret SA formations under Reich SA guidance, with the advice of a former SA and AW officer now in the SS – Hans Jüttner, the future chief of Himmler's military general staff, the *Führungshauptamt*. Plans were made for a military seizure by the *Wehrmacht* accompanied by risings of the *Schutzdienst* after the abortive Czech mobilisation of 20 May, and there is evidence that these plans extended to Bohemia and Moravia. During the hectic summer months of 1938, while all Europe hoped for peace while preparing for war, the Sipo-SD headquarters laid out the police procedures for the seizure of specific properties and personages in the vanguard of the *Wehrmacht*. Thus, the first *Einsatzkommandos* were called into existence. These police teams were to make contact with SS personnel and SD agents in the Sudetenland, who were secretly organised to take over police duties even before the arrival of the *Wehrmacht*. Liaison between *Wehrmacht* and SS, VoMi and the Foreign Office, Sipo-SD and *Abwehr* was far better than at the time of the *Anschluss*. Indeed, the atmosphere of common purpose and essential agreement – enhanced by the conferring of numerous honorary SS ranks in the Foreign Office and other state bureaus – the acceptance by the *Wehrmacht* of young SS-*Junker* (cadets) and officers for temporary duty with their units, and the sharing of espionage secrets between Canaris and Heydrich brought the SS closer to respectability than ever before. Rivalry and jostling for first place there still was, but it was subdued; the joint formulation by SS and *Wehrmacht* of the Hitler decree of 17 August 1938 illustrates some degree of give-and-take on both sides under the impetus of the oncoming crisis.

Immediately after the 17 August decree, the OKW ordered the call-up of the Police Reinforcements specified in the decree from lists supplied by the SS Main Sectors; but due to resistance and overtaxed staffs, the army corps areas refused to do the SS's work for it. Therefore, the new *Ergänzungsamt* (Recruitment Office of the SS) under Gottlob Berger and the SS Main Sectors had to improvise their own procedures in September. A total of 12,000 General SS members were mobilised by 1 October above and beyond the 15,000-strong *Verfügungstruppe* and the 8,000-man Death's Head battalions. It was on 17 September that Henlein's deputy, K.H. Frank, persuaded Hitler to approve the arming of the *Sudetendeutscher Schutzdienst*, waves of which had fled temporarily over the borders to Silesia, Saxony, Bavaria and Austria. The resulting *Sudetendeutsche Freikorps* consisted of between 10,000 and 15,000 men in four *Gruppen* (divisions, the old SA unit) of four *Abschnitte* (sectors, the current SA and SS unit formed of several *Standarten*). A strengthening of SA officers, SA uniforms and SA camping equipment was rapidly improvised – with confiscated Austrian arms, VoMi, SD and *Abwehr* advisors. General directions for these fifth-column troops came from Henlein's headquarters at Schloss Donndorf near Bayreuth, with advice from Hans Jüttner of the *Verfügungstruppe* Inspection (Replacements), Canaris of the *Abwehr*, and Gottlob Berger as the new head of the SS Recruiting Office.

Incursions across the international frontier even involving German SA elements occurred on 22 September, and by 25 September the town of Asch had been seized and transferred to two Death's Head battalions from Dachau. Next day Himmler announced that all elements of the free corps would come under the SS in the event of invasion, and although this ran counter to army orders, it was never countermanded. In fact, while *Verfügungstruppe* and Death's Head units were mixed in with *Wehrmacht* divisions, the free corps was committed on and after 30 September as independent operational units under Order Police authority. Before their dissolution on 15 October, a rapid scramble for their commanders as new SS officers poisoned relations between the two future Main Office chiefs, Jüttner and Berger. Both had come out of the SA/AW experience and both were empire-builders oriented to expanding the armed SS. Jüttner would temporarily have to accept subordination to the brusque SS recruiter during the formation of the SS-*Führungshauptamt* in 1939–40. Jüttner's vendetta with Berger in the SS Main Office was to last throughout the war, long after the SA and the Sudetenland had ceased to be important. Henlein and K.H. Frank both accepted SS generals' oak leaves, the former *Schutzdienst* commander becoming the Sudetenland *Abschnitt* commander of the SS. There was no wholesale transfer of the free corps to the SS, however, and many joined the SA.

Except in the case of Asch, SS forces entered Czechoslovakia on or after 1 October in the form of either *Verfügungstruppe* or Death's Head regiments; regular military units incorporated in *Wehrmacht* divisions; or as mixed teams of Order Police, Gestapo and SD (two *Einsatzstäbe*, each consisting of five *Einsatzkommandos*). The latter did the 'dirty work' of arresting (or killing) suspects and enemies in the name of troop security. Some SS men under thirty-five with previous military training served as ordinary *Wehrmacht* members, although there was no general mobilisation. There was no military occupation; transfer to civilian control on 10 October meant that the German divisions departed and with them the *Verfügungstruppe* and Death's Head regiments. SS and Police power was assured by the setting up of Order Police, Criminal Police and SD, as well as Gestapo headquarters by the *Einsatzkommandos* according to plan. The Border Police – a part of the Gestapo since the previous year – played a central role in the staffing of detachments for the Gestapo offices, and unpaid SD officials from the Reich (largely SS of long standing) and among the Sudeten Germans (new SS, mostly) provided much of the new SD sectorial personnel. The *Einsatzstäbe* as such were disbanded after it became clear that Hitler was not yet ready to proceed with the total liquidation of Czechoslovakia. SD efforts to assert its leadership over the teams' operations, expressed in its supplying the team commanders, were not entirely successful *vis-à-vis* the Gestapo; an Interior Ministry decree of 11 November sought to supply state sanctions for SD activities to improve co-operation by state agencies with the SD. Its agents did not thereby become state officials; the inclusion of the SD within the Reich Main Security Office (RSHA) a year later showed that the November 1938 measure was insufficient. The team approach for the 'hit squads' had proved itself, however, and even the same commanders were used again in Poland and Russia, albeit not under SD authority.

Amt III, SD-*Ausland*, was at the height of its influence that busy autumn and winter in co-operation with *Abwehr*, Foreign Office and VoMi in creating the conditions for Hitler's next move. No one knew, least of all Hitler, which of the many German folk groups in eastern Europe he would have need of next. In order to keep all options open, tighter controls and better knowledge of local conditions were necessary. Academic specialists, businessmen, state officials and the ethnic Germans themselves were recruited for the SD – and incidentally for the SS – in increasing numbers. Along with VoMi and SD went representatives of the SS Recruitment Office, for the Sudeten free corps had proved a model for combining fifth-column work with future SS recruitment, not merely for General SS expansion but for the armed SS legions otherwise so seriously limited by the 17 August decree. SS-SD penetration into the Baltic states, Poland and Rumania made good progress; but Hitler succumbed to the temptation to capitalise on the Czechoslovakian disorganisation and the need to meet the disappointment of the remaining German minority there, as well as to Slovak pressure for support. Hitler possibly lost a chance to effect a Bismarckian settlement in Europe after Munich in part due to the ambitions of the SS – Himmler, Heydrich and some of the high SS officers' corps – to engage in foreign policy intrigue and carve out a settlement area in central Europe. They were of course fulfilling Hitler's own un-Bismarckian imperial conceptions.

Himmler's entry into foreign policy matters in the Austrian case had strengthened SS ties not only to Ribbentrop's apparatus in the Foreign Office but also to Göring's operatives in the world of finance. Now both of these gentlemen had a vested interest in dominating Hitler's foreign policy moves after Munich, where he demonstrated more independence than suited either his Foreign Minister or his Luftwaffe commander. Thus, each for his own reasons was willing to assist Himmler, and the latter was glad to penetrate more deeply into foreign affairs and high finance in the interests of SS expansion. Through VoMi Himmler began to play a more direct role in discussions of foreign policy problems, while VoMi's second-in-command, Hermann Behrends, developed a network of information and influence beyond the folk groups themselves to the corresponding native governments and parties of their regions. Heydrich also engaged quite personally in foreign intrigue now, laying the foundations for German domination of fascist movements in Lithuania, the Ukraine, Slovakia, Hungary, Rumania and Bohemia. Heydrich's SD-*Amt* III agents had the advantage of co-operation with Göring's people and vice versa, since economic penetration into eastern Europe via anti-Western, anti-capitalist fascist conspirators undercut official German connections handily. Thus, VoMi Folk Group connections and SD-fascist party connections might also run together at either end, in Berlin and the field.

On the coat tails of both VoMi and SD, often in the form of a senior SS officer, the SS Recruitment Office rode into foreign capitals in search of 'human material'. The lure of the Reich was never so great as in late 1938 and early 1939 for young ethnic Germans. Four years' service in Himmler's elite guard seemed to many not too high a price to pay for a future of prominence and influence, especially as an alternative to being drafted into one's native army as a member of a minority not universally admired. Last but not least, the SS Race and Settlement Main Office – freed at last from the burden of Himmler's long quarrel with its founder, Darré, over SS ideological training – looked for new worlds to conquer for SS settlement, long stymied in the Reich by *Wehrmacht* land purchases and the needs of 'the battle of production'. The fertile soil of Bohemia-Moravia attracted the eye of the Settlement Office Chief, von Gottberg, who called Heydrich's attention to settlement possibilities there. SD agents made a careful inventory of both urban and rural prop-erties in the hands of 'enemies of Germandom' before 15 March 1939. A scheme for expelling the whole Slavic population of Bohemia to make room for German settlers found its way into SD files.

So neatly did Heydrich's and Göring's agents work, with the co-oper-ation of Ribbentrop's Foreign Office, that Hitler's own indecisive nature did not have a chance to manifest itself. His natural instinct to abuse a fallen foe was all that was necessary to prevent him from grasping the opportunity to pacify France and Britain by cultivating Czechoslovakia. Aided by tendentious reports of Czech perfidy and anti-German plans supplied through Foreign Office, SD and VoMi, Hitler went every step of the way with the conspirators without making a firm decision for himself until the last minute – probably some time on 12 March 1939. On that day, while Wilhelm Keppler negotiated in Hitler's name with the Slovak separatists in Bratislava, a week after the delivery of explosives by SD-*Amt* III agents, VoMi organised demonstrations in Prague and Brno using SS students, and SS commandos arrived from the Reich in both Bohemia and Slovakia to carry out acts of terror and provocation. Special agents within the Folk Group who carried out tasks under SD orders were taken into the SS in the next few days. The Czech army was involved in skirmishes against two different Slovak paramilitary formations and a *Freiwillige Schutzstaffel* (German Volunteer Guard Squadron) by 13 March, all under orders from VoMi, SD and *Abwehr* sources; so that Hitler's talk of 'pacification' in Czechoslovakia with forces of the *Wehrmacht* seems infinitely cynical. His invitation to Horthy to send Hungarian troops into Slovakia and Ruthenia on that date appears equally Machiavellian, unless indeed he was still really in the dark about the extent of the plot. In the early hours of 15 March before leaving for Prague with Himmler, he told Czech President Hacha that 'a few weeks ago he had really not known a thing about the whole matter. It came as a surprise to him'. Perhaps this was close to the truth. But he must have known that the mechanised *Leibstandarte* had already entered Mährisch-Ostrau 'according to plan', as Göring remarked, to keep the Poles out.

Three truckloads of SS officers seized the police headquarters in Prague early on 15 March and began immediately to work with Sudeten-German volunteer police and Czech collaborators. Himmler was quite impressed with the 'high quality' of many of the Czech police. Gestapo and SD headquarters were opened like magic in the chief towns, and arrests from pre-arranged lists began. In Bratislava a surprised Tiso was confronted by the German Folk Group Leader and VoMi spokesman accompanied by a mysterious stranger – the VoMi Deputy Chief and SD veteran – and ordered to sign a 'protection agreement' in the best gangster fashion. *Wehrmacht* forces entered Slovakia, as well as Bohemia and Moravia, but civil government began immediately in all areas. There was no military government to interfere with the SS. The partially mechanised *Verfügungstruppe* regiments of the SS had functioned well as part of *Wehrmacht* armoured divisions for the first time. By mid-April only 'Germania' was left on occupation duty along with one Death's Head battalion. The rest were already feverishly training for the Polish campaign; most of the Death's Head battalions were busy training new recruits from Germany, Austria and the Folk Group volunteers. Order Police, Gestapo and SD remained, reinforced with thousands of Sudeten-German SS co-ordinated after 5 May by a new Superior SS and Police Leader, K.H. Frank, Henlein's former deputy and now the real dictator of Prague. The figurehead protector of Bohemia-Moravia whom he represented was no more significant than Henlein, relegated to provincial Reichenberg. Gone also were many of the Vienna Party clique who had schemed with Heydrich and Keppler; but the Prague *Bodenamt* (Land Office), a RuSHa installation, remained as a symbol of SS imperial plans. To it flocked Reich SS members by the dozens, as they earlier flocked to Vienna, drawn by easy money and a chance to 'Aryanise' properties left behind by clients of Eichmann's new Emigration Office in Prague located at Gestapo headquarters. Less-coveted Slovakia had no Superior SS and Police Leader – merely a Police Attache, a Sipo-SD agent who co-ordinated arrests, deportations and seizures in Himmler's and the Reich's interest. But the Volunteer Guard Squadron remained, an unforgotten reservoir for the future *Waffen*-SS.

Northeast

A 'side show' involving the General SS of East Prussia, the SD, VoMi and another barely camouflaged ethnic German SS – the *Memelländischer Ordnungsdienst* – was ended on 22 March 1939, when the Memel territory was 'peacefully' annexed to East Prussia after Lithuania had been forced to agree to it by an ultimatum. The East Prussian SS managed the seizure and occupation without recourse to military forces, having long functioned as liaison with the *Ordnungsdienst* (Regulative Service), which was so completely under Berlin that the unusual step of transferring it as a body into the East Prussian Main Sector could occur that same day.

The Danzig SS was one of the oldest units in Germany, dating from 1926. It was unnecessary to camouflage it even before the Nazi regime began in the Free City in 1933. Indeed, from 1937 on the SS there completely controlled the police and managed liaison with Heydrich and Daluege so completely that Danzig was virtually a part of the SS and Police system. Although *Gauleiter* Albert Forster had been one of the original SS of 1925, he was not sympathetic to Himmler's ideas and ambitions. Yet his second-in-command, Arthur Greiser – the future *Gauleiter* of the annexed Polish territories around Poznań – was quite positive toward the SS. Working with Himmler in an attempt to shore up his own position *vis-à-vis* Forster, the Senate President was in a good position to aid the introduction of secret SS reinforcements for the Free City in May and June 1939, and to set up a 4,000-man Danziger *Heimwehr* with Death's Head cadre. The East Prussian Main Sector was also directly involved in *Wehrmacht* plans for the seizure of Danzig as early as April 1939. Forster could not directly resist Himmler's encroachments in his *Gau*, but making use of his own channels of influence which flowed through the Göring-Ribbentrop agents that Hitler used to prepare each of his territorial seizures, Forster succeeded in bypassing his pro-SS deputy and rival at the very last minute (23 August 1939). However, since SS lines ran through these agents as well, Himmler was merely inconvenienced by having to use conspiratorial and ancillary channels of control during the critical months ahead. Both SS and SA units figured in the step-by-step destruction of the few barriers that still separated Danzig from the Reich by 25 August.

   Himmler had had just about a year to convert an essentially peacetime General SS, with adjuncts for domestic emergencies (Death's Head and *Verfügungstruppe*), to a wartime footing. From the time of the 17 August 1938 *Führer* Order until the actual mobilisation for the war in Poland, feverish activity in the Berlin Main Offices and at the Main Sector headquarters presided over by the Superior SS and Police Leaders had shifted the emphasis from the General SS to its armed units and the police. Men of the General SS between the ages of twenty-five and thirty-five were called up under a Göring emergency service order of 15 October 1938, and trained by Death's Head cadres in Westphalia and Silesia as Death's Head Reinforcements. Those over thirty-five were also drafted for emergency service as civilians for concentration camp guard duty in wartime, already serving trial periods in 1939. Where General SS men were found unable to serve in these capacities for health or business reasons, Himmler ordered them to be discharged from the General SS, and even men over forty-five were to be discharged if they were recent transfers from other branches like the SA and grumbled about their assignments. Not many of the latter were actually 'drafted', but they often had more work to do because the younger full-time SS personnel were called up. About 10 per cent, or 30,000 men, were thus available from the General SS for occupation duty over and above the existing armed formations, which amounted to 25,000 in September 1939. The formation under Gottlob Berger of a unified recruiting system for General SS, *Waffen*-SS and Police in the spring of 1939 produced an overall increase in all three services of 15,000 youths for the calendar year, most of whom went to the new recruit training battalions of the *Verfügungstruppe* (*Ersatzbatallione*) formed after the outbreak of the war. Several thousand came from Folk Groups abroad, the majority from Hitler Youth formations as volunteers. Efforts to enlarge the Death's Head battalions proper bogged down over the twelve-year enlistment, non-recognition of this service as military service, and non-co-operation of the *Wehrmacht* in recruiting drives among two-year servicemen about to return to civilian life. In the short run this experience led to the expansion of the Death's Head Reinforcement battalions using the original battalions as cadre; in the long run the entire tie-up of concentration camp guards and the Death's Head units was dissolved. The experiment had essentially failed.

In the last week of August 1939, as the *Verfügungstruppe* regiments joined their assigned *Wehrmacht* divisions according to the mobilisation plan and the Death's Head Reinforcements reported at the Breslau camp to be formed into the new *Totenkopfstandarten* (Death's Head regiments), the *Einsatzkommandos* of the Sipo-SD began their rendezvous with other attack formations and the sabotage and provocation teams of the *Abwehr* and *Sicherheitsdienst* took up their places on the Polish border and signalled their ethnic German allies. Meanwhile Himmler remained at Hitler's side ready for a rapid change in plans, a new emergency, or a new assignment. His stock and that of the SS had never been higher with the *Führer*, but it was scheduled to rise even more in the years ahead, bringing with it vaster projects and untold suffering for millions.

Five short years had elapsed since the Röhm purge. During them the SS had made itself indispensible to the *Führer*-dictatorship. Outwardly still show-figures in their black parade uniforms, the General SS must have held the popular spotlight. But the reality of Himmler's Order for those 'in the know' must have seemed to lie in the police apparatus – Gestapo, Kripo and SD. Few would as yet have grasped the potential of the concentration camps as economic resources to free the SS of dependence on party and state – the camps seemed to be part of the terror system. Few could have imagined the *Waffen*-SS as a fourth arm of the *Wehrmacht* – least of all could the High Command itself. Whether because of their low opinion of SS military prowess or faith in their skill in starving the SS of young manpower, German army leaders did not fear the *Waffen*-SS – only the police sneaks and the party intriguers with Hitler. But another aspect of the SS must have been apparent to many Germans by 1939; what Albert Speer in his last book called 'infiltration'.

By 1939 Himmler had created a veritable second SS of honorary personnel. Perhaps to some observers he had overdone it. The wholesale award of SS Generals' ranks to the party brass could have watered down the value of the rank. The broad scale of SS colonelcies in the government bureaucracy certainly indicated some claim upon the time and attention of office chiefs and policy makers; the business world seemed to revel in SS majorities and colonelcies. Perhaps many were merely pleased to have an impressive uniform and a little 'clout' – maybe even a little protection. Realistically, no one – not even the *Reichsführer* SS – knew exactly how loyal the honorary membership rendered an otherwise powerful figure of party, state, or the economy. Rapid promotion in the SS must have been observed by the watchful – but was it an indication of the man's importance to the SS in his chosen field or of services performed? Today it is still difficult to say. Yet the impression of widespread infiltration and influence by the SS in countless walks of life could easily be gained by 1939. It served to impress, whether it was actually a genuine power or not. Whereas in 1934 the SS had merely begun to claim a special position in German society and in the state, by 1939 it appeared to have arrived – or if not quite arrived, to be at the point of arrival. Of course, the ability to continue to draw unto itself cadres of skill and competence from all walks of German life rested in part on its own intrinsic claims as 'a sworn community of blood', as a community of families; but the war would bring to the SS an external motivation – the desire on the part of the able and the ambitious to enter what appeared to be the system of power and decision in Germany. To win the war and to shape the future required membership of the SS.

THE YEARS OF TRAGIC FULFILMENT

1939–45

Seven short years had passed since Germany, torn by civil strife, had succumbed to Hitler. In those years the SS had changed from a street-fighting militia into crack military and police formations. In such a short time, much had been accomplished; yet inevitably when war came, that state of emergency for which the SS was peculiarly designed, nearly everything had to be remodelled. During the years in between the old *Kampfjahre* and the new, the SS had been prepared for war after a fashion, along with most other Nazi institutions. But the imagery of 1918 and 1932 bound Himmler and his officers within a circle that was narrower than the war they had to wage. The experiences of 1918 and 1932 were still fresh enough between 1939 and 1945 to mislead men steeped in Nazi ideology to the conviction that the chief dangers in wartime would come from inveterate enemies at home rather than on the battlefield. Rendering traitors harmless had been the chief purpose and glory of the SS. Designed for the inner-German theatre of operations, Himmler's SS found it hard to transcend the role of policeman, turnkey and hangman. Indeed, the destruction of the Jews represents an insistence on the necessity of there being an inner enemy large enough to justify the Nazi philosophy. Furthermore, the role of the SS as security forces in the occupied areas of Europe preserved among these troops the narrow, punitive and suspicious outlook of 1918 and 1932. Even Hitler had not rendered the Germans quite friendless in Europe in 1939; it was the fate of the SS, due to Himmler's and Hitler's efforts to prevent subject peoples from 'repeating the *Dolchstoss* (stab-in-the-back) of 1918', to breed hatred of Germany everywhere in Europe.

Yet, as Himmler liked to say, the SS had its 'constructive' side. Out of the settlement romanticism of 'Blood and Soil', Darré's contribution to the infant SS of the years of struggle, Himmler was to improvise an instrument of German imperialism, an SS agency for the resettlement of Germans on newly conquered soil as farmers and tradesmen – as Reich Commissar for the Strengthening of Germandom (RKFDV). The expulsion of the former residents, carried out with characteristic SS ruthlessness and brutality, was to sharpen the problems of the occupying German forces wherever Himmler located his colonies, giving rise to a partisan movement and increasing the need for retaliatory police measures of an ever more military character. Thus, a kind of self-fulfilling prophecy was at work within the Nazi imperialism as practised by the SS: believing that they lived in a Hobbesian world of enemies, they raised up opponents where there were none. Ultimately all the SS administrators and policemen had to become soldiers of the *Waffen*-SS, as an embattled Germany had to defend herself against enemies from every direction. And in the *Waffen*-SS another old Nazi theme was to be preserved and revived, the SA's ambition to outdo and replace the *Wehrmacht* as a *Volksheer*. The soldiers' plot of 20 July 1944 not only seemed to confirm the stab-in-the-back imagery of 1918, its failure appearing to augur a different outcome for Germany under Nazi leadership than in 1918; it also gave the SS under Himmler a chance to make good the supposed errors of 1934. However, the *Waffen*-SS had become by then both much more and much less than the dream of the free corps veterans. Between 1939 and 1945 the few regiments of hand-picked volunteers had swelled to many divisions – first of young Germans without SS background, soon of ethnic Germans from eastern and southern Europe, then of northern Europeans, later of allied peoples from southern and eastern Europe, and ultimately no longer of volunteers. The dream of a new community of political soldiers, European volunteers for a post-war settlement programme stretching to the Caucasus and building a Greater Germanic Reich for Adolf Hitler, went down piecemeal in the midst of a chaotic power struggle among the Nazi leaders in which Himmler too sought to extricate himself and his apparatus from the defeat by intrigue and unprincipled bargaining.

The wartime SS endured nearly six years, almost exactly as long as the *Aufbaujahre* (years of construction) from July 1934 to August 1939. During these later years the SS changed more than it had since the Röhm purge and the Seizure of Power. Just as the pre-1933 street-fighting SS stamped its image on the SS of 1933–34, so during 1939–41 up to the attack on Soviet Russia, the SS retained the impress of 1938. Lines of development which had enabled Hitler to accomplish the *Anschluss* and the absorption of the Sudetenland with minimal disturbance of the German scene could be continued. Many new features of SS activity, such as RKFDV, could emerge from the assumptions of 1938 with little relevance to the life-and-death struggle that National Socialism itself had begun.

By July 1941, however, the SS entered a new terrible phase of blood-letting – in which Himmler's dictum that the SS man does not fear to shed his own or others' blood for his cause was realised in the decimation of ranks of the original political soldiers and in the destruction of Jews and Communists on a scale so vast that the SS itself was not capable of mastering it, turning over part of the bloody work to *Wehrmacht* units and subject peoples. By the spring of 1943, the illusions involved in the earlier planning of the SS imperialists had given way to a grim determination to convert everything and everyone in their system to total war. For the men who could remember 1918 and 1932, the latter years of the war seemed a confirmation of the truth of their worst fears and deepest convictions. Conditions of total emergency seemed to justify an altering of values in which new institutions, new loyalties and new men must be born. At this time the SS came as near being a counter-state, beyond the party and beyond the German Reich, as it ever came. But in truth the SS never reached this transvaluation, though some individuals probably did. It was too much a part of the whole fabric of the German war effort, too much a part of the German state for that. Efforts to penetrate into and capture the citadels of the German social and economic system also failed at this time, although they appeared nearer to success than ever before. In many respects the war years presented opportunities for the SS to fulfil its most cherished purposes, and the evils which it perpetrated were indeed a tragic fulfilment of Himmler's oldest ambitions. Yet in another sense the war years exposed the rather young and untested Nazi institutions to a withering blast, and they did not stand up well – even before defeat wiped them off the face of the earth.

The SS and Police System

In September 1939 the SS and the police were still two very separate entities. Only 3,000 Gestapo officials out of 20,000 had SS rank; the proportion of the SS in the Kripo and the Orpo was even less, though sizeable in absolute figures. To qualify for SS runes, a police officer had to have joined the NSDAP in 1933 (or earlier) – hardly a strong basis for devotion to Himmler's Order. Other qualifications included withdrawal from Church affiliation, an 'orderly marriage' (divorce and remarriage was on the borderline) and more than one child. The sixteen Inspectors of the Order Police had long police careers behind them, rendering their high SS ranks secondary; they were officially loyal to Daluege and the Order Police apparatus in contradistinction to the Interior Ministry system of the administrative bureaucracy. Ambitious individuals among them still could on occasion choose either to work closely with the *Gauleiter* as Reich Governor or with the SS. While the sixteen Inspectors of the Security Police and SD implied in their very titles a firmer union of SS and Police, and included several old and convinced SS officers from 1931–32 days, the bulk of the Security Police were professional police officials who had risen through co-operation with Heydrich. They exemplified the traits of conscientious bureaucrats willing to serve the Nazi cause rather than of devoted SS men.

SUPERIOR SS AND POLICE LEADERS

The real focus of SS and Police fusion was the Superior SS and Police Leader (HSSPF), in every case an old SS fighter, who was the SS Main Sector commander and, after mobilisation, in emergencies the tactical superior of both branches of the police via the inspectors. But here too there was ambiguity. Not only did the formal Interior Ministry system of administration remain even after mobilisation as long as a special declaration of emergency was withheld but there was uncertainty about the nature and degree of subordination of the Superior SS and Police Leaders to the *Gauleiter* as Reich Defence Commissars and as Reich Governors. Himmler ordered them to report for duty to the latter (or in some cases to the Prussian *Oberpräsidenten*) on 25 August. An order issued by Daluege in Himmler's name on 11 September transferred authority to the *Gauleiter* in their capacity as the newly created Reich Defence

Commissars, but Himmler cancelled it on 16 October, returning to the strictly Interior Ministry chain of command. Thus, a party bid to enhance the role of the *Gauleiter* was turned aside, incidentally weakening Daluege's role as an independent channel of command and negotiating partner. This kept the Superior SS and Police Leaders within the administrative bureaucracy of the state. In fact, Himmler in his 16 October decree even used the term 'subordinate', missing in the 25 August orders. The Reich Defence Commissars might merely make use of Superior SS and Police Leaders from time to time. Himmler's caution kept these high-ranking SS officers from becoming part of party satrapies until he took over the Interior Ministry himself in 1943.

All in all, the lot of these old SS fighters was not a comfortable one, but as Himmler might say that was not what they were there for. They were to represent the *Reichsführer* SS and Chief of the German Police in the fullest sense of the word. In coming years they could assert the unity of SS and Police in a number of ways. A unified SS and Police court system was on the drafting boards, to be implemented in a matter of months, making Superior SS and Police Leaders chief magistrates for their Main Sectors and for all SS and Police units within them. As commanders of the SS Main Sectors, they had charge of admissions and promotions within the SS – of interest to ambitious policemen – and also of ideological training within the SS and by the SS for the police. Through the latter channel they could strengthen mutual understanding and comradeship.

FORMATION OF THE RSHA

Himmler's caution is also demonstrated by what he did not do either before or after the outbreak of war. Although the creation of a super SS and Police Main Office had been proposed by Daluege's Orpo Main Office in November 1938, Himmler rejected it and did not even include the latter main office in a consolidated Gestapo and SD headquarters for co-ordinating all wartime security activities. As Chief of the German Police, Himmler did not wish to have a large, ostentatious office, so he operated simultaneously out of Unter den Linden 74, Daluege's headquarters, and of course from Prinz Albrechtsstrasse 8 – which on 27 September 1939 became the headquarters of the new RSHA. This controversial agency had been under discussion during most of 1939. It certainly represented a step forward in the integration of SS and Police, inasmuch as the long-standing separation of the SD-Main Office and the Security Main Office (Kripo and Gestapo) was finally surmounted. On the other hand, the question whether the RSHA was a state agency was never resolved; and the Ministry of the Interior went on characterising Heydrich, RSHA's new chief and archi-tect, as Chief of the Sipo and SD – a designation he actually accepted in his letterheads for external correspondence. The RSHA headings were reserved for internal and SS communications. When one realises that even the geographic separation of the SD offices at Wilhelmstrasse 102 was retained, one may too readily jump to the conclusion that this dreaded new agency was merely a paper tiger.

In the discussions of 1939, one of the chief features was the problem of what to do with the SD. The evolution of the Gestapo system into an exclusive executive with the removal of all investigative, as well as arrest powers, from SD agents by 1937 had put the SD network and the SD Main Office into the shade as a truly important service. Furthermore, in spite of ambition to serve as a kind of international German secret service, Heydrich's coterie was relegated to a very secondary place by the more professional army *Abwehr*. Thus, the SD was left to cloak-and-dagger work of the oldest and meanest variety, such as the faked Polish attack on the Gleiwitz radio transmitter; to vaporous speculations and second-hand gossip about enemy and friendly countries no better than what Rosenberg's Foreign Affairs Office turned out; to situation reports about internal German conditions; and to the study and penetration of the ethnic German communities of eastern Europe. Without giving up the former preoccupations, Heydrich seems to have decided to push the latter two. The first organisational chart of RSHA, for which Werner Best was still responsible, had an *Amt* III, *Inland-Abwehr* and an *Amt* VI, *Ausland-Abwehr*. While each of these virtually reproduced the old SD-*Abteilungen* II and III, the real change occurred in the merging of the SD-*Abteilung* I with the former administrative elements of the Sipo Main Office in the Prinz Albrechtsstrasse. This consolidation, though not in its permanent form due in part to an imminent quarrel between Best and Heydrich, was necessitated by the large new tasks thrust upon the RSHA by the war. It must have been a trick of Heydrich's to carry out a reor-ganisation while key personnel were absent on temporary duty in Poland, where ever-changing conditions demanded their presence. Heydrich saw to many of the new tasks himself, bypassing Best and relaying many of Himmler's decisions directly to the special Sipo-SD units in the field.

We have seen that already in the summer of 1938, in preparation for the conflict with Czechoslovakia, the conception of special Sipo-SD teams as tactical units was developed. In the form of teams attached to the invading regiments – both SS and *Wehrmacht* – the so-called *Einsatzkommandos*, of mixed composition but essentially SD-led, ferreted out the centres of opposition to the Nazi takeover in the Sudetenland and later in Bohemia-Moravia. Mobility and independence were their chief virtues. These organs had no permanent structure, quickly giving way to regular Orpo, Kripo, Gestapo and SS structures in the course of months. Here was an executive function for the SD, which really demanded as central head-quarters an executive-type office. Thus, the RSHA owed its existence in part to the need for a co-ordinating – indeed directing – centre for the much more elaborate SS and Police invasion of Poland.

SS Occupation Forces

Since March 1939 elements of the SS, especially *Verfügungstruppe* and Death's Head regiments, had been employed as occupation forces in Bohemia-Moravia alongside *Wehrmacht* units and to some extent replacing them. The scheme for handling Poland, in whole or in part, once captured, was to turn over police duties to improvised SS (Death's Head) regiments made up of training cadre from the replacement units of the *Verfügungstruppe* and the original Death's Head regiments, to which were added General SS personnel called up for the emergency. These groups would be spearheaded by *Einsatzkommandos*, whose task was to form so-called Ethnic German Self-Defence units led by SS officers and NCOs supplied and directed by the Recruitment Office of the SS Main Office. Thus, a very intricate liaison system was evolved through SS institutions, involving the following: the SS Main Office, whose chief, Heissmeier, became for the following year 'Inspector General of the Death's Head Police Reinforcements'; Death's Head regiments; the SS Recruitment Office, whose blustery chief, Berger, was destined to become the new head of the SS Main Office for his efficient handling of recruitment and the Self Defence units; the Orpo-Main Office; and the RSHA, working through the SD network in contact with VoMi.

We know that the *Einsatzkommandos* were organised and ready to fall upon Poland in August 1939 from the correspondence of one of them with the SD Main Office regarding Jewish policy. By 19–21 September Heydrich was laying plans and sending out instructions to these units already in Poland for the concentration of Polish Jews in communities over 500 in size, the arrest of Polish intellectuals, and the clearing of residential housing (flats) in Gdynia and Poznań to make room for the first Baltic Germans being registered by VoMi for 'repatriation' from Latvia and Estonia. There were at least a half-dozen of these teams in operation in Bydgoszcz, Poznań, Radom, Łodź, Cracow and Katowice as soon as each city fell. By quickly involving ethnic German males in the Self-Defence units, they reduced the burden of the *Wehrmacht* units and even freed their own specialists for the deadly work of rounding up known and suspected opponents of Nazi Germany. On their heels came a battalion each of Death's Head Police Reinforcements for every district capital, equipped with trucks and small arms. These battalions had been pulled out of relatively recently formed Death's Head regiments, often with inexperienced officers and NCOs and sometimes with General SS personnel having no background except the memory of street fights and crude ideological training programmes.

It was from this early wave of *Einsatzkommandos*, Self-Defence units and Death's Head battalions that the SS occupation tradition took its beginning in wanton cruelty, sadism and senseless death. The *Wehrmacht* protested without effect on Hitler; most soldiers and officers were glad to be withdrawn from occupation duty in late October and early November to be replaced by thousands more of the Death's Head Police Reinforcements, a regiment of them in each district. Order Police battalions also made their appearance along with the SS units, performing the same tasks. Their personnel were drawn from regular Reich Police garrisons, replaced at home by over-age 'police reserves', often General SS. With the appointment of a Superior SS and Police Leader 'East' on 4 October 1939 – none other than F.W. Krüger, the old AW-Chief of the SA and more recently commander of the SS Border Guards and SS Cavalry – the permanent police structure in Poland began to take shape.

With the creation of another separate political entity beyond the Reich like the 'Protectorate of Bohemia-Moravia', to be known as the *General-Gouvernement Polen* (the General Government of Poland), Krüger found himself SS and Police commander of a colonial no-man's-land, a dumping ground for unwanted Poles and Jews from the Polish territories contiguous to the Reich and from the Reich itself. Lopping off Polish territories on the 1937 Reich frontiers, some of which had belonged to Germany before 1919, Hitler expanded older provinces like East Prussia and Upper and Lower Silesia. The northern portion of the Polish corridor he reconstituted as 'Danzig-West Prussia' while to the south he recreated the pre-First World War Posen district, soon expanded to include the industrial district of Łodż, renamed Litzmannstadt. While these last two *Gaue*, as they were to be called, also acquired new Superior SS and Police Leaders, the former regions fell under the command of Superior SS and Police Leaders in Königsberg and Breslau. A separate *Gau* of Upper Silesia and a Superior SS and Police Leader in Katowice (Kattowitz) came later, in January 1941. The Superior SS and Police Leader 'East' found himself confronting the ambitious Hans Frank, the so-called Governor-General. Instead of Inspectors of Order and Security Police, Himmler installed *Befehlshaber* (commanding officers) for each service, a *Führer* (independent commander) of the Self-Defence units, and *Kommandeure* (commanders) of the district police at Warsaw, Radom and Cracow (later also at Lublin). Frank regarded these police officials as strictly answerable to himself, continuing the struggle opened earlier in the Reich between the *Gauleiter* and Superior SS and Police Leaders and their inspectors.

In the other former Polish territories annexed to the Reich, there were merely the two Inspectors of Order and Security Police, but since the new *Gauleiter* and Reich Governors did not have experienced administrative bureaucracies as yet – only party adventurers and a certain number of Reich officials transferred to them 'for good riddance' – the Superior SS and Police Leaders and the inspectors rapidly became as decisive as the *Gauleiter*. In Danzig-East Prussia, *Gauleiter* Albert Forster opposed Himmler wherever he could, and Himmler prodded his representatives to ignore the *Gauleiter* as much as possible. In Posen (later Wartheland), the *Gauleiter* agreed with Himmler and was more cunning in maintaining some of his independence. Superior SS and Police Leaders sought in all the former Polish territories to maximise their powers on the grounds of emergency conditions, which certainly prevailed at the time of establishing civilian governments composed largely of 'carpet-baggers' from the old Reich and with tiny German minorities facing sullen, hungry Polish majorities.

The resettlement operation was in full swing by November and December, adding to the chaos. The Death's Head Police Reinforcements were used extensively in the expulsion of families from their homes to make way for Germans not only from the Baltic and eastern Polish territories ceded to the USSR, but also from the Reich, who streamed in now as managers of real estate, business agents and party organisers. The brutality of these SS units was no different against the innocent Polish families they expelled than against Polish patriots who had opposed Germany before September 1939 or against local and deported Jews they browbeat in forced labour battalions. Having been born out of replacement cadres for the original Death's Head regiments who guarded the concentration camps – where many an unteachable roughneck had been sent because he was hard to get along with in his original unit – these SS occupation forces of 1939 and 1940 were the last degenerate vestige of the old street-fighting *élan*, with some of the bestiality of the concentration camps thrown in. In fact, there was considerable overlap and interchange between the Death's Head Reinforcement regiments' administration and the concentration camp system in the winter and spring of 1940. Neither aspect of the SS had yet the look of cold bureaucracy as in the mass-murders of 1942–43. While some of the Death's Head Police Reinforcements went on to this 'more exacting work', the majority were doomed to death as ordinary soldiers of the *Waffen*-SS or anti-partisan police duty. The sixteen Death's Head regiments did not survive as occupation troops beyond 1940, although several were briefly employed in Norway, Denmark and Holland.

Concentration Camps

The three original Death's Head regiments were only withdrawn from the concentration camp guard duty for which they were set up when sufficient replacements had been called up from the General SS. Approximately 6,000 SS men between twenty-seven and forty were drafted (emergency service for civilians) for concentration camp guard duty during the winter of 1939–40 in SS-*Totenkopf-(Wach-) Sturmbanne* (KL *Verstärkung*). The latter units, at battalion strength and with cadre from men left behind from the departing Death's Head regiments, took over the concentration camps at Dachau, Sachsenhausen, Buchenwald, Mauthausen, Ravensbrück and

Flossenburg by early spring of 1940, directly subordinate to the Inspector of Concentration Camps, now Richard Glücks. The original Death's Head regiments in turn formed the Death's Head 'Division' of the new *Waffen-SS* under their old commander, 'Papa' Eicke, ceasing to have anything further to do with the concentration camps.

The departure of Eicke from the Oranienburg headquarters of the Inspector of Concentration Camps merely removed a source of irrational interference and flamboyant ideology from the administration. Glücks, his former deputy and successor, governed the several hundred SS *Altkämpfer* on the concentration camp staffs with the same strict, uncomprehending rigidity, aiming neither at rehabilitation nor at economic exploitation of the inmates. Little effort was made to educate the new recruits. There was not much ambition shown within the older SS of the concentration camp system. The striking growth of the war years was thrust upon them by Hitler's and Himmler's suspicious and punitive outlook and by the discovery made by Oswald Pohl, the clever and very aggressive SS Chief of Administration, that the concentration camps could be made to pay many of the SS's expenses. This notion had come first to some of the intelligent administrative personnel at Oranienburg on loan from the SS Main Office for Administration and Economy (VWHA); it took several years before it was the preponderant factor in planning concentration camps.

The first new concentration camps were quasi–illegal improvisations in the newly conquered Polish territories or contiguous German rear areas. The Superior SS and Police Leaders or their deputies, the Inspectors or Sipo-SD Commanders, set up collecting camps for persons they rounded up and arranged for guards from General SS or Death's Head Police Reinforcements. In December 1939 Himmler got around to inquiring about potential new concentration camp capacities and ordering the official transfer of these 'wild' camps into the regular system under the Inspector of Concentration Camps. Auschwitz had its beginning at this time, as did Stutthof and the Lublin complex of camps later used for the wholesale destruction of Jews. The 'euthanasia' experiment at Kulmhof (Chelmno) also fits into this early, quasi-unofficial stage of concentration camp development. So does Camp Hinzert, an SS–*Sonderlager* (special camp).

The wartime innovators and operators were not regular personnel of the old KL (concentration camp) system but a fresh wave of General SS officers and NCOs faced by a totally new, unfamiliar environment and determined to 'smash their way through' in the old tradition of civil war aggressive spirit (*Draufgängertum*). When Himmler ordered the integration of the two camp systems, the Oranienburg administrators sent some of the old Reich personnel out to the new camps. More of the old concentration camp staff were drawn off in 1940 and 1941 to set up additional concentration camps in the Reich on Himmler's orders: Natzweiler, Neuengamme and Gross-Rosen. These camps also began to show the rationalising influence of the SS Main Office for Administration and Economy in their plans, as did Auschwitz.

The process of transferring older, more experienced concentration camp administrators and establishing ever-larger camps tended to create an atmosphere in all camps of frustration and incompetence, which was taken out on the inmates. Even without an official policy of killing prisoners or working them to death, the raw newness of the camps or their personnel – or of the tasks set before them – joined with the dislocations of war and recent occupation to make all the Nazi concentration camps equally horrible, defeating Himmler's own wish that the camps be graded in terror and implication. The policy of regular transfers of staff personnel, designed at least in part to reduce corruption and maintain a high degree of discipline, spread the worst features of the old type of SS bully and increasingly the frontier ruthlessness of Lublin and Auschwitz. Thus, a kind of common denominator did develop in the war years among a few hundred officers and men who stayed in the camp administration; since preference for remaining implied disinterest in the front, there was an additional ingredient of ruthlessness in the determination to become indispensable in the productive efforts of the camps.

However, among the 35,000 who ultimately saw service as concentration camp guards, at least 10,000 were not SS members at any time. Furthermore, *Waffen*-SS units detached personnel on temporary duty to the camps as early as 1940, and wounded *Waffen*-SS personnel served as guards toward the end of the war. During the years 1940–45, there was certainly no single type of concentration camp guard, although the early SS staff personnel succeeded in putting its stamp on many of them. An additional irony which confuses matters further is the policy begun in 1940 of inducting the camp administrators, and later the guard personnel, into the *Waffen*-SS to keep them from being drafted for the *Wehrmacht*. While some of these persons certainly saw service at the front, it was not possible for Himmler to pursue his policy of wholesale rotations of even top officers through all branches of SS activity. Once absorbed into the rapidly growing system, the concentration camp SS tended to remain there, while correspondingly only a fraction of the *Waffen*-SS had any official contact with the concentration camps.

Thus, the phrase 'concentration camp SS' may be justified as expressing a common tendency even in the war years more distinct than, say, 'General SS' in the pre-war period, or even '*Waffen*-SS' after 1941. Nevertheless, organisational and functional differences persisted among: (1) the economically oriented personnel from the VWHA; (2) the two waves of camp administrators (1934 and 1939) which merged with a third wave involved in the 'death factories' after 1941; and (3) the guards, ranging from older General SS men, young *Waffen*-SS recruits – including ethnic Germans and other eastern Europeans – SA and party people hiding from the front or being disciplined, and ordinary German soldiers. Within the rapidly expanding SS officers' corps of the later war years (1941–45), the first group occupies the most prominent place in terms of rank and importance, if not in numbers. Even the second group is remarkable for its small size as far as officers are concerned; but among its captains and majors it included a very high proportion of the early pioneers of 1930–31 whose limited capacities and vices had suited them to be accomplices in evil and nothing more, although that was enough for Himmler's purpose. In spite of its relatively large size, the third group, the guard personnel of 1939–45, had very few officers, and those were of low ranks (first and second lieutenants), often of post-1933 vintage. Largely lacking even the ideology of the administrators – certainly without the education and skills of the economists – the guards were untrained policemen confronted with tasks beyond them even on SS terms. Many of their crimes were due to ignorance, fear, corruption and the bad example set by the camp administrators.

The pre-war camp personnel had been well adapted to the punitive, revenge-seeking purposes of the Nazis in erecting the camps in the first place, but increasingly after 1939 two quite different and powerful pressures were put upon them: the effort to capitalise upon the labour power of the inmates, and the drive to destroy Jews and after them other categories of humanity. Both features were known to the earlier personnel, but both had been incidental. The work before the war was often ridiculous; if practical, it was limited to camp advantages. Killing was frequently accidental or at least the random result of individuals' whims. Now SS organisations outside the concentration camp system, the VWHA and the RSHA, began to demand of the concentration camp SS – deprived of their charismatic leader, Eicke, and most of his professional guard troops – feats of production and of human destruction that were almost intrinsically self-contradictory. It is not surprising that chaos and degradation ensued beyond anything previously imaginable. Yet the relative efficiency of concentration camp production in the later years, coupled with the absolute efficiency of the killing operations, implied a co-operative achievement and a flexibility of the varied personnel that is horrible to contemplate.

The imagination and engineering skill of the 'top brass' supplemented the literal-minded and undaunted human butchers. Indeed, the arrival of the latter among the former in 1943 and 1944 (Hoess and Eichmann) signalled the completion of a process of merging and identification of SS types more effective than the SD and Gestapo or Superior SS and Police Generals and *Waffen*-SS generals. However, before this occurred numerous sharply differentiated apparatus came into existence for handling, sorting and transporting human beings as if they were so many pieces of goods. That the depersonalisation of others had a backlash on its practitioners is symbolised by the transference of the practice of tattooing prisoners' numbers on their arms to tattooing armpits of the *Waffen*-SS with their blood types. But here too there was differentiation; it is not recorded that higher SS officers, even in the *Waffen*-SS, had to submit to this indignity.

The managerial bureaucracy of Oranienburg, interested in economic exploitation of concentration camp labour for construction purposes – especially of endless *Kasernen* (barracks) and of blocks of flats and farmhouses – saw to it that Flossenburg, Mauthausen, and later Natzweiler and Gross-Rosen concentration camps were built in or near stone quarries, the original idea behind Dachau. Already prodigal in the creation of quasi-state companies, financed with party and SS funds and by borrowing from private lenders (the great D-banks), the SS economists created additional companies (*Deutsche Erd- und Steinwerke* and *Deutsche Ausrüstungswerke*) for producing building stones and bricks and for producing and distributing food, clothing and furniture for the SS, police and new settlers. The boards of directors of these companies were none other than higher SS officers of the Main Office for Administration and Economy (VWHA), who were even permitted to bring in some of their own capital, part of which they had already made through other SS enterprises, especially land sales.

These men can be described neither as ideologically motivated nor as misfits of the depression but simply as very ruthless entrepreneurs who, quite clear-eyed, saw opportunities for profit in the exploitation of concentration camp labour and were forced to share these opportunities with the SS. They began well before the war and were going strong in 1938–39 but really didn't become tycoons of vast enterprises until the conquests of 1940–42 gave them millions of human lives to play with and a patriotic justification for expanding the SS concentration camp system to squeeze the utmost from Germany's victims, beginning with the Jews. With the erection of countless 'branch camps' wherever Jews were concentrated in ghettos, and wherever 'enemy' economic enterprise could be put into operation for the war effort with concentration camp or even war prisoners (first Poles, later Russians and to some extent French prisoners of war), the men of the VWHA compelled the Inspector of Concentration Camps to develop new administrations and guard units.

Small wonder that Eicke's old chief of staff, Richard Glücks – unimaginative, lacking in energy if not lazy, even unperceptive compared to a man like Hoess – should find these men meddling in 'his affairs', regulating the new camps which had never been properly integrated into the old system anyway. But Heydrich bristled far more than Glücks at the SS Chief of Administration's minions' interference when it was a matter of state security. Yet even in 1940 after the formation of the RSHA, Himmler would not place the concentration camp system under it, preferring rather to transfer the Inspectorate of Concentration Camps and Guard Troops to the newly fashioned Leadership Main Office (FHA) of the *Waffen*-SS! Since the latter organ clearly did not care to interfere in this domain, the real effect was to force Heydrich to battle it out with Oswald Pohl, the Chief of Administration and no mean opponent, in an area now doubly consecrated to national defence. After inconclusive skirmishes as early as 1939, the battle lines were drawn in 1940 in terms of prosecutions of embezzling SS *Wirtschafter* (economic managers) in Austria, Sudetenland and Bohemia-Moravia. Before the clash reached many of the higher offices, a working compromise based on a balance of power had emerged in 1941. German conquests brought enormous possibilities for confiscation of productive properties, especially those in Jewish or enemy hands.

The RSHA was the appropriate agency for seizing this wealth but not to administer it. Heydrich was thus in a position to reward his friends with pieces of property and to punish his enemies by taking away their ill-gotten gains, but only with the co-operation of the SS Main Office for Administration and Economy (VWHA). Together they could protect the interests of the SS and the Reich (always alleged to coincide) against greedy and dishonest individuals and firms. The formation in July 1940 of an SS holding company, *Deutsche Wirtschaftsbetrieb*, to capitalise and supervise the daughter companies represents the shift to business-like management demanded by Heydrich, though in effect the small abuses and private dishonesties of individual SS officers and men were thereby erected into a state-sanctioned system of pillage and enslavement.

By late 1940 the RSHA was pressing the concentration camp administration to take ever more inmates, including Jews, and was working hand-in-glove with the VWHA to enlarge the camps and secure raw materials to be worked on therein. It is true that within the system there were still disagreements: the *Judenreferat* did not like the sorting system which preserved Jews for labour; security regulations prevented the use of able political prisoners as foremen, so that inefficient and corrupt criminals had to be used; endless reports and investigations demanded by the RSHA absorbed time which might otherwise have gone into productive labour. Nevertheless, the concentration camps had attained by 1941 a level of productivity such that with business-like management and additional investment of scarce materials, reasonably capable SS personnel, and food for the rising number of inmates, they might be regarded as sinews of the Nazi war effort. Thus, it was rumoured that Fritz Sauckel, as Plenipotentiary for Labour Mobilisation, might lay claim to the productive capacity of the concentration camps early in 1942; and to head this off Himmler finally integrated the concentration camp system into the new, consolidated Reich and SS Main Office, the renamed and reconstituted WVHA (Economic Administration Main Office).

Whereas the 1939 formulation of the Chief of Administration's powers had still conceived of two spheres – a state sphere for the police and the

armed SS (Main Office Budget and Construe Firm), and an SS and party
sphere (VWHA) – the reorganisation of 1 February 1942 clearly
combined the two and placed the concentration camps as *Amtsgruppe* D
within one unified economic administration for police, *Waffen*-SS and
General SS. In this way the camp system was brought wholly into even
more direct relationship with the business managers and supply personnel of all three systems. A goal of self-sufficiency for these three interlocking systems could now be set up as a bargaining counter with the rest
of the Nazi state and party, and especially the *Wehrmacht* – all glad to have
a larger share in what police and SS could produce with scarce resources.
Needless to say, this future SS economic independence (it was never
really attained) could become a dangerous weapon in the hands of men
disloyal to Hitler, yet given Himmler's loyalty (until April 1945), it was a
valuable aid to Hitler *vis-à-vis* the army, German business and even the
state bureaucracy.

   Thus it was that Hitler refused to let Sauckel tamper with the concentration camps' production potential, so that they remained purely SS
installations until the end. On the other hand, the needs of German industry for manpower were increasingly met by setting up detached elements
of existing concentration camps near factories and exchanging concentration camp labour for a sharply negotiated share of the production for SS
and Police purposes. General SS membership and contributions through
Himmler's *Freundeskreis* (business friends of Himmler) enhanced an entre-
preneur's chances to get this labour, but some of the best bargains were
driven by businessmen outside Himmler's influence. If the SS did not
become economically self-sufficient even in 1943 and 1944 despite even
larger investments in the camp system financed from German banks, it was
due not to Hitler's opposition but to bottlenecks of others' making, partly
even of a strictly technical character. Doubtless the formal survival of the
punitive and destructive purposes within the concentration camp system,
in addition to the informal institutional rigidities described by Hoess
(chicanery, stupidity, sadism), played a very large part in keeping the SS and
police dependent to the last upon the *Wehrmacht*, government agencies,
Party Treasurer Franz Xavier Schwarz and German big business. Killing
the Jews, starving the Russian prisoners of war and 'working to death'
persons convicted of treason was a luxury the SS could ill afford. Yet the
view that all three of these operations could be made to pay direct divi-
dends to the war effort was not restricted to the SS.

The Final Solution

There is no satisfactory history of the ghastly euphemism – 'The Final Solution of the Jewish Question'. Perhaps it dates back to the 1880s with various intended outcomes. Hitler had 'prophesied' that world Jewry would not emerge from a world war which he accused 'them' of fomenting in 1939. Göring ordered Heydrich to 'solve the Jewish question finally' in 1941. The term became widespread after the attack on the USSR.

The destruction of the European Jewish communities and their members had been a money-making operation from its inception in Germany in 1933. While the SS neither initiated the 'Final Solution of the Jewish Question' nor was its chief beneficiary, the SS in all its branches took a conscious hand in the process and sought to enrich itself collectively and individually thereby. It was impossible to keep a monopoly in Germany of so popular and rewarding an activity as stealing from the Jews. However, as Himmler pointed out, the rest of Germany and even most of the party were glad to leave the killing to the SS. Although they engaged in all the forms of official and unofficial thievery invented by others, it remained for the SS to steal their victims' shoes and underwear, hair and gold fillings. The fact that even the latter had to be shared with the Reich Finance Ministry underlines the deep involvements of non-SS sectors of German public life in the ultimate meanness of the *Endlösung* (Final Solution).

While it may properly be said that the physical destruction of Jewry was implicit in Hitler's whole philosophy, killing the Jews of Germany and Europe was not an explicit goal of the SS leadership (or of the Nazi Party) until the war years. Of course, the murder of individual Jews was a heritage from the *Kampfzeit*, concentrated in the SA and passed onto the SS glorified as political soldierdom – unflinching willingness to commit crimes, even when recognised as such, on the command of higher authority. From 1933, when they aided in 'keeping order' in the boycott of 1 April, to 8 November 1938, when they were mobilised to keep the pogrom started by others within bounds and make it pay by imprisoning well-off Jews for ransom, the SS learned to expect to do the dirty work of the Nazi leadership. As it became bureaucratised and differentiated, the SS assigned its anti-Semitism to specialists, and as is usually the case with specialists they were volunteers. Far more important in this regard than

Adolf Eichmann, Reinhard Heydrich – combining personal psychologi-cal reasons with shrewd ambition – accepted, if he did not volunteer for, the responsibility of solving the Jewish question one way or the other. Thus, the Chief of the Security Police and the Security Service (Sipo-SD), in particular the Gestapo as *Amt* IV of the RSHA under Müller, became the competent agency for Jewish matters even before July 1941, the official date of Heydrich's assignment from Göring 'to solve the Jewish Question'. While Heydrich and later Eichmann seized the initia-tive in organising the resettlement and killing of the Jews, they were continuously abetted and even rivalled by other government and party agencies. Not the least of the motives involved in this initiative was the seizure of Jewish wealth.

Austria, the Sudetenland, Bohemia-Moravia and Poland were succes-sively subjected to organised and unorganised rapine, with Jews the first and most defenceless victims. Each step of the way saw Heydrich and 'Gestapo Müller' tightening the controls which prevented 'wild Aryanizations' even by SS men and channelling the process of seizures according to pre-arranged divisions of the spoils. By the time the Germans reached France and the Low Countries, the plundering of Jews and their deportation had become a fine art, although here and there was a sense of tentativeness and experiment due to the Nazi illusion of an imminent peace treaty with France and England. The real shift to mass murder comes with the decision to destroy the Jews of the Soviet Union in the process of the invasion, a certainty by the winter of 1940–41. Now the experience with *Einsatzgruppen* in Poland; with Eichmann's emigra-tion centres in Vienna, Prague and Berlin; with killing operations at Chelmno; and with the rapid expansion of concentration camps for the exploitation of slave labour could all be combined under RSHA *Amt* IV leadership. Hitler's verbal approval seems certain at this time, but we should not conceive of one mastermind or master-plan, even Heydrich's and least of all Eichmann's. The task was chiefly one of co-ordinating initiatives of many SS and non-SS agencies and on occasion supplying initiative where reluctance was involved.

Reluctance had, of course, a moral component, especially where brutality and death were involved. Thus, it was regularly advised that Germans should not do the killing, although Germans were expected to transmit orders and, naturally, to arrange matters. Here the creation of the complex and ramified SS system, from RSHA and Superior SS and

Police Leaders down to the military framework of squad and platoon in both the old General SS and the new *Waffen*-SS, made possible the expectation that even criminal orders would be flawlessly transmitted and if not enthusiastically and imaginatively carried out, at least not sabotaged consciously or unconsciously by men in desperate turmoil of conscience. But even the Order Police, so thinly penetrated numerically by the SS, had been effectively captured and co-ordinated by the ambitious in top ranks to the degree that they too could be used interchangeably with SS units for the grisly purpose of dragging old people, women and children to their execution by 'foreigners' equipped and uniformed as policemen. Even the *Wehrmacht*, grown callous watching Death's Head and Sipo-SD brutalities in Poland, gave up protesting and knowingly turned over Jews and commissars as well as partisans to the SS for destruction.

Of course, a great deal of the reluctance had nothing to do with conscience. Himmler's intervention in the autumn of 1941 against the resistance of the mayor of Litzmannstadt (Łodż) to taking more Jews into his ghetto 'temporarily' was necessitated by a purely administrative situation. Heydrich had hoped to shift the area of concentration for the Jews from the annexed Polish territories to the 'Jewish Reservation' in the Lublin district belatedly added to the General Government in exchange for Lithuania. However, Hans Frank successfully ended the unlimited 'dumping' of Jews there begun in October 1939. So it became necessary, after all, to cram an additional 20,000 Jews into 2,000 buildings, already the dwelling places of 144,000 persons. Quite aside from the high death rate under such conditions, Heydrich meant their sojourn to be temporary, for he had set about converting the experimental 'euthanasia' operation conducted at Chelmno and elsewhere in the Reich (Hadamar, Grafeneck, etc) into mass-killing camps, not only in the Lublin district but also at Auschwitz and in the occupied Soviet Union (Riga and Minsk). Yet strangely enough the Litzmannstadt ghetto slowly became popular with its German administrators, just as later Jewish labour centres in Upper Silesia and Minsk found their German 'protectors'. The reason is not hard to find: profits for everyone except the Jews, including the SS.

It had been Adolf Eichmann who had forced the additional Jews into Litzmannstadt, and it was he in 1943 who kept insisting on the liquidation of the ghetto there against the wishes of the army, businessmen, party officials and even branches of the SS. Its survival until 1944, like that of other profitable SS enterprises employing Jews, reveals efficiency rather than inefficiency in the SS. The desire of particular SS agencies to spare 'their Jews' indefinitely did not prevent the rapid liquidation of all the rest of the Jews; and ultimately Himmler's and Hitler's backing for the indomitable Eichmann resulted in the withdrawal of these last remnants, usually after replacements from other slave-labour reserves had been found or the raw materials and fuel had disappeared which alone had made their labour profitable. Thus, a tangled web of guilt and responsibility was woven right within the SS itself in regard to the destruction of the European Jews, hardly different from that enmeshing countless officials of the government and industry. Hundreds of thousands knowingly exploited the desperate fight for life of other human beings in order to reap profits, resisting Adolf Eichmann's importunities to the last with an easy conscience. Many SS members had their Jewish protectees, as did other Germans – and perhaps some who were not even profitable, except in terms of assuaging consciences. However, the SS system made these practices 'harmless', since over the long run the vast majority of these Jews would surely die.

The 'death factories' were basically the same at Chelmno (a 'small operation'), at Auschwitz-Birkenau (the largest), and at the network of camps at Belzec, Maidanek, Sobibor and Treblinka in the General Government. Common features were an 'assembly line' procedure, a sorting operation which saved for a time the able-bodied of both sexes to do the actual work of destruction, and a salvage operation (*Aktion* Reinhardt) to get the last usable bit of clothing, combs, false teeth, hair and gold fillings from the victims. This co-ordination was superimposed on very different establishments even run by different parts of the SS and certainly by SS officers of varied background; it was made possible by the planners and administrators of the SS WVHA. The skills involved were those of accountants and economists. While such persons had to oversee the operation step-by-step, they could leave the enforcement and dirty work to officers and men of *Amtsgruppe* D. Many of these people also might be regarded as 'specialists' at solving on-the-spot problems of killing, with the typical craftsmen's rivalry about alternative methods (carbon monoxide versus hydrogen cyanide).

Yet they too had a most varied background. Discernible are (1) *Altkämpfer*, (2) young intellectuals, (3) strict technicians – from police and business backgrounds and (4) underworld characters. Inasmuch as service in this exclusive group (no more than 100 officers can be identified) was in some degree a kind of sentence, as well as a trial, it is not surprising that so many of them ended on the gallows themselves. The SS and police courts thus provided a kind of alibi for 'decent' SS officers even during the Nazi era by destroying the destroyers, though not of course for their chief crimes but for stealing.

There were naturally more SS officers and men involved in guarding the death factories than in their operation, and indeed many of the worst excesses were performed by just such guards. They were in fact precisely the same kind of excesses that had occurred in concentration camps since 1933, although few if any of these guards were the *Altkämpfer* of 1933. It was not the kind of SS men which was decisive; it was the situation SS bureaucrats had created in the camps that made these excesses possible. Indeed, the excesses were more 'normal' than the fact of the death factories itself.

Eichmann's team of 'emigration specialists' of RSHA *Amt* IV-B-4 travelled about Europe in 1942, 1943 and 1944 enlisting the support of high and low officials of the SS and police system in tracking down the Jews of France, Holland, Belgium, Italy, Greece, Slovakia and Hungary, and then shipping them off to the death factories. Only because of this extensive network of co-operating officialdom could a dozen men arrange for the destruction of 1 million people. Yet it is vital to our understanding of the SS system to realise that Eichmann's teams were not necessary for the destruction of the Jews of Yugoslavia, Romania and the Soviet Union, who never saw the inside of a death factory run by the WVHA. These Jews died at the hands of the SD-*Einsatzgruppen*, whose organisation and management lay in quite other hands, though the line of authority traces back to the RSHA and Reinhard Heydrich.

The model for the 'mobile killing operations' of the murder battalions attached to the German *Wehrmacht* in Russia lay in the ad hoc teams used in the Sudetenland, Bohemia-Moravia and Polish invasions. Temporary duty and a mixture of elements from Gestapo, SD, Orpo, Kripo and *Waffen*-SS characterised the teams of battalion strength put together for Operation Barbarossa. At the top levels, in command positions, men were placed who were to prove their absolute loyalty and dependability to Himmler and Heydrich. Many of them were academic and professional people with an 'idealistic' interest in SS ideology, Bolshevism, the 'Jewish question' and Russia. Above them, in charge of planning and liaison with

the *Wehrmacht*, were the officials of the RSHA (IV-A-1). The lower officers were usually ordinary policemen. There is no evidence that they were
especially selected; the great likelihood is that these men too were simply
gotten rid of by their superiors. Thus, it is not surprising that an atmosphere of devil-may-care, of determination to prove just how ruthless and
inhuman they could be, permeated these groups. While the killing was
played down in the death factory system, partly to make it easier, the
butchers of the *Einsatzgruppen* 'showed off', creating problems for
German army commanders who wished to remain in ignorance and keep
their troops 'innocent'. It was not long before the *Einsatzgruppen* were
ordered to employ non-Germans as killers, a procedure extensively used
in Yugoslavia and Romania.

The SS Occupation Bureaucracy

What made it possible for relatively few inhuman killers like Hoess and
human bloodhounds like Eichmann to mesh with another brand of
butcher in the *Einsatzgruppen*, and to destroy efficiently without upset-
ting the very system in which they were nourished? In part the answer
lies in the evolution of the SS and Police framework that supplied them
with directives and shielded them from conflict and prying eyes of the
rest of the bureaucracy. The lack of a central SS and Police Main Office
made itself felt in failures of co-ordination, but the fact that Himmler, a
kind of universal spider, sat at the centre of all the systems equipped with
an efficient team of busybodies in his Personal Staff offset the intrinsic
rivalry of the RSHA and the Orpo Main Office. Himmler was clever
enough to permit Daluege to handle an increasing amount of the organisational growth of the SS and Police system in 1939 and 1940, so that
even Heydrich did not have control over everything. After the move of
Heydrich to Prague in September 1941, the two offices were better able
to work together on a routine basis, a procedure enhanced by the development of a couple dozen police generals as truly SS and Police Generals
at both staff and field command levels.

    The spread of occupation responsibilities in 1940 and even more so in
1941, until large stretches of Europe were subjugated to SS and police
rule – embodied in SS and Police Generals as Superior SS and
Police Leaders (HSSPFs) – actually created the opportunity Himmler

and the SS had worked for since before 1933. One universal net or web of influence and control was to be set up in which police responsibilities and SS growth could take place surmounted by the position of Superior SS and Police Leader, the highest and most honourable field command in both systems – the prize to be sought by *Altkämpfer* and police newcomer alike. The position had from its inception within the Reich in 1938–39 been tied to the notion of emergency conditions; and its evolution outside the Reich, where normal standards of government, security and individual rights were in abeyance, was both rapid and fruitful.

If the Superior SS and Police Leaders in the newly annexed Polish territories had more powers than their brethren in the old Reich, the position of the Superior SS and Police Leader in the Protectorate of Bohemia-Moravia and in the General Government was vastly more influential still. It was enhanced in the latter case by the creation in 1940 of SS- *und Polizeiführer* out of the police commanders at the *Distrikt* level, for which there was no comparable, fully integrated position in the Reich. But it was to be in the occupied countries, especially Russia, that the system could flourish with the least competition from Reich officialdom and in closest co-ordination with the defensive and settlement functions of the SS as envisaged by Himmler and Darré in 1932. It was in Russia that some of the oldest SS officers became SS and Police Generals responsible for: the military defence of their regions, against not only partisans but even incursions of the Soviet armed forces; resettlement and expulsions from their regions to create settlement areas for Germandom; the setting up of SS organisation and recruiting; and last but not least the order and productivity of the occupied territory and the subject populace. Truly satraps out of ancient times combined with the notion of political soldierdom from the Nazi struggle for power, this segment of the higher SS officers' corps most fully represents the ideal toward which Himmler and his closest advisors had been striving. More rounded and actively engaged than the SS bureau-generals or the pure soldiers of the *Waffen*-SS, they bear the largest burden of guilt for the total implementation of Nazi purposes in wartime Europe.

It is scarcely an accident that the fullest development of the mature SS officers' corps occurred in the imperialist venture of 1941–42 in the east, parallel with the military phase and with the extermination of the Jews, resting upon but essentially different from both. SS political soldiering in Russia in that period really entailed a fundamental land seizure, in the language of Carl Schmitt, followed by a pacification of the *imperium* and a reconstruction in the spirit of the conquerors. Furthermore, the higher SS officers' corps assigned to Russia did not come there as the agents of the German government merely as hangmen and policemen for other decision-making agencies. They themselves were supposed to be the bearers of the forming culture, the rivals and opponents of erroneous conceptions of administration and colonisation. The story of the German occupation of Russia is thus entwined not only with SS brutality and atrocities, but also with the running battle fought from top to bottom of the SS and Police hierarchy with Rosenberg's Ministry of the East and with other Reich agencies. It was of utmost importance that the SS was responsible for the policing of occupied territories, yet a 'mere' police agency within the German government could not have succeeded in acting so independently in so many areas. Far better co-ordinated than its rivals, the system was nonetheless too new, too ambitious, too steeped in illusions to succeed in building half so well as it destroyed. However, as a system for exploiting the land and labour resources of conquered areas, while seizing those resources for itself and its collaborators, the SS and police of 1941–42 had advanced far beyond the SA amateurs of 1933–34. Perhaps it had advanced not quite far enough, for the aberrations of hubris and furore so characteristic of the SA pursued some of the most prominent of the *Altkämpfer* SS generals.

The SS and Police had been kept in its place, in the background, among the occupation policies of Germany in Norway, Denmark, Holland, Belgium and France. The evil reputation that followed the Death's Head Reinforcements and the Sipo-SD-*Einsatzkommandos* from the east made army, foreign office and party officials chary of granting Himmler a free hand in 1940. Moreover, while Hitler reiterated his own stand against SS military proliferation, emphasising precisely the future police role of the post-war SS, Himmler had begun to implement his old dream of a Germanic aristocracy of blood and soil drawn from soldier volunteers of northern Europe. Consequently, Himmler himself did not wish to unloose the Death's Head units on Norway, Denmark and Holland. Temporarily stationed there, a few battalions were readied for regular combat duty and kept off the backs of the populace. Sipo-SD-*Einsatzkommandos* made a brief appearance in Norway and then disappeared. Denmark and Holland went over immediately to regular police administration, while Belgium and northern France under military government virtually excluded the

Sipo-SD system at least for a time. Although Superior SS and Police Leaders were indeed appointed for Norway and Holland, their hands were tied by powerful party-oriented *Reichskommissars* and Hitler's policy of courtship of the Nordic countries with which Himmler could hardly disagree. Separate treatment for Alsace and Lorraine also dictated that Superior SS and Police Leaders in Strasbourg and Metz (also responsible for the Saar) made their appearance, but both were overshadowed by the Old Reich *Gauleiter* who were given authority over the French provinces in addition to their former *Gaue*.

Himmler was all the more resolved, with Hitler's full approval, to apply the most ruthless repressive measures in the initial stages of occupation of the Soviet territories. In *Mein Kampf* Hitler had sketched just the combination of depopulation and resettlement for Russia which Himmler contemplated. In March 1941 Himmler could gather at a meeting a preselected group of SS colonels and generals at Wewelsburg – the 'SS castle' at Paderborn in Westphalia used as a council hall for the future knights of blood and soil – and initiate them to their future duties as Superior SS and Police Leaders or those of their subordinate SS and Police Leaders (on the model of the General Government). One of their number, Bach-Zelewski, has testified that Himmler spoke of eliminating millions of Slavs and Jews to make room for Germanic settlements. In April 1941 Hitler appointed all Superior SS and Police Leaders within the Reich and outside as generals of the SS and also as generals of police, with police epaulettes and field-grey uniforms.

Thus, a powerful institution had come of age, and the way was prepared to co-ordinate and protect the most daring and reprehensible actions in the east from intervention and sabotage by other parts of the German state and society. Through their hands were to run all the threads, of both information and control, of Himmler's web dealing with the most delicate and political matters, including relations with the party – especially the *Gauleiter* – the army, the state bureaucracy and leading figures of Germany's business and professional world. Through their position as Main Sector Commander of the General SS, which retained its character and significance as an SS community both within the Nazi Party community and well beyond it in the general civilian sector until 1943 or 1944, they had access to channels of influence and information of strategic importance to the SS. Through their control of countless auxiliary forces – such as *Technische Nothilfe* and the air-raid wardens, beside all armed SS units not transferred to OKW authority (replacement and training battalions) – they had emergency strength independent of party controls. Moreover, their virtual command over all police forces via the Sipo and Orpo inspectors (Sipo and Orpo commanders outside the Reich) gave them a reasonable chance even against *Wehrmacht* power in a political showdown.

Within the Reich their importance lay chiefly in supplying alternative power centres and channels of command for Hitler beside the *Gauleiter* and corps area military commanders. In a sense, they even became intendants of the state system, superimposed upon the rest of the old bureaucracy and the new party men. They were gradually to bypass much of the state bureaucracy, while their relations with the party group depended heavily upon the personality of the *Gauleiter* and on their own natures. Quite a few quickly became embedded in the party fabric of mutual favours and antipathies and were removed by Himmler. Unlike the *Gauleiter*, whom Hitler could remove but not move about, the Superior SS and Police Leaders – like the army corps commanders after which they were copied – were at least ideally and theoretically available for many different kinds of assignments. Only rarely did their power and influence rest on local ties, and when it did Himmler usually saw to it that they were weaned away from their home grounds, even if new assignments were thoroughly uncongenial.

Nomination by Himmler to one of the higher SS and police posts outside the Reich represents an accolade for dynamism and ruthlessness. Only six or seven *Altkämpfer* of the original Reich Superior SS and Police Leaders remained at their posts throughout the war, the rest being 'promoted' to imperial proconsulates in Russia, the Balkans, or the west. Those who remained behind (one was killed in an air raid) were either too dynamic and restless to get along with the *Wehrmacht* or a bit stodgy and unimaginative. Another nine or ten assigned to inner-Reich higher SS and Police commands were of the younger generation of pre-1933 SS officers, largely on the way up after more or less distinguished apprenticeships; a few were 'put on ice' after some fiasco. Three police generals figured in the wartime ranks of the home front Superior SS and Police Leaders, one-sixth of the total.

A great deal of the power on the home front, however, rested with the professional policemen, for the ranks of the inspectors of Security Police and Order Police were also raided of their SS-*Altkämpfer* for assignments abroad and replaced by a new generation of jurists (*Kriminalräte*) and police bureaucrats with nominal SS rank, rising through Gestapo and SD regional commands. The latter positions too, filled during the war with men of assimilated SS ranks from captain to lieutenant-colonel, became more and more the key positions in a unified SS and Police administrative hierarchy calling less for aggressiveness and ruthlessness than for systematic hard work and sensitivity. Although these men, in their thirties and forties, had not fought in the brawls of the *Kampfzeit* or attended the endless roll-calls of the General SS after the Seizure of Power, the SS was still their ticket to success because its expansion during the war called their superiors to the far-flung battlefronts and offered them a dream of power as well. Many did indeed go off before 1945 to occupation assignments, and more fell in battle as *Waffen*-SS officers. Repression, torture, all the evils of the police-state were in their power; taught by their *Altkämpfer* superiors to regard themselves as soldiers in a permanent civil war with an implacable enemy, they found justification in the real battles in Russia and their own likely commitment. They lacked the self-justification in their own past, however, which played such a large role in the men of Himmler's generation. What they shared with their mentors were large ambitions and a willingness to satisfy these upon the bodies of the weak and defenceless. Partly because the war ended before many of them reached high positions, and partly because they were indeed not Nazis by conviction, this generation had no progeny. The younger survivors of the *Waffen*-SS, while perhaps also reviled and shunned in post-war Germany, are nevertheless able to identify with the SS traditions in a way that the police segment never could. Yet political soldierdom was far more fully embodied in the SS and Police officer than in the 'pure soldier' of the later *Waffen*-SS.

Himmler and Heydrich had to fight their way into Russia as much against other Nazis as against the Russians, but this time the *Wehrmacht* was on their side and for much the same reasons that it had conspired with them in 1934 – the soldiers did not want to be soiled with the blood of civilians. The *Wehrmacht* had enough to do just in conquering the Soviets; there would be no troops left over for the tasks of repression. SS fighting units were even welcomed; the spurned and hated police units from Poland and Bohemia were good enough to hold a rebellious Russian countryside in check. It still took hard negotiations by Himmler to keep the murder commandos in the forefront of the battle area in order to catch the commissars and Jews before they vanished, but ulti-mately *Wehrmacht* commanders realised they thus spared men for battle and stayed out of a messy business. The Russians could then reserve their hatred for the SS. Rosenberg, and behind him Bormann, Göring and Goebbels – and sometimes even Hitler – were to be the real obstacles to absolute SS power in the east.

Nowhere is Hitler's policy of 'divide and conquer' within his own ranks more apparent as a force for evil for all concerned than in Russia. While it is too much to say that Hitler defeated himself in Russia, since Stalin, the Red Army and the Russian people surely made a big difference, neverthe-less Hitler's determination not to let any one part of his power system have its way greatly weakened the German conquest of the east. Freedom to kill Russians the SS won easily; but even if the SS had had the skill and organisation to control and exploit the vast reservoir of manpower and resources of occupied Russia, it would have had to devote half its skill and energy fighting other Germans for its share. As it was, the SS proved far from ready for the scope of the operation, so that skilled personnel had to be stretched very thin – until the old Reich was drained of its SS and Police cadres even before the climax of the military phase in 1943–45 when so much of the SS went into army and *Waffen*-SS uniform.

In the short run, however, especially in 1942–43, the SS was able to take advantage of Hitler's predilection for disorganisation. Already in occupied Yugoslavia and Greece in 1941, it seized additional police powers because authority there was so widely diffused by excessive partition, military and civilian rivalries, and above all a general lack of fixed ideas about such new and distant lands starting with Hitler and including many Nazis. Although Hitler and Rosenberg certainly had fixed ideas about Russia, Hitler's scheme of assigning wide authority to Rosenberg's nominal subordinates – the *Reichskommissars* – and the army's insistence on controlling the forward areas for logistical reasons meant that the conspiratorial schemers in the SS from Himmler down past Heydrich to the Chief of Administraton (Pohl) and head of the SS Main Office (Berger) found ample opportunities to worm their way into very strategic offices. This occurred despite chiefs of those offices actually opposing SS expansion and its ruthless philosophy of a sub-human east. Boring from within, SS policy makers broke down the opposition to wanton acts of Superior SS and Police Leaders in the pursuit of an SS empire. Almost every year there was an additional breakthrough. In 1941, after months of

careful effort to limit Himmler's power in Russia to the level he had elsewhere, Hitler cut the Gordian knot on 16 July by giving the SS authority
to act 'on its own responsibility' for the maintenance of order there. In
August 1942 Hitler authorised the SS to conduct military operations in
the rear areas, especially against partisans. By the summer of 1943, Gottlob
Berger, the agile head of the SS Main Office, had persuaded Rosenberg to
place him in charge of political operations in the Eastern Ministry, where
he could sabotage any remaining resistance to SS exploitation of the
countryside and its human burden. In September 1944, after the 20 July
coup and in the expectation of reconquest, Himmler sponsored Vlassow's
Russian Liberation Army and a whole series of puppet exile-governments
for a *cordon sanitaire* from Estonia to the Ukraine. The SS was making
foreign policy right and left, but of course it was too late.

Russia was the grave of between 2 million and 3 million SS officers
and men. Most of these died, weapon in hand, as soldiers of the *Waffen*-
SS or the army. A much smaller group of SS officers and men constituted
the repressive forces who did so much to make the Germans hated in the
hamlets and cities of the Soviet Union. A figure of 10,000, even including
the *Einsatzgruppen*, is ample to include the anti-partisan SS units; the
concentration camp administrations at Riga, Kaunas and Minsk; the
network of Order Police and Sipo-SD officials; the SS administrators of
farms, mines and factories; and the staffs of the Superior SS and Police
Leaders and their regional subordinates. Fewer than 2,000 SS officers
were involved, even if we include those commanding non-SS units of
police, both German and foreign – and a great many of these officers
would have to be termed 'nominal SS' members. Truly, a few hundred
officers at the rank of major and above were the deadly means by which
so much havoc was wrought. From the grisly mass murders of 1941 to
the routine execution of hostages and prisoners of war, from the liquidation of all living inhabitants of 'partisan' villages to kidnapping hundreds
of thousands of slave labourers, from the systematic looting of Soviet art
treasures and museums to the brutal destruction of every productive
facility and living thing before it cleared out – the gestating SS officers'
corps let itself be represented by a fraction of its membership. But that
fraction was damned by its training, its selection and the condition of
unrelenting warfare to be devils incarnate.

Initially an elaborate differentiation marked the SS occupation policies. Heydrich himself sought to steer a different course *vis-à-vis* the

Czechs from that toward the Poles. The Serbs were repressed without mercy while the Ukrainians of Galicia were 'liberated' by the SS administrators at Lemberg (Lvov). Beside the underlying distinction between western and eastern peoples, which gave even Frenchmen rights before SS and police authorities, the Nordic lands like Holland, Denmark and Norway were especially to be favoured. There was of course also the distinction between allied peoples like the Slovaks, Magyars, Croats, Finns, Italians, Romanians and Bulgarians, and conquered groups like the Greeks, Albanians, Estonians, Latvians, Lithuanians and Turkic peoples from inner Russia. Racial theories and evolving recruiting practices for the *Waffen*-SS conflicted; the consequence was a familiar one with the Nazis: without modifying the theories but simply by ignoring them, the regulations were stretched to make room for more foreign recruits, and with them came relaxation in the negative differentiation for their relatives and even their home communities. At the same time, however, spasmodic exhibitions of resistance multiplied in favoured western areas. The *Nacht und Nebel* (Night and Fog) decree with its ultra-punitive response to any attacks on Germans in occupied areas helped to reduce the level of the treatment of western and northern Europeans by SS and Police officials to a common denominator with eastern peoples.

Naturally, a vicious circle of retaliation by resistance groups set in, so that by late 1942 the number of Superior SS and Police Leaders equipped with tyrannical powers was on the increase, not only in the west but in the Balkans. Himmler had also increased the number in the former Austrian areas, to which former Yugoslav (Slovene) territories had been joined. A cautious system of partial concealment in nominally independent areas led to the withholding of the actual HSSPF title in Albania, Greece, Slovakia, Croatia, Hungary and Belgium until as late as 1944. Although designated as plenipotentiaries of the *Reichsführer* SS and Chief of the German Police, leading SS and Police Generals were very obviously powerful channels of German influence. They facilitated the implementation of the Final Solution of Eichmann in these areas. There were two examples of an even higher SS and Police rank created in 1944: *Höchste* (Supreme) SS and Police leader. In the first case, the position was assigned to Hans Prützmann, one of the oldest and most deadly serious of the younger *Altkämpfer*, who was placed in charge of all South Russia during the scorched earth phase of the evacuations there. The second time the title was used was in Italy, during the successful resistance to allied invaders and the formation of the Republic of Saló. The post went to Himmler's own personal staff commander, Karl Wolff, an indication that it was a political rather than a military appointment.

The subordinate position of SS and Police Leaders was introduced into France and Norway in 1944, showing that Himmler had finally determined to consolidate the two arms even at the risk of disturbing relations further with the *Wehrmacht* and the subject populace. These posts went largely to products of the police career; the era when deserving SS-*Altkämpfer* could be 'rewarded' with important police posts was long past. Indeed, as the war years passed, the sequence of crises had offered so many challenges and screenings of SS and Police personnel that even the selection process of the growth years after 1934 had become irrelevant. The *Altkämpfer* who had risen through the 1930s to police ranks of prominence were few by 1939; they were certainly reinforced by the addition of a sizeable number from the General SS in the course of the war, selected for abilities demonstrated during the 1930s.

But the preponderance of the officialdom responsible for the police activities of the SS during the war, and especially the rising generation of new talent aged under forty, were not the products of the General SS and its vicissitudes. Numbers, of course, do not tell the whole story. The leavening of General SS veterans, and especially of a few thousand fanatical and competent pre-1933 fighters and killers, was indeed decisive in warping and constraining hundreds of thousands more who passed through the police system. The influence of formal indoctrination in the form of training programmes and published materials like '*Der Untermensch*' ('The Sub-Human') surely must take second place to the power of a totalitarian system to create a milieu of terror and disregard for human life in which even the moderately healthy adjust themselves to injustice as a matter of course, and the neurotic and asocial are in their element.

The RKFDV System

A particularly telling example of adjustment and rationalisation occurred in the case of the several thousand SS officers and NCOs who constituted the staff of the government agencies known collectively as the 'Reich Commissar for the Strengthening of Germandom' (RKFDV). Himmler had invented for himself the grandiose title of Reich Commissar for the

Strengthening of Germandom in October 1939, when he won from Hitler the authority to supervise and implement resettlement of ethnic Germans 'rescued from Bolshevism' in the Baltic states and eastern Poland. Himmler liked to say that he had his good side and his bad side, and that if the police duties were his bad side, then the creation of new German *Lebensraum* in the east was his good side. Thus, Himmler himself created for those SS officers and men whom he employed for this purpose a very special alibi – a defensive interpretation of their activities, essentially police in nature, which extended even to the removal of less fortunate peoples from their homes and farms, the rejection of 'racially inferior' stocks for the future settlement areas, and the kidnapping of 'racially superior' children from their parents.

Hitler had begun by giving the resettlement task to the Party-Foreign Office bastard agency, the VoMi, the Liaison Office for Ethnic Germans; but Himmler rather easily seized the reins from Werner Lorenz, the SS colonel-in-charge, the more readily because of the penetration into VoMi of Heydrich's SD agents. Himmler's ploy with Hitler was precisely the need for police supervision, and he inserted Heydrich decisively into the operations in the newly occupied Polish territories to make way for the new settlers. VoMi retained the subordinate organising responsibilities for 'bringing them back alive' and for their care and feeding in camps while awaiting settlement. Before 1939 the Liaison Office's network of officials and employees abroad wherever ethnic Germans were to be found was only lightly sprinkled with SS, usually doing double duty as SD agents. However, already in the case of the Sudeten crisis, the value of more extensive SS contacts to start the fledgling SS in motion in the new area was made apparent. VoMi therefore developed an SS and a non-SS wing in 1939, but more and more of the employees and officials joined the SS.

The arrival into the *Altreich* (Reich proper) of many ethnic German refugees from Poland, even before the outbreak of the war, gave rise to the organisational innovation of Liaison Office branches in each party *Gau* responsible for the necessary camps. Naturally, the closest co-operation with regional Sipo-SD headquarters became de rigeur, so that the *Gau* VoMi offices needed SS officers to handle their business more expeditiously, and preferably SD officers. The VoMi developed teams to go into newly conquered areas (Yugoslavia, Russia) to evaluate and earmark ethnic Germans and Nordic types, including children of partisans, for resettlement. Naturally, they needed or at least wanted field-grey uniforms, of either the police or the *Waffen*-SS. Consequently, VoMi came to form a constituent of the RKFDV system after mid-1941, and the SS part of VoMi was organised as an SS Main Office (*Hauptamt* VoMi). The SD component gradually became less important as better intelligence channels opened up for SD-*Ausland* (RSHA *Amt* VI), although VoMi remained an important pipeline for Himmler and later Kaltenbrunner, Heydrich's successor, to and from party and Foreign Office branches. Rightly or wrongly, VoMi personnel were regarded as 'the SS' and as tale-bearing fanatics.

In the reorganisation of the *Sicherheitsdienst* accompanying the formation of the RSHA, a Main Section III-ES (Germanisation settlement) was formed in *Amt* III (SD-*Inland*), headed by Hans Ehlich, an SS colonel who specialised in nationality problems. His office thereupon received the assignment from Heydrich to supervise the processing of the potential settlers in elaborate 'immigration centres' (*Einwanderungs-Zentralstellen*, EWZ). The first of these was located at Gdynia (or Gotenhafen), moving to Poznań (Posen) in November 1939; yet the most active was situated at Łodż (or Litzmannstadt) with branches at Berlin, Stettin, Cracow and later also at Paris. The staff of the centres were chiefly non-SS and largely not even police but instead governmental clerks and bureaucrats representing relevant ministries such as Interior, Transport, Food and Agriculture, Labour, Finance, Economics and Health. They were, however, all under the RSHA in their immediate duties along with a registration bureau of the Order Police, a Race and Settlement Main Office team charged with racial examinations of the settler families, General SS (later *Waffen*-SS) physicians, and *Waffen*-SS recruiters. The managers of the centres were officers of the Sipo-SD system whose job was to keep smooth the flow of resettlers; inevitably a degree of intervention in the decision-making process resulted from their powerful connections *vis-à-vis* the non-SS personnel and even RuSHa examiners.

An even more direct integration of RKFDV activities into the Sipo-SD system occurred in the Resettlement Centres (UWZ) set up in the spring of 1940 expressly for the processing of evicted Polish families. Although here too there were problems of sorting out persons for 'Germanisation' and ultimate Reich citizenship by the use of racial examinations and other checks, the operation was conducted almost entirely by Security and Order Police, with RuSHa teams called in rather than being assigned. All involvement of non-SS agencies was avoided until the few 'Re-Germanisables' arrived back in the Reich, where the Security Police still was responsible for pushing their cases through the relevant agencies, including VoMi and RKFDV representatives. The heads of the UWZ were, of course, Sipo-SD officers, reporting directly to the inspectors of their regions but in closest liaison with VoMi camp administrators and RKFDV representatives in their *Gaue*. As the war reduced the number of RuSHa officers and men available for racial selection, the UWZ even carried out the crude separation of expellees for eventual re-Germanisation, slave-labour in Germany, or shipment to the General Government. In other words, the very same type of procedures used in Eichmann's operations crept into the handling of Slavs, and in fact the EWZ and UWZ administrators landed quite regularly in the *Einsatzgruppen* and in Eichmann's *Sonderkommandos*. The RKFDV operations were no more hermetically sealed off as Himmler's 'good side' than was the *Waffen*-SS from Himmler's genocidal activities.

On the other hand, it was possible for RuSHa personnel to blame Heydrich and later Kaltenbrunner for the executions and other suffering resulting from their negative verdicts on people, since the former were merely making a 'scientific' evaluation of some Pole accused of sexual intercourse with a German woman, or of some Jew who had smuggled himself along with a transport of Ukrainian metal workers to the Reich. While they used and were aware of the true meaning of the term *Sonderbehandlung* (special treatment: death) in certain cases of 'racial inferiority', RuSHa examiners were largely spared the grisly context of their activities. Indeed, wartime RuSHa devoted only a small part of its time to such work, though of course the absolute amount increased considerably. The absolute growth of RuSHa officers did not keep pace with the enormous increase in the SS due to the expansion of military and police branches, all of which required racial examinations for admission to the SS. Hundreds of General SS officers and NCOs had to be recruited for RuSHa posts in 1940–41 and given rather short, inadequate 'anthropological' training. Crass ideology, simplified biology and pseudo-genetics were crammed into six weeks' basic training – with the result hat later positive and negative verdicts were likely to be reached under the impulse of some extraneous factor, like the need for more *Waffen*-SS recruits or the desire of the Security Police to be rid of a case. Most of the examiners were men of relatively low rank compared to *Waffen*-SS and Sipo-SD officers in whose bailiwicks racial examinations were merely an added complication.

Many high-ranking, older RuSHa officers had little to do with this routine matter, whether 'bad' (condemnation to death as sub-human) or 'good' (admission to the *Waffen*-SS – for many also a condemnation to death). The task of the RuSHa colonels, and of many clever younger officers also, was to devise schemes for a RuSHa comeback to prominence as a settlement agency in Russia after a period of eclipse owing to Himmler's quarrel with Darré – caused in part because Himmler thought RuSHa's ideological training for the SS was too 'intellectual and impractical'. Thus, RuSHa was instrumental in the development of settlement plans for Russia, entailing the acquisition of large collective farms to be established as training farms for wounded *Waffen*-SS veterans with farming backgrounds. RuSHa also won for itself the right to select and supervise the assignment of all SS men to agricultural management positions under the WVHA-economic managers, even when they remained in the *Waffen*-SS and were also subordinate to Pohl, the jealous Chief of Administration. Ultimately in the winter of 1942–43, a complete breakdown in the rate of racial examinations resulted from overtaxing an already thinned-out system. New recruits and thousands of settlers could not be processed while RuSHa bigwigs and junior officers drove around Russia inspecting settlement sites. Himmler lost his temper and fired the acting head of the Race and Settlement Main Office, Hofmann – the third man to fill the post since 1938. Richard Hildebrandt, one of his most trusted and ruthless Superior SS and Police Leaders, was given the post with a top Sipo-SD officer as his deputy. They were to reduce red tape, stop the empire-building and hold the line till the war ended.

A new large task gradually devolved on RuSHa, or rather on the Main Sector RuS-officers: caring for the families of the *Waffen*-SS casualties. There were a number of reasons why Himmler picked RuSHa for this duty. RuSHa had traditionally a responsibility toward the SS *Sippen* (clans) reflected in the *Sippenamt*. While there was a separate SS Maintenance and Welfare Office and, of course, *Lebensborn*, both soon became technical bureaucracies that needed a regional channel to the SS home front via the still existing, skeletonised General SS-*Standarten*. For this purpose the SS *Pflegestellen* (care centres) were set up at each General SS headquarters under a wounded *Waffen*-SS man responsible to the Main Sector RuS-officer. Through these miniature welfare bureaus passed the major and minor tragedies of SS widows and orphans, wounded SS men seeking a pension and farm in the east, a mother whose fourth son had been called up, and unmarried girls with babies due.

Procedural directives from *Lebensborn*, the Maintenance and Welfare Office, and other SS Main Offices were channelled through RuSHa to the care centres along with the regulations of Reich ministries, and the implementation was left to the young *Waffen*-SS junior officer-in-charge, with perhaps assistance from some overage General SS personnel and, in delicate cases, the regimental commander. Himmler was forced to insist a number of times that the latter must personally notify parents and wives of sons' and husbands' deaths. Inevitably the tragedies and incongruities of war led to mistaken and unsuitable treatment by the inexperienced and untrained 'welfare' personnel, but mingled with complaining recriminations the correspondence of these offices contained many letters of heartfelt gratitude and simple faith. At a time when some SS men were killing the innocent, others were succouring and giving solace. Certainly these home front positions were not matters of personal choice, although an element of preference seems to be associated with the type of man who insisted on returning to his comrades on the front. With the increase in allied bombing of German cities in 1942 and 1943, there was not much hope of safety and a great deal more horror at home. On the other hand, the close collaboration of RuSHa and the care centres with the SD, and probably also the Gestapo, sheds an eerie light even on this 'decent' SS role. SD procedures were primarily informational in character, but the Gestapo 'warning' was a regular method of pressure during the later war years if widows and parents complained too loudly of mistreatment. The concentration camps were never very far away from any SS bureau.

Threats of punishment for rumour-mongering had to be increasingly backed up as the war progressed, among them the persistent story of the SS 'breeding homes' associated with half-knowledge about *Lebensborn*. A girl who wrote to Himmler to learn about them in 1944 was ordered committed to a concentration camp, yet there is not a shred of evidence that there ever were such places. We have seen that *Lebensborn* expanded its system of lying-in homes greatly after 1937, and Gestapo seizures of Jewish properties in Austria were the basis of *Lebensborn* expansion there. Similarly, *Lebensborn* entered Poland with the *Einsatzkommandos* to help the ethnic Germans and incidentally to seize whole warehouses of supplies. The multiplication of such homes in far-flung places like Norway and Holland, the General Government (of Poland) and Russia may have been an indirect encouragement to SS men to sexual indulgence with the local population, but the homes were strictly for pregnant women. Admission to them involved an elaborate health and police check, with racial evaluation formally included if not always done by an 'expert', so that the SS did not sponsor just any liaison. The staffs in the homes outside the Reich were not all officially part of *Lebensborn*, and the Munich headquarters of that organisation was not really capable of keeping a check on every place that bore its name. These homes too, being run by the Nazi Party, may have winked at illegitimate pregnancies in cases where the SS might have frowned – but they were not brothels.

Aside from the operation of a dozen or more official lying-in homes, *Lebensborn* grew into a large-scale adoption agency. Starting with the placement of illegitimate children born to German girls and women, largely in SS officers' families, *Lebensborn* soon branched out to combing orphanages in occupied Poland and other lands for 'Germanic' children under seven. Secrecy used to protect the unmarried mothers was readily adapted through SS ties with the police authorities to name-changing and record alteration which concealed the whereabouts of these children from relatives. The children were well treated even though many of them had to be taught German. In 1943 legal changes were brought about to equip the SS, acting through *Lebensborn*, to act as guardian for the children during a period of adaptation until final adoption; and authority was vested in the SS care centres to function as *Jugendämter* (Youth Protection Offices) instead of the regular state offices. Thus, the SS could exclude the state from all inquiries into dubious cases at all stages of the proceedings. The *Lebensborn* headquarters was even given a kind of fictitious status as a branch of the Ministry of the Interior (*Amt* L), so that the identities of the children could be legally falsified without interference.

Lebensborn became a huge financial operation as well, taxing all full-time SS officers inversely in proportion to their progeny and conducting its own health and death benefit insurance for its charges. When Himmler extended *Lebensborn* responsibilities to the care of selected children of partisans, even those who had been shot or committed to concentration camps, he burdened its personnel with tasks too far removed from their original assignment to succeed. The children from Slovenia, the Ukraine and Bohemia (e.g. Lidice) were often much older than seven; they were aware of what had happened and miserable. SS families did not want them. In this way an added *Lebensborn* responsibility evolved: supervision and even operation of children's homes or boarding schools into which unwanted and unplaced 'valuable' children were placed. Here, as in so much of *Lebensborn* activity, the major roles were women's, although SS officers held formal responsibility. The functions of *Lebensborn* were certainly caritative from beginning to end, although its chief personnel were quite clear that they were co-operating with other SS personnel who had in fact kidnapped many of the children and even killed their parents. *Lebensborn* officers sought to increase their 'empire' and fought the splintering of the original procedures into non-SS hands, so their plea of utter innocence and disgust with the taking of older 'non-German' children 'by mistake' and through 'excessive administrative zeal' rings hollow. Since they were business managers and lawyers rather than social workers, the children were probably incidental.

Strictly speaking, none of the foregoing groups of SS and police personnel had duties limited to the RKFDV. At the core of the imperialist project but by no means always 'in' on the whole scheme as Himmler evolved it was the staff of the office (*Dienststelle*) on the Kurfürstendamm set up by Ulrich Greifelt, an SS colonel whom Himmler had used as a liaison man with Göring's Four Year Plan Office. This headquarters, known from June 1941 as the Staff Main Office to give it equality with other SS Main Offices, was a Supreme Reich Authority as well as an SS Main Office. Its personnel were a judicious blend of professional SS officers (though by no means *Altkämpfer*) experienced in SS administration since 1933, including lawyers and economists lacking previous SS ties. The latter were soon 'assimilated' to SS rank without significant duties beyond RKFDV, while the former soon acquired high police ranks. Beginning rather weak *vis-à-vis* the Superior SS and Police Leaders and the Police Main Offices, the RKFDV Office rose to prominence in the heyday of settlement fervour and enthusiasm in 1942, thrusting aside such ancient SS citadels as RuSHa and challenging Sipo-SD planners for hegemony. Its strength rested on the control over landed property in the east, in collaboration with Göring's installations, and on a network of executive personnel in the settlement areas who were assigned by Berlin and able to offer Superior SS and Police Leaders additional power over their rural areas in exchange for police support at the evacuations and settlement stage. Most fully developed in the 'settlement *gaue*' of Danzig-West Prussia, Wartheland, East Prussia and

Upper Silesia, they penetrated successfully into the Slovene borderlands but were ineffective in the General Government, the Baltic states, the Ukraine and Alsace-Lorraine – where powerful Superior SS and Police Leaders and *Gauleiter* acted without consulting the 'planners'. Neither Himmler nor even Heydrich was ever capable of drawing up a blueprint or master plan of imperialist settlements or of vesting central authority in one SS Main Office, least of all in this *ad hoc* creation of 1939.

Improvisation was often the chief strength of the middle-level SS officer-bureaucrat, and the RKFDV officers had to be good improvisers. Ideological trimmings of 'blood and soil' were less important than simple faith in ethnic German abilities, in Germany's winning the war, in Hitler, and in the SS as a team. After that technical know-how, imagination and energy made RKFDV junior officers in the field a kind of Nazi Peace Corps. Naive concentration on helping new settlers establish homes and put down roots could obscure for many the intimate tie with the genocidal expulsion of Jews and Poles. The men in the field had to see the connections more vividly, but they also had the compensation of direct knowledge of their own 'good' efforts. The higher-ups in the desk jobs could be blissfully unseeing when it came to the disposal of the wastage of human lives, even ethnic German lives, caught up as those officials were in working out a big picture of a Greater Germanic Reich of the German Nation.

The Waffen-SS

One of the most vigorous planning agencies of the SS in this last regard was not part of the RKFDV at all: the *Germanische Leitstelle* (Germanic Guidance Office) founded in March 1941 by the former chief recruiting officer for the *Waffen*-SS and wartime chief of the SS Main Office, Gottlob Berger. It was not merely his energy, which was bottomless, that gave the Germanic Guidance Office its importance and prestige. This forty-man organisation, nominally within the SS Main Office, became the apple of Himmler's eye because it combined his Nordic preoccupations with a primary purpose of finding new recruits for the *Waffen*-SS. Far from having things his own way, Himmler had a long struggle with the *Wehrmacht* to get sufficient recruits for more than one SS combat division in wartime. The person who achieved a final breakthrough in the winter and spring of 1941–42 was Berger, the new chief of the SS Main Office since August 1940. The former SS Main Office chief, August Heissmeier – after an unimpressive year in charge of the Death's Head Reinforcements over which he had little real control and interest – was made Superior SS and Police Leader of the Berlin area, and the 'new broom' of the vigorous SS chief recruiter soon swept out many of the place-holders of the 1930s from the SS Main Office. His bombast and fits of temperament turned the SS Main Office's quiet bureaucracy inside out. Ineffective negotiations that had rumbled on for months or even years with *Wehrmacht* offices were stepped up, and amid a great deal of noise and smoke, the *Waffen*-SS got more recruits as Operation Barbarossa took shape in the autumn of 1940.

Initially weakened by the loss to combat command of their chief, Paul Hausser, the old Inspectorate of the Special Duty Troops at Oranienburg gravitated back to the SS Main Office at Berlin, as the *Kommando* (*Kommando-Amt*) *der Waffen*-SS. But the skills and specialities of the staff officers of the former inspectorate threatened to be dissipated under the crude and reckless hand of Berger at the Recruitment Office, so Himmler – never one to allow one SS office to become too strong – raised up Hans Jüttner, the chief of the *Kommando-Amt*, to be head of the independent Leadership Main Office in August 1940, practically an SS general staff for military training and operations. Thus, by 1941 the revitalised SS Main Office was freed, much against the will of its ambitious new chief, of the all-consuming responsibilities of immediate military policy making and the training of replacements. Instead, the Main Office could turn to making the SS a truly Germanic and European order by finding the replacements – first among the youthful age group of rural Germany; secondly among the ethnic Germans 'returning' from areas ceded by Hitler to the Communists and from other German folk groups in the Balkans and eastern Europe; and lastly, though equally vital, among the Dutch, Belgians, Norwegians, Danes and Finns.

We have seen that even before the outbreak of the war, Himmler tied up recruitment procedures for the *Waffen*-SS with penetration into the ethnic German groups. By 1939 the future Main Office chief was pulling in ethnic Germans from Estonia, North Schleswig, Rumania and Slovakia. His daughter's marriage to Andreas Schmidt, a Nazi Party chieftain in Rumania, made easier a haul of more than 1,000 ethnic German volunteers from Transylvania in February 1940. After the outbreak of the war, his network of ethnic German Self-Defence units located able young volunteers for formal military training in the Reich as soon as local situations stabilised. A main disadvantage, however, was the lack of regular recruiting organs and special replacement training units for personnel with specific linguistic and other cultural differences from Reich Germans. The new Main Office chief had to battle not only the foreign governments loath to part with cannon fodder and jealous party and even VoMi officials who did not like to see their best young men spirited off, but even *Waffen*-SS training officers and the new Leadership Main Office general staff, who disliked making special arrangements for ethnic German recruits. Since the *Wehrmacht* dragged its feet in co-operating with Himmler to get Reich Germans, the SS would have to get along with ethnic Germans as manpower. The conquest of the Low Countries, Denmark and Norway was what really opened up the possibility of a Germanic-European *Kampfgemeinschaft* (combat community) which would justify special organisations and special training for the non-Germans. Even so, it was not until Barbarossa loomed up large before the top military planners both inside and outside the SS that the Germanic Guidance Office was authorised.

While Himmler had talked proudly of twenty Germanic volunteers in the *Verfügungstruppe* at an SS Generals' Conference on 8 November 1938, and the figure had reached 100 before the 1940 campaign in the west, this trickle of enthusiasts was unimportant compared with the larger recruitment problem of the *Waffen*-SS. Since the summer of 1938, Himmler had been determined to break through the one-division limit on his forces, if only to be prepared for the double duty of policing the home front and handling occupation responsibilities as foreseen in the Hitler directive of 17 August 1938. His tactics and those of his chief recruiter had been ones of conspirators. By creating as many different kinds of unit as possible, they could tap different sources of personnel and also conceal the growth ratio of the whole force. Thus, the SS retained the distinction between the motorised *Leibstandarte* Adolf Hitler (LSAH) and the *Verfügungstruppe* after the latter too became motorised in 1939; the former kept its special height requirements and its right to be committed integrally when the *Verfügungstruppe* was made into a division in the winter of 1939–40. The LSAH could be committed in the west as a reinforced regiment, while the *Verfügungsdivision* would be cannibalised to form another SS division, the 'Fifth' or *'Wiking'* division.

Himmler converted the original three Death's Head regiments into the Death's Head division during the autumn and winter of 1939–40 and furthermore pieced together a Police division from 150,000 of his younger Order Police officers and NCOs. Moreover, in the Death's Head Reinforcements, which he organised into twelve regiments during the Polish campaign – swelling their numbers to 50,000 or 60,000 by June 1940 – he had a force of General SS led by *Altkämpfer* officers from the original Death's Head units, supposedly occupation police but as conscripts subject to transfer to the *Waffen*-SS. He now introduced ethnic Germans, non-citizens and thus not yet subject to a German conscription law, as a sixth ingredient.

Clearly, Himmler's problem in 1940 was that while he succeeded sneaking in more *Waffen*-SS volunteers under Hitler and von Brauchitsch's noses, he risked destroying what unity had evolved in the SS before 1939. The term '*Waffen*-SS', which he himself coined that winter of 1939–40, represents more than an obvious subterfuge in dealing with an OKH jealous of every attempt to increase the *Verfügungstruppe*. It encompassed in its 75,000 men the *Verfügungstruppe*, the Death's Head troops – both twelve-year enlistments in the Death's Head division – and emergency service men drafted for the duration in the Police Reinforcements. But its charisma, harking back to the oldest theme the SS shared with the Nazi movement – *Frontgemeinschaft* (the front soldiers' community) – succeeded in bridging the gulf between young and old, Reich German and ethnic German, fanatic Nazi and ordinary patriot, and ultimately among the soldiers Himmler enlisted from Norway and Holland, Rumania and Croatia, Estonia and Turkestan.

Heavy losses by the SS units active in the Polish campaign were no secret. This did not make the SS campaign for youthful volunteers or older party volunteers any easier, but Himmler managed to convert the spilt blood into a badge of honour for the widely proclaimed *Waffen*-SS. The right merely to draft his own General SS for the duration as 'police reinforcements' could now be combined with a claim on ever so small a fraction of German boys of eighteen to twenty-two and sealed with the charisma of blood. The OKH reluctantly approved in principle the right of the *Waffen*-SS to have *Ersatz-Bataillone* (replacement battalions) just like the German army; this meant that if Himmler and the SS Main Office chief could find the men, they could channel them wherever they wished. The sharp separation between Death's Head units for non-military duty and *Verfügungstruppe* for the front was chipped away in 1940 even before the organisational lines were destroyed. Thus, the OKH gave the *Waffen-SS* a share of the precious right to be a part of the *Wehrmacht*, retaining merely formal qualifications excluding the Death's Head units *per se*. Himmler would go on drafting his 'police reinforcements' among the General SS, even retaining the Death's Head designation throughout most of 1940; but the conscripts went along with the volunteers to the new replacement battalions and from there to new units of the *Waffen-SS*.

Once the conception of the *Waffen-SS* had taken root in Hitler's mind, and the recruitment and replacement channels were laid down, Himmler could proceed to the formation of foreign volunteer units. Although he had assured von Brauchitsch on 6 April 1940 that no additional units would be formed, Himmler wrote to Hitler ten days later stating that volunteer units from the Germanic countries would be recruited. On 20 April he secured Hitler's approval for a VT-*Standarte 'Nordland'* made up of Danish and Norwegian volunteers; by 25 May Hitler had approved a *Standarte 'Westland'*. A fifth *Waffen-SS* division ('*Wiking*') might be carved out of the *Verfügungsdivision*; by channelling more Reich German and ethnic German recruits into the replacement cadres of the *Verfügungsdivision* so the way was paved to get the third regiment for '*Wiking*'. However, the German offensive in the west, like the Polish campaign, decimated *Waffen-SS* ranks, especially among the officers. The units had generally made a favourable impression on their *Wehrmacht* superiors, so that there would be less resistance to replacements, but replacements were needed thick and fast if the SS was to fulfil its ambition to become 10 per cent of the peacetime *Wehrmacht*, as it once had been of the SA. With a peacetime *Wehrmacht* strength of sixty-two divisions, this meant six divisions, or about 125,000 combat soldiers. Heavy weapons and vehicles were also far below strength, even including the booty of Czechoslovakia and Poland to which the SS had privileged access.

An additional anxiety in high SS circles proved groundless: that Hitler would demobilise, removing at one blow the 60,000 General SS men drafted for the duration. There actually was some demobilisation on an individual basis of men over thirty-five, and three of the Death's Head Police Reinforcement regiments were really deactivated as a consequence. But Barbarossa was sufficiently prominent at the top echelons of SS and *Wehrmacht* by August to shift the balance once more to co-operation, ending a phase of subterfuge on both sides in which the SS clearly had been the more successful. Hitler's remarks of 6 August 1940, circulated by the OKH in 1941, define the new balance: a *Waffen*-SS in wartime amounting to 'five to ten per cent' of the peacetime strength of the *Wehrmacht*, to become the future *Staatstruppenpolizei* (garrisoned State Police troops) of the Greater German Reich, relieving the *Wehrmacht* of the onerous duty of protecting internal security. Incidentally, he also designated the *Leibstandarte* to become a brigade (it was soon made into a division).

There is no reason to suppose that these remarks represent other than Himmler's own views of the future of his political soldiers. Even if Hitler did not give sufficient prominence to the occupation duties of the *Staatstruppenpolizei*, Himmler himself did so in a speech at Metz in September 1940. Stressing the harm inherent in organisational snobbery within the SS, he pointedly referred to the SS actions in Poland – expulsions, killing, the settlement of ethnic Germans from abroad, guarding Jewish labour camps – as no less important than the exploits of the *Leibstandarte*. It was portrayed as a privilege for the SS man to serve as a soldier at the front, and the SS needed to spill its blood in order to earn the right to carry out the unspeakable yet necessary police tasks which most Germans shunned. Symbolic of this mantle of righteousness which the *Waffen*-SS could wrap around SS crimes was the formal inclusion of all parts of the concentration camp system within the *Waffen*-SS. In reality, the dissolution of the special inspection of the Death's Head Reinforcements at the time of the formation of the Leadership Main Office (August 1940) along with the transfer of the Inspectorate of Concentration Camps to the latter meant very little more than the acknowledgement that the distinction between *Verfügungstruppe* and Death's Head troops had finally ended.

The Germanic Guidance Office had a very modest prelude in the setting up in late 1940 of a special training camp at Sennheim in occupied Alsace, to provide ideological and physical conditioning for non-German SS recruits. By this means Gottlob Berger, the SS Main Office chief, hoped to get around the already familiar objections of military commanders that the east European ethnic Germans, Danes, Norwegians, Dutchmen and Flemings were simply not ready for inclusion in regular German units. Particularly poor experience with the '*Nordland*' and '*Westland*' regiments seems to have motivated Himmler to approve this special treatment; and an increased flow of SS volunteers from southeast Europe after the arrival of German forces in Hungary and Rumania made it all the more necessary to prepare these volunteers physically and psychologically to share the lot of the Reich German SS. Over the protests of VoMi, the new Main Office boss was able to construct an elaborate network of specialised branch offices to look after the families of the volunteers, oversee the Folk Groups to guarantee the recruiting and mould the recruits along lines different from those laid down by VoMi in agreement with their local leaders.

To co-ordinate the activities of the Sennheim-Lager with those of field personnel in the Balkans and in the Nordic countries, Himmler authorised the creation of a new 'Office Six' within the reorganised SS Main Office early in 1941. It proliferated in the next few months before the attack on the Soviet Union to three Main Sections: Ethnic-Germanic Leadership, Ethnic-Germanic Recruitment and Ethnic-Germanic Education. Its official title was the Germanic Volunteers' Guidance Office, but the shortened form of Germanic Guidance Office became current almost immediately. The office's six regional sub-sections included the east, southeast and south of Europe. While some of the paper plans envisaging 'overseas branches' must be taken with a grain of salt, there is good evidence that Himmler supported his ambitious subordinate in his schemes to penetrate even into power structures of the party and Foreign Office such as VoMi and the *Auslands-Organisation* (AO), where the SS already had its supporters.

Like Hitler, Himmler was a thorough conspirator, who profoundly believed that power struggles even in his own ranks could be productive as long as he knew about them. The VoMi and AO chiefs had not proved sufficiently enterprising, yet he did not try to remove them or destroy them. He let his new Main Office chief, Berger, bypass them, as Berger had bypassed his former superior, Heissmeyer – the previous, ineffective chief of the SS Main Office. Himmler thus created a rival even to the RKFDV leadership, for ethnic German policy was so intimately tied to manpower problems that too much success in recruiting for the *Waffen*-SS could actually undermine the settlement efforts. This is exactly what happened, but, of course, winning the war in 1943 and 1944 was far more critical than RKFDV goals.

In 1941, however, the need for soldiers for the *Waffen*-SS created new opportunities for empire-building in the SS instead of reducing them. In at least partial competition with the recruitment of replacements for the '*Nordland*' and '*Westland*' *Waffen*-SS regiments, national legions were started in Denmark, Norway, Holland and Flanders. While the former were recruited through straightforward SS channels and were henceforth treated as *Waffen*-SS (they did not automatically become General SS members), the latter merely had SS commanders and SS NCOs, at least some of whom were their own nationals. There was no national legion for Belgium *per se* because the Nazis wished to encourage only the Flemish speakers. Later, however, the French speakers (Walloons) would also secure their own legion. Recruitment took place through native Nazi parties. It was inevitable that friction should develop even within the SS structure itself, for the Germanic Guidance Office quickly 'went underground', so to speak, so that not only local populations but also Superior SS and Police Leaders were in the dark about the source of funds, informants and the purposes of complicated intrigues. Himmler intervened sporadically and just enough to contain the bitterness of some of the oldest and most loyal SS generals in the regional commands. Clearly, he was playing for high stakes – the chance to help make German foreign policy.

Heydrich's personnel of course kept very close tabs on the native politicians used by the Germanic Guidance Office, but Berger's operatives kept their work very well concealed. The RSHA system certainly had no partiality for the new empire-builder and his charges, yet Heydrich's own foreign ambitions and his basic support of Himmler's strategy dictated a cautious pattern of weakening or removing highly placed individuals who exposed themselves, even SS officers, while permitting the empire itself to grow. The ruthless vigour of Himmler's chief recruiter was to pay off in the critical years of 1943 and 1944, when many hundreds of thousands of SS soldiers flowed through the channels he had created in 1941. The short-term advantages, as measured in soldiers, were more modest.

THE RUSSIAN CAMPAIGN

Waffen-SS strength on 22 June 1941, was 160,405, with a combat force of 95,868. Ninety per cent of these men were Germans, still largely from the Reich proper. Ethnic Germans were considerably better represented in the replacement units and field formations not under the army but under the *Kommandostab Reichsführer* SS in the new Leadership Main Office. During the period of maximum commitment and before heavy losses were reported (September 1941), *Waffen*-SS strength rose to

172,000, with the additional forces nearly all engaged. They were still Reich German units sprinkled liberally with ethnic Germans: the First and Second SS Infantry brigades, the SS Cavalry brigade, the *Kampfgruppe Nord* (Combat Group North) and the old Ninth Death's Head regiment that had served in Norway in 1940. In fact, this whole new combat element was formed from a thin Death's Head cadre, the younger Police Reinforcements and ethnic Germans. The foreign legions did not join in combat until November 1941, mostly in the Second SS Infantry brigade at Leningrad.

In discussing the shortcomings of these units, Himmler later was to observe that the 'officer-cover' for many of them, and indeed for the whole combat SS, was thin. Yet the summer and autumn of 1941 saw the SS officers' corps in its best condition. An influx of new blood from the police, *Wehrmacht* officers, party and state officials, and able young doctors, lawyers and youth leaders, as well as the rapid promotion of thousands of young SS men from ranks of the General SS had raised the total of SS officers to nearly 20,000 – of which some 5,000 held *Waffen-*SS commissions. In many ways, the latter were the cream of the crop along with the other elite of the RSHA apparatus (perhaps 5,000). Soon the bloodletting in Russia would destroy this cream, whose replacements would increase the officers' corps and the whole SS far beyond the size of 1941 until both bore scarcely a token resemblance to the pre-war body.

Three times as many SS officer dossiers (61,438) survived the war as there were SS officers in 1941. The great bulk of the remainder were not General SS expellees of the 1930s or early turnover from pre-1933 but wartime commissions in the *Waffen*-SS granted between 1942 and 1945. Tens of thousands of officers were thus added to the potential corps, whose ties to the pre-war SS were tenuous or non-existent; indeed party membership was also significantly lower in this group than in the first 20,000. Within the group of approximately 5,000 *Waffen*-SS officers of mid-1941 were not only the products of the SS-*Junkerschulen* (Officer Candidate Schools) since 1934 but the self-selected elite of the professional SS officers of the 1930s – *Verfügungstruppe*, Death's Head troops, and the battalion and regimental commanders of the General SS units who had volunteered for Police Reinforcement duty in 1938. Decimation had been their lot already in Poland; proportionately lighter losses in France and the Balkan campaign had added nevertheless to the absolute loss of experienced and committed SS leaders.

Himmler's prodigal squandering of his officers' corps in Russia after the lessons of the previous campaigns must be traced to his own convictions about the tremendous advantage which would accrue to the survivors for having shared in the bloodletting as a new 'front generation', and also his desire to impress Hitler *vis-à-vis* the officers' corps of the army and the party's *Führerkorps*. In view of Hitler's own character and that of the two rival leadership elites, Himmler's policy was not irrational; the risks involved were part of the SS charisma. It was essential, however, that enough of the leaven of the officers' corps of the 1930s survive to produce a post-war crop with qualities similar to those of the front generation which had built the SS. Still quite possible in 1942, this necessary process became more and more attenuated in 1943 and 1944; even the police and concentration camp systems were inundated with officers from outside the SS, although this leadership preserved itself better while giving up much of the ideology of political soldiering for an empty bureaucratic consciousness of duty.

In the *Waffen*-SS the Germanic idea merged in 1942 with a pan-European concept of anti-Bolshevism which survived the war, largely through the medium of the *Waffen*-SS front soldiers' community. But the bearers of this concept had little in common with the administrative bureaucracy of the SS that predominated in the police, in the RKFDV system, and in the Main Offices, including the Leadership Main Office which supposedly ran the *Waffen*-SS. Indeed, because the Germanic Guidance Office preserved a good deal more of the amateur spirit of the pre-war and even pre-1933 SS, it was still able to innovate and grow with the tasks of the war, thus bridging the gulf between the political soldier-dom of the SA from whose ranks its founder came and the European *Landsknecht* of 1945 and after.

Success in breaking down the resistance of Hitler and the OKH to enlarging the *Waffen*-SS in the winter of 1941–42, due in part to its demonstrated 'aggressiveness', meant that a battle royal broke out between the SS Main Office and the Leadership Main Office over the management of the huge increment. While the doughty chief of the SS Main Office claimed the whole credit for the breakthrough, there was little question that the growth in 1941 of a real SS general staff made up of military professionals for whom the organisation of new units, their training, management and staffing was routine reassured the *Wehrmacht* professionals – and perhaps Hitler too. The SA background of this headquarters, from its chief downwards, seemed ample guarantee that it was not reactionary. But the old dilemma of the SA was to be repeated in the internal quarrels of top *Waffen*-SS leaders; a revolutionary *élan* was hard to keep consonant with military efficiency, and close aping of traditional military structures too easily vitiated the special virtues of an elite guard. These quarrels reverberated into the combat officers' corps in terms of titles, saluting, uniform, decorations and – far more important – non-co-operation with other branches of the SS such as the Superior SS and Police Leaders.

The Leadership Main Office captured the General SS, strange as it might seem – since the chief functions of the skeleton structure remaining by 1942 were pre- and post-service military training and the care of dependants. Outside the Reich, however, the Germanic Guidance Office maintained its lead in the care and development of the new SS and captured strategic positions originally held by the Leadership Main Office, such as the Censorship Bureau of the SS *Feldpostprüfstelle* (military postal system), through which it could build up a strong case against any practice which seemed inimical to recruiting success in non-German areas. Himmler and Hitler showed an avid interest in this intelligence operation, which was kept entirely separate from the RSHA.

Yet the Leadership Main Office managed to develop a pattern of *Waffen*-SS *Standortkommandanturen* (command posts) within the Reich and *Waffen*-SS commandants abroad, nominally subordinate to the Superior SS and Police Leaders – actually their close collaborators and aides – who often could 'freeze out' a delegate of the SS Main Office chief (Berger) bent on increasing the role of the Germanic Guidance Office. The creation in 1942 of a separate *Waffen*-SS Welfare and Maintenance system independent of both the state system and the old General SS network signalled another attempt of the SS to operate beyond party and state, but it was equally a result of internal rivalries within the SS system itself. It was not long before this potentially strategic sluice-gate of favours and rewards was detached from the SS Main Office and reassigned to the Race and Settlement Main Office, where it was removed from the control of both jealous chiefs.

When Himmler toyed in 1942 with the penetration of Rosenberg's dilapidated empire by sending the inventor of the Germanic Guidance Office to be Rosenberg's lieutenant, he considered giving the Main Office to Richard Hildebrandt, another aggressive SS general and Superior SS and Police Leader; but instead he kept the SS Main Office chief at his old post and used the other SS general as a troubleshooter in the tangled affairs of South Russia, where Erich Koch was outdoing the SS in ruthless barbarity. It was not accidental, then, that Hildebrandt became the new RuSHa chief as well, since RuSHa had been made responsible for the post-war settlement of SS veterans and already had begun to set up large SS-run collective farms to train personnel and supply food for the troops. This whole operation fell outside both the SS Main Office and the SS Leadership Office, just as did the anti-partisan operations.

SS ANTI–PARTISAN CAMPAIGNS

While Himmler had underestimated the extent and toughness of the partisan movements, he had provided initially for their control by the Death's Head Police Reinforcements. When these units had proved inef-fective in Poland and Norway, he substituted an extensive system of police formations drawn first from Reich police reserves and later from Baltic and Balkan volunteers not yet considered eligible for the SS. He supplemented these police battalions (later police regiments) with *Waffen*-SS Training and Replacement battalions under Leadership Main Office control after 1940. However, by 1942 it was clear that in Russia and Yugoslavia use of these types of unit by Superior SS and Police Leaders was not sufficient to check the growth of partisan-controlled areas. Co-operation among HSSPFs, the Leadership Main Office and the Order Police headquarters was weak.

So Himmler created yet another elaborate command system under one of the oldest SS generals, Erich von dem Bach-Zelewski, a former Superior SS and Police Leader both in the Reich and later in Russia. This time Himmler arranged – perhaps out of necessity – that the Plenipotentiary for Anti-partisan Warfare had no permanent troops but drew *Waffen*-SS troops and police formations on an *ad hoc* basis. Operationally, however, this new command was free even of *Wehrmacht* control. A series of campaigns in 1942 and 1943 was conducted so brutally and ruthlessly that nothing living was left in vital communications zones.

As in the case of *Waffen*-SS and Police units temporarily assigned to Sipo-SD-*Einsatzgruppen*, criminal acts were demanded of the personnel, and these acts occurred as a matter of course; yet the troop units assigned had not been designed for this purpose, and few of the personnel intended such acts to be part of their service. It would be exceedingly difficult if not impossible to establish participation in specific acts by specific units, since the turnover of these units was probably even greater than was intended, due to military exigencies. Himmler clearly preferred to keep such operations from resting on the conscience of his crack troops or coming to the knowledge of the German population; still, while rotation was regular practice, it had limits. Sadly enough, it appears that it was often easy for many Germans within the SS and outside – in the *Wehrmacht*, the state and party sectors – to see and look away, thankful that they were not called upon. An increasingly large number of SS officers and units did, however, need to become involved with the failure of these 'pacification drives', so that in 1944 the division between *Bandenbekämpfung* (anti-partisan measures) and other assignments broke down. *Wehrmacht* units were increasingly involved from 1943 on, and thus the special status of Leadership Main Office units outside the OKH sphere disappeared.

EVOLUTION OF THE WAFFEN–SS DIVISIONS

The Russians mauled the *Waffen*-SS so badly during the winter months of 1941–42 that a total rebuilding of all outfits was necessary. In preparation for the 'final' summer offensive of 1942, Himmler and his Leadership Main Office pumped men into eight field divisions, four of which received tank battalions so as to become armoured infantry. The *Leibstandarte* Adolf Hitler finally attained division strength as 1. SS-*Panzergrenadiere* (First Armoured Infantry division), but its exclusive 1.72m height requirement had to be abandoned. Sepp Dietrich, its dashing commander, and a sprinkling of pre-1939 officers were left to carry on the 'aristocratic' tradition. Of course, not all the rest were dead – some had been taken out as early as 1941 to supply officer cadre for other units, especially those formed from Death's Head Reinforcements. '*Das Reich*', formed out of the '*Deutschland*' regiment and '*Der Führer*' of the old *Verfügungsdivision*, had already added a regiment of Death's Head Reinforcements in 1941 (the Eleventh Death's Head regiment), renamed simply the Eleventh SS Infantry regiment). Now the Second SS Armoured Infantry division, '*Das Reich*', acquired Georg Keppler as its commander by New Year's Day 1942, Paul Hausser having been pulled back to the Leadership Main Office for staff duties. Keppler perpetuated what Hausser had made a firm tradition among the officers' corps from the *Verfügungstruppe* of the 1930s – a strong orientation to the *Reichswehr* tradition and anti-party resentment.

On the other hand, the Death's Head division with Eicke, its intrepid Nazi commander who hated brass hats, still consisted in June 1941 of its three original regiments created in 1937, though without the regional designations. Its devil-may-care spirit and versatile military prowess contrasted favourably with army divisions, according to non-SS military specialists. An original disfavour associated with its concentration camp origins, reflected in a dearth of decorations after the western campaign, was reversed in 1941–42, so that the divisional officers' corps had an enviable record of decorations but also of losses. Himmler had to write very sharply to Eicke, who would not part with his old regimental commanders in exchange for *Verfügungstruppe* 'brass hats'; and the second regiment had to be cannibalised to preserve the other two regiments as early as July 1941. Attached to it during the gruelling winter campaign in the far north were the *Freikorps Danmark*, a Danish legion under *Waffen*-SS officers, and the Ninth Reinforced Death's Head regiment, renamed '*Thule*' for its valorous role in northern Finland.

The Fourth or Police division – unofficially a *Waffen*-SS division since April 1941, officially in February 1942 and publicly in September 1942 – languished in comparative obscurity with its old-fashioned horsedrawn vehicles and artillery, and its strictly police replacement system (contrary to Himmler's own stated policy). It had the distinction of being the first SS division to have its commander, Arthur Mülverstedt, one of the crop of 1938 police generals, killed in action. Due to its character, it could only be used for besieging Leningrad, not conducive to the winning of *Ritterkreuze* by its police officers' corps.

The '*Wiking*' division and its commander, Felix Steiner, was the special favourite of the Germanic Guidance Office and its chief for the obvious reason that the bulk, although not all, of the Germanic volunteers were in the division's regiments '*Westland*' and '*Nordland*'. Its third regiment had been part of the original *Verfügungstruppe*: SS–*Standarte 2*, '*Germania*'. With the strongly profiled character of the division commander, who had transferred out of the *Wehrmacht* into the old AW in December 1933 and risen through the *Verfügungstruppe* from its inception, the 'Germanic division' acquired a marked spirit of soldierly independence and even insubordination which gave Himmler many attacks of stomach cramps and provoked his most choleric outbursts. After all, here was an officers' corps of political soldiers par excellence – and in their officers' casinos 'not even the *Reichsführer* SS was spared.'

Since in 1941 a stark contrast existed between the lower middle-class officer and NCO personnel of the German cadres and the upper middle class enlisted men from the Scandinavian and Lowland countries, Nordic dissatisfaction made it obvious that the officer replacements for this division should come from within rather than by transfer from other German units. Himmler was very reluctant to accept this separateness, as was the Leadership Main Office, while Steiner and Berger – with the latter's Germanic connections – pressed for field commissions and Officer Candidate School appointments. Himmler only succumbed in the winter of 1942–43 after desertions and public unrest in the volunteers' homelands made clear the danger of treating this elite as second-class soldiers. But by then the volunteers were going into national legions, and the '*Wiking*' division drew its replacements from wherever they were available, '*Reichsdeutsche*' and '*Volksdeutsche*' included.

The 'Sixth', or 'Northern' ('*Nord*') division, got off to a bad start. Established in the autumn of 1940 as a motorised mountain combat group from the Sixth and Seventh Death's Head regiments of Police Reinforcements, these troops were placed under army command in Norway as early as 4 November 1940, where they got little training and plenty of guard duty. The soldier personnel were almost all General SS who had been called up under the 1938 emergency service law; officers and NCOs were personnel combed out of the original Death's Head regiments preparatory to the constitution of the combat division and from the *Verfügungstruppe*. Thrust into battle after marching 600 miles across Lapland, the battle group collapsed; its company and battalion commanders lost control of their units, and the two regimental commanders, both former police officers, also had to be relieved. Karl Demelhuber, the combat group commander who only assumed command a few days before the battle, was a *Verfügungstruppe* veteran who later demonstrated great military competence; but he too had to be pulled back to the Leadership Main Office.

In August 1941 Himmler persuaded the army group commander to reassemble the remains of the unit, which had been distributed in battalions; and with an all-new officers' corps from *Verfügungstruppe* veterans robbed from other units, the *Gebirgs-Division* '*Nord*' was created. Initially it was given as a backbone a third regiment, the better trained and outfitted Ninth Death's Head regiment from Kirkenes. The new division, especially the latter regiment, gave a good account of itself in Finland. When the ninth regiment was removed to join the Death's Head division as *Standarte* '*Thule*', the Sixth SS Mountain division became a fast, light (*Jäger*) unit with a reputation for being northern specialists.

The formation of the Seventh Volunteer Mountain division 'Prince Eugene' sheds additional light on the improvising, not to say conspiratorial, tactics of Himmler and his recruiters. Immediately after the occupation of Yugoslavia, in the military government district of Serbia the ethnic Germans who were concentrated in the area called the Banat were directed to form the familiar Self-Defence units which had become the hallmark of SS and more especially SS Main Office penetration. After a combing out of genuine volunteers for the *Waffen*-SS by Recruiting Commissions, Himmler simply ordered that ethnic Germans in Serbia be subjected to compulsory military service. Since the Serbian Banat had once been part of the Austro-Hungarian empire, Himmler hit upon the ridiculous subterfuge that they were still subject to 'the Tyrolese *Landsturm* ordinance of 1782'. In spite of serious objections from VoMi and the Foreign Office, the Self-Defence units were made the cadre of a new mountain division to be made up entirely of ethnic Germans. Its purpose was anti-partisan warfare, and its theatre was to be the Balkans, as revealed by its name and its first commander Arthur Phleps, a K.u.K. (Austro-Hungarian) and Romanian army veteran. Recruited and committed as it was, it is not surprising that the division gained a horrible reputation for cruelty.

Himmler's Eighth division 'Florian Geyer,' a cavalry unit, began as two Death's Head Cavalry regiments of Police Reinforcements set up in Poland early in 1940. As the SS Cavalry brigade, they were thrown into Russia in the dead of winter; what was left over by the spring of 1942 became the cadre of the new division. Ethnic Germans increasingly replaced the Reich German General SS personnel from the fashionable *Reiterstandarten* (Cavalry regiments). Ethnic Germans, especially from Hungary and Rumania, also preponderated as replacements in the two SS Infantry brigades formed out of Death's Head Reinforcement regiments. Himmler and his recruiters resorted to the meanest kinds of trickery in these nominally independent lands, against the advice of the Foreign Office and the protests of VoMi and the Leadership Main Office. Men were told they were going to the Reich for brief sport training or were being hired as labourers; those who caught on and hid had their homes destroyed by gangs of the party-led Folk Group. The Hungarian government also retaliated by denaturalising the 'volunteers' and their families. It is little wonder that their Reich German officers tried to get seventeen- and eighteen-year-olds fresh from the Hitler Youth instead. Their initial experience with the small foreign legions in the Second brigade (Norway, Netherlands and Flanders) was also unimpressive; unlike the western volunteers for the *Waffen*-SS, these legionnaires were younger members of the fascist parties whose eyes were constantly turned back to their homelands, where vicious and deadly power struggles went on among the collaborating factions.

The *Waffen*-SS had a strength of 222,000 men at the opening of the summer 1942 campaigns, of whom approximately 90,000 were recruited in 1941 or later. Between 30,000 and 40,000 of the new recruits were ethnic Germans; there were some 10,000 additional western volunteers. All the rest were German boys born between 1921 and 1924 channelled to the *Waffen*-SS through the Hitler Youth. They were still volunteers, many with extensive political indoctrination; but after February 1942 their parents' approval was no longer needed, opening up the possibility of intense pressure on seventeen-year-olds (class of 1925). The appeal of joining a first-rate military formation especially approved by the party and the *Führer* had to be balanced against the grim knowledge of SS losses. The SD reported that from the winter of 1941–42 on, the German population also regarded the *Waffen*-SS as capable of being used against other German formations or in other capacities (anti-partisan warfare). Parents' refusals were of critical importance, since the SS was still trying to recruit the boys before they could be drafted by the *Wehrmacht*. Some of these boys had been recruited while still in the *Reichsarbeitsdienst* (labour service), away from home and without a chance to be influenced by parents or clergymen. Later this tactic was to become a favourite method of SS recruiters. In the spring of 1942, however, Hitler still exercised a moderating influence, as can be seen in his table remarks about the necessity of keeping the *Waffen*-SS an elite guard by limiting recruiting. He explicitly alluded to the heavy losses as a badge of honour, as if to counteract implications of incompetent leadership.

A larger incompetence, that of Hitler and his military professional advisors, soon overshadowed any question of the SS's technical competence. With scarcely enough time to rest from gruelling defensive operations for which the mobile divisions of the SS were not especially suited, they were thrown into the July 1942 offensive under strength and without operational training in any unit larger than a company. After brief triumphs, due in part to a shift in Soviet tactics from sacrificing large units in initial holding actions to extensive withdrawals to the Volga and the Caucasus, the SS divisions began to bleed to death in fruitless attacks along with the rest of the German army.

But the SS losses had not even begun to show up before Himmler began to cash in on them and on Hitler's faith in the SS. It was only 15 July 1942 when the *Waffen*-SS examiners already began to apply the lower *Wehrmacht* standards to new 'volunteers'. Largely in deference to Hitler and because he alone could force a change on the *Wehrmacht*, Reich German youths still had to volunteer for the SS for another year. Especially for officer replacements and specialists, the struggle for volunteers continued hot and heavy.

The General SS superstructure in 1942 was still largely intact, and even expanded to include not only annexed territories (Main Sectors 'Vistula', 'Warthe' and 'Westmark') but occupied countries as well (Main Sectors 'North' and 'Northwest' for Norway and Netherlands; 'Ostland' and 'Ukraine' for the Soviet Union). This superstructure, minus the intermediate or Sector level, continued to play an important role in recruitment through liaison and propaganda in pre-military training camps, farm and labour service units, and Hitler Youth security patrols. It could also be tapped directly for older personnel until eventually it became so hollow in 1944–45 that it no longer functioned.

SS ARMOUR AND AN SS ARMY CORPS

In the autumn of 1942 in the midst of the heavy fighting that led up to the battle of Stalingrad, Hitler gave Himmler permission to make the First, Second, Third and Fifth SS divisions *Panzer* (armoured) divisions, and to motorise the Fourth or Police division. He also approved the formation of an SS *Panzer* corps superstructure. He does not appear to have authorised the formation of any more SS divisions, still clinging to the elite concept with which the *Panzer* formations were quite consistent. The SS *Panzer* corps was a tribute to SS loyalty; the time had passed when the army and Hitler himself would fear to concentrate so much fire power and *élan* under one SS commander. A powerful combine in the hands of a competent commander, the SS *Panzer* corps of the *Leibstandarte*, '*Das Reich*' and Death's Head was constructed in the heat of combat around Kharkov in January and February 1943. Light on personnel and *panzers*, it nevertheless proved the advantage of larger operational SS units and made the last successful German counter-offensive on the eastern front at Kharkov an SS triumph. Yet the Fifth or '*Wiking*' division did not get its tanks until another year had passed, and the Police division only became armoured infantry in 1944.

The explanation for this is not far to seek: the SS triumph at Kharkov supplied Himmler with the justification he needed to compel the *Wehrmacht* to let him create more SS divisions. Three more armoured SS divisions were called into existence in the spring of 1943, the Ninth SS or '*Hohenstaufen*', the Tenth SS or '*Frundsberg*', and the Twelfth SS- '*Hitlerjugend*'. Actually the Tenth SS was formed from the remnants of the First SS brigade, while the first of several new armoured infantry divisions was made out of the Second SS brigade (II.SS). The Ninth SS and Twelfth SS, however, were brand-new constructions, with an SS- *Führerkorps* exclusively from the younger generation of the *Junkerschulen*. The fresh personnel of all these new divisions were Reich German volunteers aged between seventeen and nineteen, products of the Nazi educational system par excellence (they had reached puberty between 1936 and 1938). The SS recruiters found them ideal for *Panzer* troops. Often more patriotic and healthy than well educated, and usually without any earlier contact with the General SS, they were as different a breed as the ethnic Germans or the Germanic volunteers.

Speaking in October 1943 at Poznań, Himmler claimed that as early as December 1942 Hitler had ordered him to put together two additional SS divisions in France by mid-February 1943 in order to cope with an allied invasion. Up to 27,000 of the class of 1925 in the Reich Labour Service camps were promised, although only 15,000 had become *Waffen*- SS by February. The notion of armour was born even later, of course, made feasible through a loosening up of SS weapons procurement in 1943 in return for increased use of concentration camp labour for war production. It is typical of this latter-day SS growth that it preserved an elite character of sorts (armour), was improvised from the external necessity of Hitler and the *Wehrmacht* (fears of allied invasion), was carried beyond the original authorisation (from two infantry divisions to three armoured and one armoured infantry or *Panzergrenadiere*) and was given a 'new look' which added further to the bewildering multiplicity of the SS. Every one of these units became crack divisions, respected by their *Wehrmacht* comrades-in-arms and by the enemy. There was no sense yet of 'scraping the bottom of the barrel'. On the other hand, efforts to turn these young people into political soldiers were necessarily minimal.

FOUR MORE SS PANZER CORPS

An additional factor in the forming of these units was the new military doctrine, absorbed by Hitler and Himmler from unit commanders, of the value and even necessity of *Panzer* corps as relatively independent operational units. The First and Second *Panzer* corps, under Sepp Dietrich and Paul Hausser, were set up as pairs of *Panzer* divisions. The Third *Panzer* corps was designed to realise the ambition of *Wiking*'s commander to command a Germanic corps, albeit with only one armoured division, *'Wiking'* itself. The new *Panzergrenadier* Division Eleven '*Nordland*', consisting of Danish, Norwegian, Flemish and Walloon legions, the refurbished '*Nordland*' regiment, and the SS-*Freiwillige* (Volunteer) *Panzergrenadierbrigade* '*Nederland*', provided motorised infantry. Himmler even looked forward in October 1943 to two more additional armoured corps! The new Ninth and Tenth Armoured divisions had not even received all their armour yet, but he was planning to match each with a new armoured infantry division in January 1944, '*Reichsführer* SS' and 'Götz von Berlichingen' (SS nos 16 and 17).

For this purpose, Himmler was counting on the Reich German class of 1926, part of which was already drafted that same month. The sole survival of SS criteria in this case was a height requirement: 166cm for those under twenty. This reduction in SS height requirements from 168cm had applied since January 1943, on the grounds that the boys had not reached their full growth. The drafting of youths for the *Waffen*-SS had begun without fanfare in the spring of 1943, the final breakthrough occurring at *Wehrkreis* levels responsible for the call-up procedure. Such personnel, as indeed the vast majority of the ethnic Germans and volunteers from eastern countries discussed below were, strictly speaking, 'nominal SS'. They had special SS numbers or none at all, while General SS personnel – including eighteen-year-olds who volunteered and Germanic members who were not even in the *Waffen*-SS – continued to receive SS identity cards in the #400,000 series on into 1945.

Thus, although the SS 'victory' over the *Wehrmacht* was pretty hollow at this juncture, since the new recruits were scarcely elite in any sense, the General SS as a future potential elite still loomed large in Germany's future in the event of a negotiated peace or a German victory. In fact, Himmler envisaged twenty to thirty SS divisions in arms at the time of the peace or armistice, and from then on he would draft annual classes for *Waffen*-SS service on the military frontier, an SS preserve. In this way, the General SS would always be the product of survival of the fittest and always have a 'front tradition'. In the meantime the SS got an even wider range of choice for its future elite; they had access to the whole class of 1926 instead of merely those addressed by SS recruiters.

A EUROPEAN SS?

The term 'European SS' occurs for the first time in Himmler's conversations with his masseur, Felix Kersten, on 6 March 1943 – although the term 'European volunteers' occurs earlier, especially in 1942. The shift in emphasis from a Germanic SS – for the two concepts had continued side by side since 1941 – corresponds to the development in 1943 of *Waffen*-SS units which were definitely not claimed to be Nordic. When we recall the gradual evolution of the Germanic Guidance Office and with it the notion of a 'Community of Arms' as the basis for a political union after the war, it is clear how the racial theme and even the General SS as the vehicle of unity could be eclipsed, though not eliminated, from the minds of Heinrich Himmler and his close associates.

Himmler even alluded at Poznań in October 1943 to the formation of a fifth and sixth SS army corps, neither of them armoured – composed in the first case of the old Seventh SS Mountain division (all ethnic Germans) and a Bosnian Mountain division, and in the second of a Latvian brigade (already in existence) and a future Latvian division. In the background of these units already lay more than a year of bitter SS factionalism and indecision on Himmler's part.

HIMMLER AND HIS 'GENERALS'

Himmler had always needed practical advisors with realistic plans because of his tendency to substitute his wishes for present realities and his grasshopper mind, which conceived a thousand schemes only to forget them. He seems to have lost Heydrich even before Heydrich died in June 1942, out of mutual suspicion and rivalry; three or four less able men took Heydrich's place, so that never again did Himmler have the certainty that comes from a single planner at the helm. Since late in 1942 Himmler kept having disappointing encounters with his *Gruppenführer*. In plain terms, Himmler 'could dish it out' – meaning harsh truths – 'but he could not take it'. The result was the pursuit of unrealisable and even inconsistent goals rather than give up any avenue of power. Paths of least resistance were chosen without his conscious awareness because men who survived as his advisors succeeded in tricking him simply in order to enhance their own power and to 'show results'. Individually these men, chiefs of the SS Main Office, the Leadership Main Office, the Reich Security Main Office and the Economic Administration Main Office, were tough and shrewd. But pitted against one another, their practicality was used up enhancing the viability of their own sectors, often only in the short run. The foreign SS legions were a typical product of 'hard-headed SS realism' gone berserk. Not all were unsuccessful in military terms, but they cost the SS a very high price.

Inroads on the Nazi-SS gospel of genetic purity came from several directions, but in the last analysis the force of necessity lay behind all the breaches. As early as 1939 the Czech police were utilised in the 'Protectorate' of Bohemia-Moravia as one aspect of indirect rule, clearly with the approval of Himmler and Heydrich if not on their initiative. In Poland 'direct rule' was believed necessary, through the use of Death's Head Police Reinforcements and German police battalions. The horrible consequences led even Hitler and Himmler to moderate this policy in the Scandinavian and the western-occupied regions, through extensive use of native police. Initial plans for Russia, however, suggest the intention to follow the Polish pattern except to emphasise German police units and rear-echelon *Waffen*-SS troops instead of the nearly worthless Death's Head Reinforcements. Yet in practice Russia was the theatre where the most extensive use of native police units took place. The second such theatre was the Balkans. In both cases, the manpower problem in juxtaposition to technical difficulties of controlling vast partisan-filled territories with second-line German troops led both Himmler and the *Wehrmacht* to employ native forces. The SS actually lagged behind the *Wehrmacht* in 1941–42 in the willingness to use such personnel, and it was partly because of competition with the *Wehrmacht* for power in these regions and for prestige with Hitler that Himmler had to bow to improvising suggestions among his own SS staff and grudgingly permit police units of Ukrainians, Russians, Lithuanians, etc.

When we recall the ideal of a future *Staatsschutzkorps* (Corps for the Protection of the State) of SS and Police, it is not very difficult to see the dangers of admitting the camel's nose under the tent. However, the rationalisation employed by Heydrich and Himmler with regard to the Czechs was applied first to the northern Baltic peoples, Finns, Estonians and Latvians – that a winnowing process involving service or being put to a test might eventually make a certain portion of these peoples worthy of assimilation. With a thin underpinning of racial theory and history – and an element of willingness to collaborate on the part of certain segments of these populations – the analogy of elite formation from SS practice in Germany and subsequently in Scandinavian and western countries helped SS planners in 1943 and 1944 convince Himmler, Hitler and themselves that they were still operating consistently. Only when their inconsistency became visible to everybody else late in 1944 did they accept the fact that they themselves had wiped out the SS elite concept in the process – the SS becoming in the minds of Germans and non-Germans merely another part of the German forces, and for many an evil part.

FOREIGN SS LEGIONS

Thus, the SS Main Office moved imperceptibly from the creation and use of police and special anti-partisan units separate from the *Waffen*-SS to the creation of *Waffen*-SS units for special use in partisan-filled areas (the Bosnian unit, later SS division 13 '*Handschar*'). The notion of converting a police unit, after being put to a test, into *Waffen*-SS was already present in the development of the Fourth or Police division. Similarly, the assignment of 'nominal' *Waffen*-SS status to police formations guarding the concentration camps (increasingly ethnic German and even non-German) for the convenience of pay, welfare, rationing and privacy from *Wehrmacht* prying had made a precedent ready to hand for units like the Bosnians, which by no stretch of the imagination could be considered Germanic. The technique of using *Waffen*-SS cadre had been perfected by the Leadership Main Office not only for the handling of the young German recruits but also for the ethnic Germans after 1940. Thus, ready at hand were many of the forms and patterns out of which Himmler's technicians, far more than he personally, improvised division after division for him to 'present' to Hitler. He did not even dare to tell Hitler in 1945 just who all the thirty-eight-odd SS divisions were, not to mention Bulgarian and Rumanian battalions, Indian, Turkoman and Transcaucasian legions, and three Cossack Cavalry formations.

In order to have a *Waffen-SS-ist-Stärke* (actual strength) of 330,000 men in 1943, the SS Main Office had had to add as many men as comprised the whole *Waffen*-SS in September 1941 (172,000) – estimating losses during the winter of 1942–43 conservatively at around 60,000. Thus, a swamping of the Reich German personnel had to occur in 1943. Ethnic Germans from Hungary and the Balkans as well as the resettlers of 1939–41 taken from their new Polish farms and VoMi camps amounted to over 40,000; western volunteers, largely from Holland and Belgium, amounted to another 40,000 or more; Letts, Estonians and Bosnians already under arms in *Waffen*-SS units must have totalled at least 40,000 – all compared to new Reich German additions of some 50,000.

A NEW SS OFFICERS' CORPS?

The *Waffen*-SS officers' corps available to train and lead this motley array consisted almost entirely of Reich German personnel, 10,702 as of 1 July 1943. Of these, only 4,145 were designated as career or professional officers, about 1,000 of whom held ranks above the rank of captain. The latter were in effect the military elite of the SS. A year later a quarter of the officers had fallen, with losses of professional and field grade officers at a not appreciably lower rate than reserve and company officers. Thus, a figure of 5,102 professional *Waffen*-SS officers on 1 July 1944 meant an addition of some 2,000 new officers including field grades. The 'military elite' commanding the European SS of 1944 was, then, far from congruent with the SS officers' corps of the later 1930s. Former *Wehrmacht* and police officers stood shoulder to shoulder at high officers' conferences with the younger generation from the *Verfügungstruppe* and Death's Head troops of the 1930s, NCOs then at best, who had passed through the *Junkerschulen* or had no special training at all. Neither their exploits nor their crimes as perpetrated through their units can be traced directly to the *Kampfzeit*.

Indeed, more of the General SS officers' corps of the 1930s were in the *Wehrmacht* than in the *Waffen*-SS, and most of the latter were reserve officers. It is probably true that their training duties and command responsibilities toward rear-echelon replacement units were the real vehicle for transmitting values and techniques of the *Kampfzeit* to thousands of *Waffen*-SS recruits. Political soldiering, in terms of the old values, survived in the boot camp and the garrison, the replacement depots and infamous special duty units like the SS-*Bataillone* z.b.V. *der Waffen*-SS, the 'Kaminski' brigade, and the 'Dirlewanger' brigade. The newer officers' corps either had a conception of the political soldier associated with the imagery of a Germanic or European comradeship-in-arms, or had none at all. In fact, the *Nur-Soldaten* (only-soldiers) preponderated in the *Waffen*-SS. Himmler's betrayal of Röhm's SA avenged itself upon the SS by the AW 'refugees' of 1935 becoming the worst offenders in shedding the political. Could it have been otherwise? This was the would-be officer-elite of the SA; when Himmler let the SS become 'a department store where anything and everything could be found' – like the SA of 1934 – the *Nur-Soldaten* recognised a familiar milieu and acted accordingly. They retreated into the 'inner emigration' of the front.

By the autumn and winter of 1943, 'the front', now in Italy as well as in Russia and the Balkans, extended far behind the chief line of battle (*Hauptkampflinie*, HKL). Partisans and infiltrators made 'rear echelon' an almost meaningless term. The conditions of the *Kampfzeit*, of civil war, returned, for which the *Nur-Soldaten* were ill-equipped. The inner emigration was hard to practise for an extended length of time; nevertheless the determined SS officer could now get to the front much more easily than before, since it was harder for Himmler or the Main Office chiefs to hold such a man back due to the burning necessities of the battlefield. Sooner or later such men were struck down, eliminating selectively a vital part of the *Waffen*-SS. The officer records for the whole year of 1944 are mute and tragic evidence of the disappearance of *Nur-Soldaten* and the survival of political soldiers. Naturally, the deepening front took its toll of aggressive spirit in rear-echelon special units, police formations and anti-partisan defence operations closer to home in the General Government and the Slovene marches. Still, even with heavy allied bombing creating 'battlefield inner Germany' for which, after all, the SS had been developed, the home front was still safer and more rewarding in promotions in 1943 and 1944.

Thus, the nature of the SS and of its incipient officers' corps was contradictory to the very end; there was an increasing alienation of its combat forces from the goals of its political-soldier leaders. Its mass armies of foreign mercenaries and *Landsknechte* had more in common with the *Nur-Soldaten* who led them than with Main Office chiefs and the Reich German honorary SS whose profits and prestige were increasingly tied to a victory for Himmler's empire. The task on the home front of staving off popular revolution and foiling putsches called for very different sorts of men; by their very nature these men were better equipped to survive even defeat.

Even on paper Himmler's acquisition of the title Reich Minister of the Interior in August 1943 and Commanding General of the Home or Reserve Army after the 20 July 1944 fiasco contributed remarkably little to the long-dreamed-of fusion of party and state, SS and police, into a political soldierdom – State Security Corps. The curse of the SA of 1933 and 1934 pursued the SS of ten years later. Overloaded with opportunists, top-heavy with staff positions, dependent on and therefore afraid of its combat forces, and above all lacking the self-discipline which sets limits to ambition and commitment, the SS of 1943 through 1945 failed to 'shake down' as a functioning institution. In spite of last-minute abortive efforts on the part of individuals, even Himmler himself, the SS failed to consolidate. Efforts to transcend its own past, the shortcomings of the state and party to which it was bound almost against its will, and the grim realities of unconditional defeat simply tore the SS apart.

Dénouement

At the time of the allied invasion in the west, the *Gesamt*-SS (entire SS) had reached its maximum size – 800,000 men, not counting strictly police units of all kinds and subsidiary foreign mercenaries like the Cossack divisions. At least 1 million SS men had already fallen as *Waffen*-SS; more than that many of the General SS were serving with the *Wehrmacht*; and no separate record was kept of SS casualties in army, navy, or air units. Some effort to maintain contact with General SS personnel in the *Wehrmacht* continued in 1944 by means of newsletters from the Berlin offices and regional commanders; and, as has been noted, notification and care of the spiritual and physical needs of survivors was supposed to be extended to General SS casualties in the *Wehrmacht*. However, these duties were being neglected already in 1942; in later years when the bombings destroyed the Berlin offices, scattering records and personnel widely over Germany, and local and regional staffs were reduced to the bone, the casualties of the General SS went unnoticed unless some wounded soldier made his appearance on furlough. Such individuals were quickly caught up by frantic home front administrators, the soldiers' old General SS status giving one or another agency connected with the SS and Police first claim on them. Often they were added to the *Waffen*-SS precisely to keep them on the home front instead of returning to their *Wehrmacht* unit.

The General SS itself was partly run by such severely wounded men, as well as by those temporarily returned to active General SS duties from *Stamm-Einheiten* (SS reserves over age forty-five). The 64,000 General SS men not in the *Wehrmacht, Organisation Todt, Technische Nothilfe*, RSHA, or other organisations for which one could be drafted were in fact largely members of the overage SS reserves, a kind of vestige of *Altkämpfertum*. That Himmler was quite interested in preserving this remnant and was far from abandoning the concept of a General SS is shown by the plethora of his orders in 1943, 1944 and even 1945 solely for the purpose of defining some feature of it or making changes surely meaningless in a dying structure. It is hard to avoid the conclusion that the General SS was headed for political oblivion along with the SA, and for the same reasons.

Himmler did not relish the truth that all of his real power apparatus lay, after all, within the state sector: the police, RKFDV and *Waffen*-SS. The General SS had been a vehicle to carry him into and not out of the state apparatus. What remained of that vehicle was a mere *esprit de corps*, the SS spirit, transmitted from the *Altkämpfer* to the *Waffen*-SS and the younger administrators of the Main Offices. Perhaps still viable in the Germanic conception – with its claim to transcend the German state system – as the *esprit de corps* of a European SS, Himmler's realm was now little more than a comradeship-of-arms, unsophisticated anti-Bolshevism and a *Landsknecht élan* which fought to avoid dying.

Scattered about the Reich and its shrunken empire lay the fragments of the future State Security Corps in the form of many hundreds of sepa-rate *Waffen*-SS units ranging in size and complexity from armoured corps to temporary companies in transit; Security and Order Police headquarters as well as police regiments, battalions and hundreds; Superior SS and Police installations with RKFDV, SD and *Waffen*-SS rear-echelon command posts; and the dozen or more SS Main Offices, each already split between Berlin and countryside locations. The co-ordination of this hydra's many heads should have occurred in the personal staff of the *Reichsführer* SS and Chief of the German Police. However, what co-ordination occurred was largely the work of the adjutants of the Main Offices and of Rudolf Brandt, the deputy chief of the Personal Staff. Karl Wolff, the actual chief of that organisation – no match for the 'rival satraps' vying for Himmler's ear – had not unwillingly taken his leave of 'Byzantine' Berlin to become the Supreme SS and Police Leader of Italy in 1943. His deputy, Brandt, was an affable nonentity with a talent for getting along with everybody and especially with other adjutants whose horizons were no wider than their filing cabinets. To this latter-day breed of SS bureaucrats posterity owes the *Schriftgutverwaltung* (Records Administration), which preserved the 'Himmler files' so rich with trivia for the years 1943–45.

Co-ordination in the form of *Gremium* or advisory council of Main Office chiefs, Superior SS and Police Leaders, top military commanders and the like hovered in the plans and projects of the men around Himmler; but the *Reichsführer* SS himself could only talk of an Arthurian Round Table 'after the war' and gather together 150 or more *Gruppenführer* to digest his rambling pronouncements instead of talking back. Modelling himself after Hitler, Heinrich Himmler denied the SS a chance to depose him and thus also a chance to coalesce sufficiently at the top to avoid being broken apart by the successive blows Hitler's Reich experienced.

As it broke, the SS and its officers' corps fragmented along lines of class and regional cleavage that had never quite been sealed over: SS soldiers went with non-SS soldiers, SS bureaucrats with non-SS bureaucrats, SS fanatics with non-SS fanatics, and SS opportunists with non-SS opportunists. The political soldiers of the SS who were still alive in 1944–45 did not have enough in common to transcend these fractures, especially since they lacked a leader. Himmler allowed himself to be caught up in the state apparatus, first via the police and the Interior Ministry, reforming German justice out of existence; then in the military arena, playing at generalship without regard for the military potential of his troops – thinking only of 1918 and determined to slaughter hundreds of thousands rather than yield territory. The high quality of many SS divisions and the SS armoured corps did much to prolong the war which was to have been fought till 'five minutes after twelve', in Goebbels's classic phrase. But Goebbels and Himmler lacked the willpower to depose Hitler and join what was left of their respective power systems to preserve Germany within the frontiers of 1939, the goal of the vast majority of German fighting men and of the Resistance itself.

Even if this goal was not achievable, neither the allies nor the Germans in 1944 doubted the capacity of the Reich to stave off defeat for a year or two, inflicting terrible casualties on both sides. Thus, Himmler had something to bargain with as he picked up the threads of the *Abwehr* and Resistance ties to the allies, only to stampede the plotters into precipitate action on 20 July due to arrests made necessary by their ineptitude. The SS had been founded to prevent just such a counter-revolution against Hitler and the party; the imagery of 1918 had often played its part in strengthening Himmler's hand over the police and the *Waffen*-SS. Yet when the long-feared stab in the back occurred, its main effect was to interrupt Himmler's own feeble efforts to cast the SS itself in the role of a counter-revolutionary junta! The RSHA was barely efficient enough to prevent other elements of the SS from collaborating with the Resistance and with foreign intelligence – including Himmler and his former chief adjutant; it did not figure in preventing Hitler's death.

In the aftermath of the plot – which resembled the atmosphere of the summer and autumn of 1934 when SA and SS purged their comrades in nervous anxiety that they should not be next – the SS leadership assisted in the purge of business, bureaucracy and military comrades with mixed emotions, even heavy hearts, believing that the victors this time were Goebbels and Bormann. Instead of reaffirmations of SS unity that autumn and winter, the purges brought new splits in the Main Offices. Rather than sticking together, the State Security Corps broke up into rival intrigues, with Himmler heading the pack.

While some SS military leaders, bureaucrats and policemen contributed to the bestiality of the German efforts to keep Finland, Hungary, Slovakia and Romania in the war, others with Himmler in the lead sought to trade Jewish lives and other 'expendable material' for trucks, food, passports, time and good consciences. Himmler meddled in foreign policy far too long, yet there was no uniform SS foreign policy in Italy, the Balkans, Scandinavia, or the west. Eichmann complained that he got better co-operation from the Foreign Office than from the Superior SS and Police Leaders. They in turn waged their own wars with the

Foreign Office, High Command and the SS Main Offices increasingly manned by SS lieutenants and captains – the adjutants determined to go down with the ship. Few Superior SS and Police Leaders died with their boots on, preferring to save their skins by collaborating with the invaders. However, *Waffen*-SS officers were prominent in the kangaroo courts hanging army deserters and shooting civilians who talked of surrender.

Needless to say, there was nothing cohesive about the death throes of the *Waffen*-SS. With a paper strength of nearly 500,000 in spite of losses totalling 300,000 the rag-tag units of grounded Luftwaffe and sailors; the sallow, starchy-complexioned boys of sixteen and seventeen; the confused and frightened eastern Europeans with only a dozen words of halting German; the grimy, tired *Kampfgruppen* of thirty or forty veterans of too many winter campaigns – this *Waffen*-SS was no longer an elite corps of political soldiers. Bravery and self-sacrifice grew apace in some units, under commanders who had learned how to lead – some in the *Kampfjahre*, others in the *Junkerschulen* and far more on the battlefield. Cruelty and sadism, useless destruction and pillage multiplied in other units whose leaders as often as not were on Himmler's blacklist for drunkenness, neglect of duty, corruption and cowardice. Both kinds of SS officers had their counterparts many times over in the *Wehrmacht*; it was merely that 'when they were good, they were very very good; when they were bad, they were horrid'. The Sixth SS *Panzer* army in the Ardennes offensive was merely a moderately well-equipped German military formation; and even the trick formations of Skorzeny's American-speaking jeep drivers only preserved the *élan* of their fathers in the free corps. These were not political soldiers. The much-feared Alpine Redoubt, with its intrepid SS divisions, was a better trick, which Himmler and Goebbels perpetrated with Göring's help. But in the end the hardest fighting SS units were chewed up in Budapest, the Baltic states and Berlin, so that Himmler knew better than to migrate south to a defenceless land of pretty scenery. In strange contrast to the corps anthem, '*Wenn alle untreu werden*' ('If everyone becomes disloyal'), Himmler, his Supreme SS and Police Leader in Italy, several army corps commanders and assorted division commanders, numerous Superior SS and Police Leaders, and countless Sipo-SD officials bartered with the allies for a negotiated peace – not for Germany but for their own immediate entourage. The SS had ceased to exist.

8

CONCLUSION: BEHIND THE
MASK OF POSSESSION

Scholars and non-scholars alike have had a field day assessing the Nazi SS. For more than a generation now, the men in the black coats have been weighed in the balance and been found wanting. The ineradicable fact that their most decisive activity was the death-machinery that destroyed many millions of helpless and harmless Jewish men, women and children has led to monolithic condemnation and sweeping generalisation about 'the SS'. Here we cannot and must not reverse that condemnation of the system and the men who ran it. Yet it seems that our last remarks should be devoted to a deeper understanding of the forces and mechanisms that made possible the 'tragic fulfilment' of Hitler's and Himmler's theatrical fantasies. Considered in that attempt is a need for differentiation among those men in the black coats, a return to the German and European social and economic context referred to at the beginning, and some insight into our own times with their own dreams and illusions.

It should not be forgotten that the history of the SS is fundamentally a part of the history of the National Socialist movement and that this movement lasted only twenty-seven years. On the one hand, then, both the SS and the Nazis went through very rapid development, changing and growing so fast that generalisations for periods shorter even than a decade are often inadequate. On the other hand, the whole evolution was truncated by total disintegration caused by massive military defeat, partition of their geographical base and systematic proscription of all National Socialist writing or political activity. Processes of change, whether of adaptation or internal decay, were thereby cut off absolutely.

The whole trajectory of SS experience, of SS thought and of SS plans can be followed for less than a quarter-century, which even for a human lifetime is not very long. In our kaleidoscopic century the twenty-one years, 1925–45, of the *Schutzstaffel* risk being taken out of context, isolated and reified as some sort of epic – albeit of evil, for most observers – and incorrectly used as a lesson. Without doubt there are lessons in the history of the SS, but we should take care that we learn them from stubborn reality, not from images and theatre.

'The SS' was anything but a monolith. Though sometimes presented as such during its lifetime, and excessively thereafter, the SS was more often manipulated to appear to be different things to different viewers. The mask of possession was merely one of these manipulations, though it rested on some features of the Order. But the substance of the SS did change – so much that it is tempting to say that it was never one specific phenomenon at all. Still, at least from the early 1930s, in the mind and at the hands of Heinrich Himmler the SS developed continuity. Some of this continuity came from the vision he shared with Hitler and with countless Germans: the wish that in 1918 there had been strong men with authority who could have struck down the rebellious soldiers and sailors and their civilian supporters, rallied the German armed forces, and fought until 'five minutes past twelve' – thereby securing a peace more consonant with Germany's posture in Europe, especially eastern Europe. The illusion of 1914 that victory could be willed, and that German institutions had the inner resilience to withstand anything their combined enemies could direct against them, was a dogma of the nationalist right. But the idea of creating more popularly based German institutions and a band of political soldiers to defend those institutions was Hitler's own contribution, even if it was the Storm Troops and not the SS that Hitler had originally conceived for this role.

Another part of the continuity came from the intrinsic need in a pugnacious and violent movement not merely to have a headquarters guard but even more to have a body of committed roughnecks who could be asked to do quite literally 'anything'. This also was Hitler's own conception, for he had no use for the liberal utopia of John Stuart Mill in which truth and good judgement can battle it out, using words and logic alone. The war, the revolutions and the post-war European political milieu all gave the lie to expectations of a return to pre-1914 conditions. Hitler had recognised the falsity and superficiality of the genteel and intellectual tradition in German politics in any case. Again, the original version of these roughnecks had been the SA, who were to guard the meetings, protect the speakers, beat up opponents – and very literally commit any imaginable crime on orders of the *Führer*. Hitler, not Himmler, had already singled out a headquarters guard and then a *Stosstrupp* in 1923; and in 1925 the SS was called into being not so much as a replacement for the SA but as Special Duty units, again antedating Himmler.

Yet Heinrich Himmler definitely put the impress of his own enthusiasms on the 'permanent SS' in two regards: the role of snoopers within the party and in German life, high and low; and the task of being a future gene pool for the German people. Here we find Hitler in the background. While he authorised Himmler's detective proclivities, it went against Hitler's grain to give any Nazi a monopoly of anything – Himmler built up a mere police potentiality into so deadly an instrument that nearly all rivals were intimidated out of existence. Goebbels and Bormann did keep systems of their own but did not quarrel openly with the SS; Hitler parried Himmler's investigative power by enlisting Ernst Kaltenbrunner of the RSHA to watch Himmler. It is doubtful if Hitler ever took the SS gene pool seriously. Nevertheless, the general Nazi support for eugenics, 'race purity' and biological viewpoints ('Blood and Soil', body-building, nature religion) helped make the peculiarly SS version of racism seem very appropriate.

The SS, then, reflected Adolf Hitler's world view, not merely by being his sworn liegemen in a feudal sense but by evolving under Himmler's hand into a State Security Corps – a corps of state guardians willing and able to carry out any task, abominable or disgusting, on orders from its leader. The SS was made by Himmler into a network of influentials, of spies and of lodge-brothers (in spite of the alleged SS hatred of all lodges), each of which overlapped the others. This aspect of the SS did not reflect Hitler; it reflected Himmler – and, more than Himmler, the unmodern bourgeoisie of post-world war Germany. In its world view the failure of Germany to win the First World War, the mishandling of the German revolution, the depression and SS members' own chequered careers must imply a fundamental faultiness in the twentieth century. To such men, as to Himmler, the 'rottenness' was everywhere; they imagined conspiracy and enemies of Germany, of its ways and ideas, in each social class. They had been taught that obedience and diligence was everything, but they had learned in war and business, in politics and human relations that more was needed. That 'more' was perceived as a blend of volunteer spirit and personalised loyalty, of ruthless self-seeking and the harshest self-abasement. In the fantasy of a future biological community of clans, Himmler and his generation indulged in a reversal of their fears of being inadequate and degenerate. As a 'sworn community of superior men', SS volunteers imagined that they had been coopted by Adolf Hitler's truest henchmen into becoming the ancestors of the better Germany they projected into the future. The unreachable, just and moral society which had failed to emerge after 1918 – or even after 1933 – could be something they carried in their loins! The destructive urges and hatreds born of their frustrated lives were channelled outwards away from those near and dear to them toward the foreigner, the alien and those symbols of awakening self-doubt – the Jews and the Catholic clergy. Anti-clericalism was almost as strong in the SS as racism, but this trend also was only partly Hitlerian. The SS was kept tethered *vis-à-vis* the Church, though only up to a point.

The mental furniture of Himmler and his intellectual cohorts was the warmed-over folkish world view that well-educated Germans regarded as slightly ludicrous. National Socialism itself was not a set of ideas at all but a set of attitudes and aspirations, covering what political scientists like to call primordial feelings – such as fear, resentment, envy and rage. In its earlier versions (1919–23), National Socialism was relatively naive and honest – and hopelessly crude. Its political soldiers were soldiers or if not they were young men who thought soldiering was breaking heads, and politics was shouting and booing. After its refounding, National Socialism slowly took on the trappings of middle-class sophistication in the form of a Goebbels, the Strassers, or even a Hermann Rauschning. Yet clever slogans, cartoons, posters and handbills were only means to a single end, the ballot box and electoral majority. In this respect, the Nazis were in their element, for their ultimate goals and their fundamental world view was well concealed by this resort to the enemy's weapons. It was in this double game that the SS began – hardly more than local *Stosstrupp*s but with the difference that as picked men from the party, they could be stamped with the pseudo-superiority of the 'Master Race'. The best of the Nazis must thus be racially superior – if not wholly by external hallmarks at least by behaviour, bearing and attitude. It was virtually inevitable that such a group would find its Himmler, a devotee of human breeding and Nordic archaeology, an amateur detective and would-be officer. He was a good bureaucrat, at least for many years – though ultimately the very antithesis of orderliness and routine. Himmler had the skills to organise the primitive SS units into a unified system of party security in a no-nonsense fashion admired by Hitler and many other bigwigs; yet he was, or seemed to be, relatively harmless as a man or a thinker. His predilection for a certain amount of racial hocus pocus, cephalic indexes and marriage approval for his charges, did not seem to matter much.

Few of us are wise enough to invent new institutions; the Germans tried, and their copying was very well meant. The breakdown of their electoral system took some time to register, and as it broke the tremors benefited the Nazis. The Nazi strategy was itself clumsy and contributed to the general chaos without necessarily furthering the Nazi goal of a seizure of power, because they did not know where to turn for support at the polls. Gradually they put together a reasonably strong coalition of voters from the country, the small towns, the comfortable (yet frightened) suburbs and among the unorganised unemployed; but they were stymied by the toughness of the political institutions so recently erected, notably the presidency and the chancellorship. End-running these institutions, occupied by none-too-intelligent human beings, the Nazis succeeded in frightening the business and financial world with exaggerated images of a *Götterdämmerung* of private property during a bloody civil war with the Communists. Thus, the nationalist right was persuaded by its financial supporters to let the Nazis pretend they had made a seizure of power, the famous 'taming' manoeuvre, which gave the Nazis a chance to seize actual power in stages from within. For this strategy the Nazis were quite well prepared, but here too the crudity and indiscipline of the movement threatened to give away the game before the victory. It was to be the SS that kept the game alive when Röhm and the SA became impatient.

The SS that took part in the conspiracy to destroy Röhm and his top brass already had some of the features of the State Security Corps towards which Himmler had been heading his unified *Stosstrupp*s since the early 1930s. From being merely local groups to protect speakers and spy on party goings-on, the SS was made into striking forces in 1931 and 1932 which could aid and stiffen Storm Troop expeditions and street warfare, and which it was thought might combat a Communist coup or carry out a Nazi seizure of power after some landslide victory. Its units were often simply slightly more respectable (and more dependable) Storm Troops. Some of their number misbehaved according to Nazi standards, but others could be used to 'clean out' pockets of 'Stennes SA' in 1931. In the actual seizure of power, the SS role was absorptive: to sponge up the business and professional classes, the bureaucrats and the academics, the police and the jurists turned off by Storm Troop hooliganism yet still anxious to jump on the most likely bandwagon. This sponging up had begun at least two years earlier and was part of the NSDAP strategy of creating their version of the leftist 'front organisation', known by the Nazis as 'auxiliaries'. In 1933 this process gave the SS access to money, influence and power – without confrontation and bad blood. In this respect, it resembled the party itself, which also absorbed many times its weight within pre-existing organisations; but unlike the party, at least for the peacetime years, the SS did not swell up with fellow-travellers. The SA, on the other hand, had already swelled rapidly in 1932, if not earlier, and in 1933 became a monstrosity by adding the *Stahlhelm*. Yet its leadership preferred the confrontational style, defiance and contumely. If SS men regularly joined with SA men in headbreaking, housebreaking and drunken escapades, the former did not boast – did not make speeches for the press or challenge editors to fisticuffs. They were kept silent, and a few were punished.

Above all, Himmler had systematically created a state apparatus for himself in the secret police units of the *Länder*, capping the edifice with the Prussian Gestapo. This network was in principle detached from the authority of local administrations and was united only in Himmler's person. Thus, the feudal features of the *Führerstaat* (which would be reproduced and ramified from 1933 to 1945) appeared very early with respect to the secret police. It may also be noted that here the SS – and especially the SD – were essentially growth points, organising centres, pressure groups, or entry facilitators. The police units did not become SS nor did the SS become the secret police. However, control over the Gestapo and other secret Political Police made rivalry with the SA for influence over the rest of the police at least an equal match for Himmler.

The Röhm purge cannot be divorced from the intimidation of the German right at the same time, and in this respect the usability of the SS against all designated enemies must be emphasised. The SS may have seemed for a time to be a refuge and rallying point of the upper classes,

Culture and Property, and even a potential fronde – there is evidence that the right-wing resistance still thought so in 1943! They were in deadly error, and this was already true in 1934. Here the name of Heydrich must figure, for while we now know he was always loyal to Himmler and certainly did not push him around then or later, Heydrich had the brains and imagination that were lacking in the majority of the SS officers of 1933. Specifically, he helped Himmler to 'frame' Röhm and other SA leaders, which was highly necessary in view of Hitler's ambivalence about striking them down. Again, the police apparatus available to Himmler to strike at the SA was partly the work of Heydrich. Here, though, we must mention both Kurt Daluege and Sepp Dietrich as well. Daluege was the conduit through which Himmler developed his connections with Hermann Göring, all-important in gaining the Gestapo in Prussia – although without Heydrich, Himmler might have been outmanoeuvred by Daluege, who was there first. Göring was Himmler's co-conspirator against Röhm; indeed without Göring, a Himmler initiative against Röhm even supported by Heydrich was unthinkable in 1934. Thus, Daluege was the tie that bound Göring and Himmler together. On the other hand, it was Sepp Dietrich to whom Himmler entrusted the *Stosstrupp* functions at Bad Wiessee, using the embryonic *Leibstandarte* to do the very dirty work of the 'long knives'. The three men, Heydrich, Daluege and Dietrich, were movers and shakers in a corps that prided itself on the gung-ho spirit. But none of them contributed any ideas to the SS.

It was Richard Walter Darré who enriched the SS beyond Himmler's own brand of blood-and-soil agrarian mysticism. Not Darré alone but his coterie of young and middle-aged agricultural romantics, with their biological racism and confidence in human breeding, provided the SS from 1931 on – and especially after 1933 – with a pseudo-scientific rationale for SS exclusivism, elitist ambitions and penetration into the field of real estate. Although Darré himself would become more and more preoccupied with short-run policies designed to prepare Germany for war, his personnel, his friends and his disciples would continue to give the SS the patina of science at least for the ordinary German, including party members. Even the Ancestral Heritage Foundation with its sepa-rate academic ties and its own ambitious strivers and schemers could never replace or erase the decisive impact Darré had had through the RuSHa. While the formal focus of the Ancestral Heritage Foundation on ancestors could have suggested a fructifying historical enrichment of SS, Nazi and German ideology, Walter Wüst and Wolfram Sievers chose to chase down Himmler's will-o'-the-wisps and to toady for Himmler in the field of military medicine (the experiments on concentration camp inmates). Nor was the work of Günther d'Alquen at the editor's desk of 'The Black Corps' of any substance. That journal remained a shadow of the *Reichsführer* SS, in spite of apparent efforts to express the aspirations of a younger intellectual generation. Perhaps the ideas of Otto Ohlendorf and his friends concerning a centralised, planned economic system to replace the allegedly planless and selfish capitalism of German big business deserve to be classed as both theoretically interesting and of possible importance had the SS survived the war in a Nazi state. The trouble was that Himmler was a little too powerful, both in the SS and in the Nazi state: his crotchets and his judgement acted to stymie development of a systematic and consistent intellectual agenda for the SS. Ohlendorf was tried and executed for having commanded a killing unit in the USSR – one of his sidelines.

It is often remarked that totalitarian systems, no matter how inefficient and clumsy they are in areas related to caring for human needs, are quite effective at repression and war. In these latter areas, the name of Theodor Eicke stands out for his contributions to SS 'achievement'. For Eicke made the SS concentration camps the horror that they were, reducing opportunities for inmate self-protection and designing a system of brutalisation for guards that totalitarian Communism has never surpassed. Balkan, Latin American, Chinese and Japanese prison camps, not to mention North American 'chain-gangs' and other dehumanising improvisations, all have demonstrated that human systems of torture and the destruction of personality are world-wide. Still, the SS was forever imprinted through Eicke with a style of dehumanisation involving the perpetrators, as well as the victims. This style was carried over into the wartime Death's Head regiments, and, through the so-called 'police rein-forcements' which they trained as replacements for regular divisions, it was carried into the field. It would, of course, be wrong to 'blame it all on Eicke'. Yet it was specifically Eicke who earned the sobriquet 'Papa Eicke' which carried over into his Death's Head division until his death in 1943. Why was this? Perhaps because his unique brand of primitive appeal to the emotions, his eyeball-to-eyeball violence, and his apparent lack of discrimination in punishments and rewards (resembling the stereotypic German father-figure) was congruent with the immaturity of the kind of volunteers drawn to the SS. This is not an argument for a special kind of German personality but rather a commentary on the apparatus that National Socialist seizure of power had made possible, for which the SS supplied the raw material. Like so many other *Waffen*-SS generals, Eicke was long on courage and aggressiveness; he 'looked after' his unit when it came to stealing from other units (even SS) and refusing to give up personnel to them, but he sacrificed his men wantonly to the Moloch of battle. He became in death a *Waffen*-SS legend that survived the war and in which his concentration camp feats were, it would seem, forgotten.

Oswald Pohl also contributed to the reality of the SS in the slave-labour empire of the wartime concentration camps. Albert Speer insists that the whole enterprise was a terribly inefficient operation, yet even in his last work, Speer makes it clear that Germany needed and used those wretched, starving men and women for its war production. Like Eicke, Pohl was not a man of broad mental horizons. But, again like Eicke, he was entrepreneurial. In fact, his staff – partly from the camp administrators, partly from the General SS business managers and administrative officers – knew how to make personal fortunes out of their SS economic activities, and that quite legally and above board by prevailing standards. Their theft of human labour for their own advantage was combined with the theft (exploitation) of labour for SS advantage above and beyond that of the Reich. 'Aryanisation' was hardly an SS and Police monopoly and, when privately practised to excess, was sometimes punished; nevertheless the profitability of the Final Solution – both for individual personnel and for the SS in general – is important for understanding the intimate relationship between the SS willingness to 'do anything for the *Führer*' and the probability of pay-off. Indeed, the whole integration of the concentration camps with the world of industry and finance, the co-operation of so many branches of the non-SS bureaucracy with the destruction of European Jews, brings us close to one of the secrets of SS success. Even before the seizure of power in Germany, the SS gave itself out as somehow near the seat of power, in fact as wielders of that power 'on orders'. Once the Nazis had power in plenty, the SS became identified with enforcement. Its manner of silent reserve was the direct opposite of the Storm Troops' noisy clamour for a share in the spoils. Yet the SS did get its share, and it let the business and professional world know that co-operation with the *Reichsführer* SS was minimally a token of safety from harassment and potentially a connection worth money. The judicious use of the carrot and the stick did the rest. It would be too simple to say that the SS was a Mafia or even a conspiracy to muscle in on the spoils of the German economy by sharing them with the more co-operative members of the economic ruling class. The SS took a good while to develop its blackmail methods, and perhaps if Ohlendorf and the younger generation of SS economists had ever risen to the top of the SS empire, their second seizure of power might have resembled Stalin's methods of destroying potential opponents. National Socialism was a truncated episode in which the total war economy was of very short duration. It is a mistake to single out any one trend or phase in that kaleidoscope as determining.

We have observed that Himmler liked to say he had both a good and a bad side. Ulrich Greifelt of the RKFDV and Adolf Eichmann of the RSHA – each stands for the banality of a side of Himmler and the technocratic social engineers who served him. Neither Greifelt nor Eichmann moulded the SS. Rather, they were moulded by their experience and the opportunity it gave them to solve technical problems in which human beings were a matter of numbers. But the problems and the solutions became different from those encountered in the exploitation of prison camp labour or even in Aryanisation, each of which found their ecological niche in the rapacious Nazi economy. The effort to collect, 'evaluate' and resettle many hundreds of thousands of 'valuable' Germans in time of war – locating them in homes and shops and on farms of displaced Poles and Frenchmen – plus the commandeering of scarce transportation to cart off Jews to death camps while ammunition and replacements were waiting for trains entailed the use of SS and Police methods that flew in the face of the war effort, often went against party and surely military intentions, and cost the SS money and personnel. In Greifelt's case, the man co-ordinated a vast network of underlings and equals without much personal ego or effort at self-aggrandisement. In the case of Eichmann, another man was swelled with pride although only a lieutenant-colonel due to his ability to 'get things done' in the face of all obstacles. Both were social engineers. Each is conceivable outside the SS – even outside of Germany, for instance, since Vietnam in the United States – but the SS created for them, and for thousands like Greifelt and Eichmann, a field of operations in which power was available in quantities not ordinarily accessible to such limited personalities.

The role of '*Wölfchen*' ('Wolfy'), Karl Wolff, in moulding the SS is quite a different matter. The chief of the Personal Staff of the *Reichsführer* SS illustrates the Byzantine aspect of the whole National Socialist edifice. More than any of the chiefs of the SS Main Office with the exception of Gottlob Berger – whose role was never determined by that post – Karl Wolff managed the SS. He did not do this by decrees or organisational changes. He did it through communications or the interruption of communications. Fundamentally, Himmler, like Hitler and most of the leaders of National Socialism, realised that regular bureaucratic structures were straitjackets. Therefore, they practised 'authoritarian anarchy' in exercising the privileges of spontaneity available to the powerful. But Himmler had evolved from a highly bureaucratic individual, so it was as he was approaching age forty and had already created quite systematic repressive agencies as well as top-down chains of command in the police and military SS (*Leibstandarte* and *Verfügungstruppe*) that he gradually relied on the Personal Staff to sift and winnow SS problems for him. Thus, matters that should have gone to the Personnel Office, the SS Main Office, or even the Race and Settlement Main Office found their way to Karl Wolff, who became a sort of 'SS post office' – routing and rerouting inquiries and suggestions, complaints and gossip. Wolff posed as the 'friend of all', and indeed he was not malicious, though certainly self-aggrandising and dishonest. By wartime, persons outside the SS knew of his critical role and also knew that Himmler himself consulted Wolff frequently, with the result that the latter became much more than a 'post office'; he was a sort of *eminence grise*, a mellow and occasionally sardonic critic of the foibles and insufficiencies of the great and near-great. He seemed to many 'their friend in court' – and to many a dangerous enemy. It is not so easy to describe what he did to the SS; he helped to make it even less a rational system of command and policy than Himmler's basic design – yet in fact he did essentially what Himmler wanted. He smoothed and softened the rougher edges of the *Reichsführer*'s moods and reactions, thus tending to encourage higher ranks to think they could 'get away' with whatever they wanted to do. Of course, he humoured Himmler and went to great trouble helping him carry out many of his fantastic schemes and whims.

The creation of the *Waffen*-SS cannot of course be credited to any single man. Bernd Wegner has argued that Himmler himself planned from 1934 on to create an alternative to the *Reichswehr* tradition of *Nur-Soldaten* in the form of a cadre for a future National Socialist army. While persuasive, Wegner's thesis rests on circumstantial evidence. The formation of a highly creditable trio and then quartet of crack regiments by 1939 was accomplished by Sepp Dietrich, Paul Hausser, Hans Jüttner and several dozen other officers, of whom many joined the SS after 1933, often with pre-war or Weimar experience in the German army. The work of the staffs of the *Junkerschulen* before 1940 should also be mentioned as forming a type of military officer respected and valued beyond ranks of the *Waffen*-SS. While *Waffen*-SS boot camp was perhaps akin to that of the US Marines, the ignominy and dehumanisation characteristic of the Guard batallions and Death's Head regiments should not be attributed to these commanders. There is little doubt, however, that *Waffen*-SS units were designed and trained for use against 'traitors' – as in the case of 30 June 1934 – and against a German insurrection, whether from the left or right. Thus, the principle of absolute obedience and perfect loyalty, though not yet further perverted by being employed against helpless prisoners, was prepared ideologically and morally. Recognition of what Sepp Dietrich had expected his men to do at the time of the Röhm purge could not have been omitted from *Verfügungstruppe* education. Still, this ruthlessness seems to be of a different order from that of the camps, and we should be careful as historians to keep the intentions and practices of 1934–37 from all blending together as indeed they did after 1939. That they did so may be readily attributed to Himmler, to the 'nature of the SS', to National Socialism, or to the demands of war; all are partly to blame. It is less certain that something called 'the SS mentality' should be added, made up of the determination not to let anyone stand in the way of the *Führer* or of a German victory, steady indoctrination with the importance of obedience and local unit pride. Himmler gradually merged the Death's Head units, the Police Reinforcements trained by them, and the crack *Verfügungstruppe* regiments not systematically, as if by policy, but instead by improvisation. It would seem that the *Waffen*-SS was never born but, like Topsy in *Uncle Tom's Cabin*, just grew.

The 'Almighty Gottlob' – Gottlob Berger, sometime SS recruiter, chief of the Germanic Guidance Office, last head of the SS Main Office – certainly would not agree that the *Waffen*-SS 'just grew'. For Berger the care and feeding of the infant institution was a twenty-four-hour job. He did not really enter the scene until 1938, at a time when the probability of war with the likelihood of severe casualties had become pressing for Himmler. It was also a highly delicate time for the *Waffen*-SS because mobilisation spelled dominance by the *Wehrmacht*; in fact SS units were to come under the army's disposition in time of war. Berger was not only instrumental in developing and co-ordinating the Ethnic German Self-Defence units in Czechoslovakia and Poland (which fell outside the *Waffen*-SS proper and also were not subject to army control); also the chief recruiter laid the foundation for a 'Nordic SS' before the Nazis had conquered any territory in western Europe. Thus, Berger unquestionably shaped the future of the wartime SS, both in the use of non-citizens as recruits and in the conception of a European SS. Berger was the chief agitator for a multiethnic SS from 1942 on; no other SS leader came near him in responsibility for this feature of the later *Waffen*-SS.

Here again we come to the knotty issue of the immanence of a European SS within the ideology and make-up of the 'Order'. National Socialism had a love-hate relationship with everything foreign, perhaps an exaggeration of a form of insecurity not limited to Germans. The foreign admirer of the Nazis was much appreciated but was usually discounted. The Italian fascist, though theoretically a 'brother-in-arms', was often ridiculed. True admiration seems to have existed for the 'Nordic specimens' among the Scandinavians and for certain of the English aristocracy. There is little in the evolution of the SS to prepare us for the European SS; it appears to have been the improvisation it has usually been painted. And yet… there was the intrinsic appeal of a racial elite, the fundamental doctrine of 'good blood' scattered throughout Europe and the SS as an anti-Bolshevik, 'classless' lodge. It would seem that in the National Socialist dream of an 'Order' – certainly not an invention of Himmler – there lay half-concealed, half-revealed, the potential of a pan-European rather than merely pan-German (or pan-Germanic) rallying point for the old elitist strivings of so many ethnic traditions. From such a vantage point we might be inclined to ask not how Berger and Himmler could come upon the European SS ideal but rather what features of the German SS got in its way.

The answer is that most of all the institution was itself unripe. The burden of assimilating ethnic Germans into the Reich as a whole, not to mention into the party and the SS, required time. Of course, the heat of war did something toward amalgamation, but the reverse was also true: the war generated suspicions and jealousies which all too easily could be discharged against the less than 100 per cent German human being. SS training and spirit were not particularly well designed for assimilation, even though 'strict orders' required it. The case of the Nordic recruits seems to have been doubly complicated by language difficulties and their expectations of autonomy. Unlike the ethnic Germans, the Nordics 'got their way' after a fashion, or at least caused the uncompromising SS to compromise. After experimenting with a dual system of regular (German-led) units and foreign legions, the *Waffen*-SS developed the German-led but linguistically and culturally homogeneous division, which by 1943 could be applied to other than Nordic groups. Much of this experimenting and adaptation was engineered by Gottlieb Berger, who shared with Himmler the dishonesty and intrigue necessary to suck these men up from other employment in the Reich, from their home-lands, or from the *Wehrmacht*.

Berger's and Himmler's expansion of the *Waffen*-SS, more especially by its internationalisation, was certainly opportunistic in so far as they created a non-elite military system. It could only be justified within SS tradition as an extension of the elite, racial idea to all European societies. Probably the idea of a western European comradeship-in-arms with or without the anti-Bolshevik crusade can be seen as consistent with the pacification of that region concomitantly with the expected armistice with Britain. Here there is no necessary contradiction with the picture of a future National Socialist army being groomed to replace the *Nur Soldaten* who did most of the fighting. The racial-ideological reinforce-ments from western Europe might have been allies in this ambition. However, the fateful attack on the USSR, more improvisation than inevitable fulfilment of Adolf Hitler's fantasy, doomed the SS as it doomed National Socialism. It is probably a mistake to look for some profound or Machiavellian reason for Himmler's turning to quantity more and more between 1939 and 1942: he was a 'true believer' in his *Führer*. While Hitler had not needed the numbers Himmler provided him before 1941, that was not known ahead of time. In 1941 those numbers were not enough, so Himmler with the help of Berger got more – many more – even at the temporary cost to the 'SS idea' of consistency. After all, the *Waffen*-SS uniform did not supplant the membership card from Munich. Or, we may ask, did it? Certainly not in Himmler's mind – even in 1944!

It was left for the thousands of *Waffen*-SS officers of 1941–45 to shape the military aspect of the corps. Largely men aged between thirty and fifty, they were often but not always Nazis, some but not all veterans of the street fighting of 1930–32, and a great many doing what they had always wanted to do – command men in a war 'for Germany'. Common denominators other than these are few and far between. Many were impatient with Himmler, whom they regarded as 'unmilitary', and they had little use for the racial or historical education the SS Main Office still supplied as late as 1944. They gave the *Waffen*-SS the reputation as a 'fire brigade' for threatened sectors of the front, they had less than their 'share' of cowards and turncoats in adversity, and they worked very well with non-SS units and officers. They also included more than their share of 'last-ditchers' who led their men to useless death and executed civilians who flew white flags.

In analysing what the SS 'was' and what it became, it is critically important, then, to specify time periods and viewpoints. Viewing the SS from the inside first, and from the centre outwards, so to speak – Himmler's conception of the SS certainly evolved between 1929 and 1945. In the *Kampfzeit* (before 1933), its small size and pick of relative quality among party stalwarts – who were after all themselves volunteers under conditions of a wide range of political choice – made the SS for Himmler like a personal troop. This troop he hoped to pound, squeeze and hone to an instrument of power for Hitler, for the party and for his own ideas – especially as an embodiment of his dream of a future racial elite. Gradually from 1933 on state power lured him into becoming the Reich's policeman but not before he had used the SS to construct that state office and in such a way as to retain in branches of the SS various reserve strengths – even striking power – and, equally important, refuges from the exercise of state power against him in the form of the concentration camps, the Gestapo, the SD and even the General SS. It is doubtful that any or all of these could really have secured him against Hitler had the *Führer* turned upon him; in fact they might not have even protected the *Führer* against a determined military coup, as was shown in 1944. However, neither eventuality disturbed the peacetime evolution of the edifice, so that by 1938 Himmler's view of the SS and Police structure increasingly appears to be that new National Socialist breed of institution, beyond party and state, a *Führer*-institution. However, he continued to nourish and develop the SS as a community of families, still with the gene pool in mind – although it is clear that in view of the numbers involved, he tended to think in terms of his officers' corps, more especially the higher officers (*Standartenführer*, colonels and above).

As the war years came and multiplied, Himmler was increasingly dejected about his conception of the SS, for although the war had seemingly brought wonderful opportunities for international expansion and the 'blooding' that he felt necessary to justify the existence of a troop with such elite claims, he felt the SS slipping out from his control. He often spoke with satisfaction of the instrument he wielded against the internal enemies of the 'movement' and was proud that in the SS and Police he truly did have an institution capable of doing the dirty work despised by everyone else in Germany – killing the Jews. Yet he was always fearful that '1918' would come again and the SS would not be quite united enough or selfless enough. Through the SD system, indeed through the whole network of contacts he had in business – the *Wehrmacht*, academia and the media – already in 1942 he had become all too aware how much depended on the *Führer*, the armed forces, the SS and Police to stave off an inner collapse. He complained that the *Waffen*-SS, which he had allowed to overshadow everything else except the police in his system, was going its own way; its officers' corps was becoming *Nur Soldaten*. Still, he was bewitched by power potential, and he followed out every lead in international politics – now using the SS ploy, now the police, and inevitably the *Waffen*-SS. As Minister of the Interior, and even more as Commander of the Home Army and Army Corps, Himmler showed that he had wandered beyond his own design for the SS and beyond his own ingenuity in adapting it and his new positions to the *Führer*-constitution. But by this juncture (1943 and 1944), that half-myth and half-aspiration was itself showing signs of cracking under the burden of defeat. Strangely enough, Himmler in 1945 thought his police powers would be most appealing to the western victors, although no doubt he still imagined that an anti-Bolshevik crusade 'five minutes after twelve' would find use for what was left of his 'European' SS. He may even have had the conspiratorial experience of the first SS up his sleeve for post-war years. His suicide remains enigmatic; the same uncertainty and ambiguity which apparently lay behind his stomach cramps dogged him in the last hour of his captivity. He chose to disguise himself as a member of the Military Police (a category liable to be detained), then voluntarily identified himself as Himmler and only bit the cyanide capsule when he was sure he was going to lose it.

Among the *Altkämpfer* (those who had joined before 1933), the view of the SS changed with their degree of adjustment to its changing demands. For the many 'losers' who had to be consoled with becoming unpaid SS lieutenants in 1933 or 1934, and retired by 1935 with the job of a factory night watchman or meter reader, the SS had become another part of the uncaring 'Rule of the Bigwigs'. For some who found a good civilian job and 'connections' through the SS after 1934, the SS remained essentially a lodge, which sometimes took too much time and made inconvenient demands such as leaving one's Church. Many of these became reserve officers or NCOs in the *Wehrmacht* and had little or nothing more to do with the SS. But others climbed from rung to rung of business and SS rank, of state office or party hierarchy, and adjusted their official and unofficial views of the SS accordingly. There was a wide spectrum of loyalty to the Himmlerian ideal; minimal official loyalty meant responding positively to requests from SS headquarters, not just from Himmler personally – paying the numerous exactions required (which kept going up) and being 'active'. The latter meant more than attending a monthly meeting: it meant wearing the uniform, making appropriate appearances and speeches, getting one's family and relatives out of the Church, and getting married and having children. Unofficial views of the successful *Altkämpfer* who did not make their living as SS officers range from deep personal commitment to Himmler, to the 'Idea', and to the SS as shown by unstinting voluntary activity and dangerous service at home and at the front, to callous use of SS friend-ships, the uniform, position and ideology for crass personal aggrandise-ment. As the war came, more and more SS members experienced the moment of truth, when talk of sacrifice and parallels with the *Kampfzeit* became very real and immediate. In 1943 and 1944 Gottlob Berger was still routing out of comfortable rear-echelon posts some of these types; he and others were still preserving others at home for the sake of SS power and influence in 1945.

At the very core of the SS between 1933 and 1945, there were a few thousand *Altkämpfer* with paid positions. Already by 1939 their numbers were diluted by paid personnel who had joined in 1933 or later, espe-cially in the military and police fields. As the war years continued, more and more of the paid positions went to men who had been in the SA or to those not even in the party before 1933. But it is this first group of *Altkämpfer* which should have been the leaven that gave the SS of 1937,

1940 and 1942 unity; and several hundred, perhaps even 500, of them did. Yet they were not enough; the other paid *Altkämpfer* succumbed to the 'evil' which Himmler identified as breaking up the SS into soldiers, police, doctors, lawyers, business managers and worst of all 'SS bureaucrats'. It is doubtful if even the possible 500 shared the whole dream of the SS, but they showed by their evolution that they comprehended that it must become an SS and Police to withstand the fate of the SA and perhaps the party as well as becoming an adjunct to a reconstituted Wilhelmine state. They did not treat the police as an apparatus of the state only but as fighters for National Socialist measures, no matter what those might be. Similarly, as soldiers they did not recognise the rights of civilians, of prisoners of war, of neutrals, or of the clergy. Victory at any price, the virtual rejection of a calculus of costs in blood and material – these were the attitudes of the minority of *Altkämpfer* commanders. Again, as policy makers and regional managers, this type of Old Fighter thought of the SS first, last and always in comparison to the self-interests of the civilians, the party, or the state bureaucracy. Such men were a thorn in the side of many other Nazis, and in their ruthlessness often seemed and sometimes were less interested in German interests (meaning those of the German people) than in SS interests. However, there were three or four times as many top SS leaders with SS numbers below #200,000 who did not fit these terrible – nay, damning – characteristics. And of course the joiners of 1933, 1934 and later did include men with many of these ruthless traits, although rarely in the breadth and depth necessary to bridge the orientations of police, soldiers, administrators, doctors, lawyers and so on.

So to summarise the view of the SS from within among the top brass who were not Himmler's ideal: between 1929 and 1933 the SS was a 'cause' that paid and promised to pay even better. Its doctrines and methods were all intended to be taken literally and internalised like a catechism. As fellows SS members were mostly a good sort, better than those of the SA, much better than the so-called party comrades… thus went the litany. In the early years after the seizure of power, the *Altkämpfer* in paid posts groused about the newcomers who got better positions in the SS while the newcomers groused at the incompetence of the 'dead wood'. There was nevertheless a lot of hope for expansion and for just rewards of hard work and devotion to the SS rather than one's family, a job in private industry, or a civil service post. This brand of SS staff person could always be trusted to flaunt his uniform, fight for his 'rights' and 'honour' on every conceivable occasion, and after some complaining pick up and move his family to a new city when ordered to in the interests of SS geographic coverage.

The years 1936 to 1938 truly did bring good jobs and prestige to these SS officers (and brought some newcomers into officer ranks as well, though not as many as had come in earlier or as came in after the outbreak of the war). They now began to become quite differentiated one from another, specialists of many kinds – although as we have seen, they tended to think like soldiers, policemen, business managers, administrators, doctors, lawyers, etc. Their promotions began to be more closely related to their expertise, as well as relationships within their own bailiwicks, whether topical or regional. The SS 'began to look like a department store'. There appeared the first signs of rivalry of one sub-group with another. Intrigue, always present, began to be a full-time occupation for some. It looked as if intrigue was necessary to get things done with some superiors – perhaps with Heinrich Himmler. As the signs of war began to multiply and some paid personnel began to desert the ship, jobs opened up even better for the rest. Some began to think in terms of empires abroad and of using international connections to lay the foundation for greater things to come. Himmler favoured such activity.

Lastly, this group experienced the bloodletting of the war, at first in a proportion to be borne. Later the losses at the front, in occupied Europe and in bombed-out German cities began to make being an SS officer a very exposed role. These men did not desert the SS. As police, as soldiers, as administrators, they killed, they tortured, they seized and operated, they designed and built, they inspected, and they investigated. Many were quite selfless, but many were very venal. They simply kept their noses to the grindstone of war and devastation, without too much thinking except to survive, get a furlough, a promotion and a rise in pay , and to live a little. They were rarely wrestling with the future of the SS – as was Himmler – and they rarely wondered if the SS had got lost somewhere before the war – as did some of the *Altkämpfer* who stayed true believers. They were critical of Himmler for taking on too much; they were critical of much more than Himmler – of the party, the *Wehrmacht*, the other branches of the SS – but not of the *Führer*. (Naturally, paper records would only show this of someone who was later in disgrace. I do not doubt that *Altkämpfer* could privately doubt the *Führer* – we know others at their level did.) The essential thing about them is their lack of a *leitmotiv* at any time other than doing the job they saw before them without much imagination. It is doubtful if they can be said to have had an overall view of the SS during the war years; if so, it would have been heavily coloured by their own interests and that of their branch of the service.

What, then, can we say about views of the SS and its importance from outside its own ranks? Here also we need to distinguish among friends, enemies, victims and the disinterested observers. In the years of struggle, Hitler and the Munich party leadership had had a soft place in their hearts for Himmler and his minions. They found the SS to their liking for its manageability. But they saw it as merely one among many party organisations. Himmler did not get his way especially often – not nearly so often as SA commanders. Regional and local party chiefs had closer ties, more intense relationships of like and dislike, most of them personal. Many but not all preferred the SS to the SA, again because the SS was disposable. The SS before 1933 certainly was neither feared nor treated with kid gloves. It was in the radical SA that SS men were detested as stool pigeons and spies. Yet many in the SA merely regarded the SS as another branch of their own service, to be roundly cursed, envied and perhaps fought with on occasion but not especially respected – or hated. The German left sneered at the SS for its *petit bourgeois* pretensions, its (greatly exaggerated) capitalist supporters and wire-pullers, and the absence of 'real workers' from its ranks. Unlike the SA – which the Communists wooed and even the SPD acknowledged contained workers – the SS was regarded as monolithically middle class. This was a mistake, but the class-conscious worker was indeed totally out of place in the SS, which could not be said of the pre-1933 SA. The workers and other victims of the SS before 1933 hardly distinguished it from the SA; except for the 'Stennes SA', their victims in the movement rarely could single them out from other spies and intriguers of the party. Disinterested observers (ourselves) would have to add that the SS was largely under-appreciated and under-feared before 1933. Its impact was small upon German life, certainly compared to the party propagandists and the mass mayhem of the SA. Yet inside the movement and as an attraction for the potentially useful doctors, lawyers, civil servants, writers, academicians and police, the fledgling SS of 1929–32 provided reserves of strength against dissidence and disorganisation. Still, had the party foundered as it threatened to do, the SS neither could have saved it nor could it have survived its demise. At best it could have offered a shipwrecked Hitler a nucleus with which to start over.

Slowly, in fits and starts, Hitler came to see Himmler with his SS as pieces useful in checkmating Röhm; but Hitler allowed nature to take its course with indirection. Göring seems to have given Himmler the strength to take risks about Hitler's intentions, but in truth Hitler clearly chose to happen what did happen at the hands of the SS. Thereafter, the rest of the party leadership and its regional staffs regarded the SS with awe and respect, though the loathing widespread in the SA must also have existed in the party as well. The SD, Heydrich and the state apparatus (Gestapo and concentration camps, as seen from the party side) were powerful arguments with party leaders who did not like Himmler or the SS. The SS could become a bogeyman to frighten others with. The civil servants, judges, academicians and writers hesitated to criticise SS lawlessness, although some did resist 'legally' for some time (in some cases years). Now the victims knew their tormentors, and it is from this era (1935–39) that the monolithic image of the black-coated fiends arose. Actually, the SS was still largely confused with the Gestapo, and anti-fascists generally regarded the SS and Police system as fully unified and integrated with the National Socialist one-party state long before it was. In our judgement, the period 1933–36 should be regarded as extremely tentative for the SS, a period of trial and error; its impact on the Nazi movement was to strengthen Hitler one more time against the grass-root forces which had made his rise to power possible. As for the impact on Germany, the SS power system gradually fastened itself by 1936 on the political and social order to such an extent that few processes could occur without SS surveillance and intervention. Since these effects were largely negative, the impact was cramping and warping toward outward compliance; but for that period it would be a mistake to magnify or reify a totalitarian Big Brother in place of the essentially unimaginative and repressive police mentality which was the SS and Police reality after 1936. There was room for intelligent and creative resistance, yet the mood of the German people did not promise much support for such resistance – and the SS had only a modicum to do with that mood.

As Germany prepared for war from 1937 on, Hitler and the Nazis valued the SS as security against a recurrence of internal resistance. Hitler cautiously gave Himmler the means to set up striking forces for internal security, as well as for mopping up after a seizure of territory. The State Security Corps idea seemed to recommend itself in the face of a reluctant army leadership; and, as in 1934, Hitler arranged to be surprised by revelations concerning von Blomberg and von Fritsch supplied by Heydrich. By now the army leaders might fear and detest the SS – much as had their erstwhile enemies, the SA leaders of 1934 – though some anti-Hitler conspirators imagined the SS as an ally against the party. The victims of the State Security Corps in Austria, the Sudetenland and Bohemia encountered a smooth and Machiavellian instrument which from their viewpoint was an agency of the Reich – and Hitler – and so it was. That it was also feathering its own nest by seizing properties and laying the foundation for an imperial rule of its own was rarely perceived. But observers can record that now the SS was functioning on all cylinders, genuinely preparing the Reich for imperial conquest, giving Hitler that margin of assurance of domestic security he needed to make the Stalin Pact and to start what was known to be an unpopular war. The SS of 1939 was doing just what it was set up to do – and a little more, with regard to its own imperial ambitions arising from its plethora of technicians and dreamers.

Hitler was slow to realise the military usefulness of the *Waffen*-SS, and the army was even slower. The army was upset by SS behaviour in occupied Poland and to a lesser extent in the Balkans. Hitler, on the other hand, entirely approved and 'understood' the reasons for SS terror. There is every reason to believe that he ordered it. Similarly, he gave Himmler *carte blanche* in the rear echelons of Barbarossa; he wanted the State Security Corps to kill and torture. With respect to the Final Solution, there is only a shadow of doubt; it is probable that Göring arranged matters with Heydrich as he had both in 1934 and 1938, so that the *Führer* could by indirection alone secure his ends with 'clean hands'. The slow improvisation of the killing operations and the intricacies of collaboration give the lie to an internal conspiracy within the SS, of a segmented evil within an evil. Rather, it was a task thrust on the men in the black coats, wholly consistent with their cultivated image at least since 1933 within the party and German society. The mask of evil which the SS donned at this time was desired for them by all who were in the know. Individuals themselves may not have felt or acted as ones possessed, but the attribution of total perversion to the perpetrators – incorrect as it was then or now – reveals how much the onlookers always have to distance themselves from such behaviour. The whole SS did not do the killings, but the whole SS knew of them, and few could stand aside when called to participate. Aside from the murder of the Jews, the German people as a whole knew the SS as the deadly executioners of eastern Europe, and the guardians of law and order in western Europe. Its members were inevitably seen as 'different from ourselves'. This was despite the reality that few showed such differences. The SS for the victims of 1941–45 were all that the word 'fiend' conveys, undifferenti- ated and unforgivable. For the Russian soldier 'SS' meant no quarter on either side. During the battle of the Bulge, American interrogators of prisoners of war had to go to the company command post for SS prison- ers because GIs beat them so badly they were worthless. The prisoners were greatly feared, being readily (and incorrectly) identified with spies and infiltrators. Some of them were shot. *Waffen*-SS soldiers in 1944 and 1945 had the reputation of committing outrages against civilians on all fronts. And some of them had, although the majority had not.

Thus, the SS of wartime became an alibi of a nation. The real SS was more multiform – though always subject to the total power of a dictator- ship – in special ways not equally and usually applicable to men of the *Wehrmacht*, civil servants, or ordinary Germans. SS members were pledged to obey; they were organised in handy units which everyone expected to be ruthless and terrible. The impact of the wartime SS was at times as terrible as its reputation: certainly for the Holocaust the SS deserves all the blame it has received, if not the exclusive blame some- times bestowed. The *Waffen*-SS undoubtedly prolonged the war; it bought the Nazis time they did not know how to use – perhaps the time bought by so many deaths would have been wasted in any case, for nothing could have bought the Nazis enough time. This was not then something men of the SS could decide. It was their tragedy that they had previously surrendered these choices to such masters as Hitler and Himmler. As sorcerers' apprentices, they found themselves in the ruins of the sorcerers' workshop – Germany.

GLOSSARY

Abteilung
means both section and battalion. A *Sport-Abteilung* was the 'Sport section' of a party local; a *Sturm-Abteilung*, on the other hand, called to mind a 'Storm battalion' used to lead a trench attack or to hold an endangered sector. The SA *Hundertschaft* (hundred) became a battalion when it outgrew (during 1922) its numerical denomination. Each battalion was supposed to be composed of four companies, and four battalions made a *Standarte* (regiment).

Black *Reichswehr*
refers to units like the one Heinrich Himmler belonged to briefly in September–October 1923. They were assembled illegally by the *Reichswehr* to help resist French, Polish, or other incursions at the time of the Ruhr occupation, to quell Communist risings and to put down various secession schemes. They were disavowed in 1924, but many of them continued in existence as combat leagues, especially within the *Frontbann*.

Citizens' Militia
local middle-class militias with a sprinkling of the paramilitary police force, formed by an order of the Prussian Interior Ministry (*Einwohnerwehr*) and the soldier leadership. Their personnel usually slept at Temporary Volunteers' homes and did not move far from their own emergency volunteers' (*Zeitfreiwilligen*) communities. They functioned as guards and as auxiliaries for the free corps.

Defence or **combat leagues**
replaced the free corps to some extent by 1923, although they were often composed of free corps

veterans and sometimes whole free corps units. Their
membership was also drawn heavily from the former
Einwohnerwehr and *Zeitfreiwilligen*. Of dubious legality,
they were especially plentiful in Bavaria, which
flouted the Republic and the Entente.

Fatherland Party   this organisation was founded in 1917 by the German
High Command to rally opinion behind a prolongation
of the war for imperialist gains. It consisted of members
of radical right groups like the Pan-Germans, Anti-
Semites, and previously unorganised superpatriots.

Feldjägerkorps   a shock formation of the SA, dissolved 1935 and
incorporated into the Police.

Feme   another resurrected historical institution, a (German
'*Fehme*', or '*Vehme*') popular lynch proceeding in the
Middle Ages, applied in the 1920s against the political
left and outspoken democratic liberals by secret clubs
operating in a gangster mode. Probably the most infamous of these clubs was the OC (Organisation Consul).

Folkish and conservative-patriotic movements
(*Völkisch und vaterländisch*)   opposed the Republic and all it stood for (particularly
the revolution).

Freikorps (free corps)   privately organised military and paramilitary units
employed by the provisional regime in Germany in
1919 to fight the revolutionary left and Polish insurgents. The term harked back to similar units recruited
to fight Napoleon in 1813.

Frontbann   a loose confederation of disparate combat leagues
which retained their individual identity throughout
1924 and into 1925. Organised and run by Röhm to
replace the Storm Troops.

Gau   region of the party run by a party leader (*Gauleiter*).

German-Folkish Protection and Defiance League (*Deutsch Völkischer Schutz- und Trutzbund*)   founded in 1919 with the explicit support of the
Pan-German League, this anti-Semitic organisation
specialised in propaganda publication and rallies among
the folkish movement in urban and small-town
Germany. The 'folkish' (populist) tradition dated back to

the 1880s among the artisans and small-business people overtaken by industrialisation and urbanisation. The system of regional *Gauleiter* of the *Schutz- und Trutzbund* was copied by the Nazis, and some Nazi *Gauleiter* came over from the *Schutz- und Trutzbund* (Josef Grohé, Ludolf Haase, Martin Mutschmann).

Jungdeutscher Orden
Tannenbergbund and **Blücherbund**

these groups were more or less conspiratorial, more or less armed, right-wing 'clubs' which flourished in urban Germany among young men of bourgeois background, both of the front generation and younger. Their political goals were opposition to co-operation with the victors, opposition to the Republic and hostility to Marxism. Not strictly combat leagues, they tended to be locally based, with local policies and interests.

Kampfzeit/Kampfjahre

years of struggle, pre-1933.

Landsknechte

the original *Landsknechte* ('servants of the country') were mercenary soldiers of the sixteenth and seventeenth centuries who were romanticised by the German Youth movement before and after the First World War, thus adding to the image of the Wars of Liberation (1813) that of the Peasant War and the Thirty Years War to blur the realities of the anti-Bolshevik free corps.

National Bolshevism

first appeared in 1923 during the Ruhr occupation. Free-corps types like Leo Schlageter combined chauvinist and militarist convictions with an essentially non-Marxist liking for Lenin-like revolutionary organisation and slogans. The second wave appeared in the agricultural north and among the Reich Defence. Some later joined the German Communist Party.

Oberleitung or **OL**

the High Command of the Guard Squadron (*Oberleitung der Schutzstaffel der* NSDAP: note the singular usage of *Schutzstaffel* here). This military term did not stick. The term *Schutzstaffel* of the NSDAP would be technically preserved but rarely used.

Organisation Rossbach
and the **Schilljugend**

the *Organisation Rossbach* was a combat league, while the *Schilljugend* was a youth contingent organised on a local basis by Heines. The two units were notorious for homosexuality and for wearing brown shirts which had been prepared for German colonial troops, acquired from the old Imperial army stores.

Reichsbanner   Social Democratic defence or combat league.

Reichkreigsflagge   Ernest Röhm's terrorist organisation. The word itself is defined as 'Reich war flag'.

Reichswehr (Reich Defence)   the so-called provisional *Reichswehr* was set up by the German National Assembly on 6 March 1919. It operated out of the General Commands of the old Imperial army corps' areas.

Roter Frontkämpferbund   the Red Front Soldiers' League had been founded to compete among veterans with the Social Democratic *Reichsbanner* and the Nationalist *Stahlhelm*. Officially illegal since 1930, the 'Red Front' was as much part of urban Germany in the depression as the SA. Its slogan was 'Kill the fascists!'

Scharführer (*Gau* SS leader)   the term *Schar* was another romantic borrowing from the pre-war youth movement, who took it from medieval literature. The SS also used *Gauführer* and even spoke of the SS-*Gauleitung*. Later the SS adopted the SA term '*Gruppenführer*' (Group Leader), but by then (1932) such commands were no longer congruent with the *Gaue*.

Shock Troop (*Stosstrupp*)   a term like *Sturm-Abteilung*, carrying the elite ethos of the trenches. It referred to small 'shock' or attack units. The term was employed in Germany after the war for strong-arm squads used by political groups; it was not unique to the Hitler movement.

Shock Troop Hitler   the enlarged bodyguard of Hitler in 1923 that became
(*Stosstrupp Hitler*)   the historical pattern after which the SS was modelled.

Sicherheitsdienst   the SS Security Service established by Reinhard Heydrich in 1931 as the intelligence organisation of the Nazi Party.

Sippenamt   office for kinship.

Soviet Republic (*Räte-Republik*)   the short-lived Communist dictatorship established in Bavaria from 7 April 1919 to 2 May 1919. Largely confined to Munich, the badly organised and led 'dictatorship' had a certain resemblance to the Paris Commune, including the execution of hostages. It was followed by a much bloodier 'white terror' in the same parallel tradition.

Stabswache   headquarters' guard.

Staffelführer (squadron leader)   the only 'SS officer's' rank until 1930 when the SS introduced *Stürme* and *Sturmbanne* (companies and battalions like the SA). Like the SA, the SS preferred the term '*Führer*' (leader), developed in the pre-war German youth movement, to *Offizier*, a foreign loan word.

Stahlhelm (Steel Helmet), also called **Bund der Frontkämpfer** (League of Front Soldiers)   this veterans' organisation was founded on Christmas Day 1918, retaining the imperial colours (black-white-red) as a symbol of its rejection of the Republic and its black-red-gold flag. *Stahlhelm* members assisted in the *Grenzschutz Ost* (Border Defence 'East') paramilitary units defending Germany's eastern frontier against Polish irregulars.

Standarte   regiment.

Sturmbanne   battalion.

Stürme   company-size units.

'*Völkischer Beobachter*'   the newspaper of the NSDAP.

Volksheer   People's army.

Waffen-SS (Armed SS)   this term was used after 1939 to refer to the former *Verfügungstruppe* (Special Duty troops), garrisoned military forces in contrast to the paramilitary and largely parade-ground General SS. The *Waffen*-SS fought alongside the *Wehrmacht* in 1939 and later.

Wehrmacht   the armed forces, consisting of the German Army (*Heer*), Navy (*Kriegsmarine*), and Air Force (*Luftwaffe*)

LIST OF ABBREVIATIONS

a.M.	*am Main*	On the *Main* (River)
AO	*Auslands-Organisation der* NSDAP	Party organisation for Germans living abroad
AW	*Ausbildungswesen* of the Storm Troops, 1933–34	Military training organisation
DAF	*Deutsche Arbeits-Front*	German Labour Front
DAL	*Dienstaltersliste der Schutzstaffel*	Officers' Rank List of the SS
DAP	*Deutsche Arbeiter-Partei*	Original German Labour Party from which the NSDAP sprang in 1920
DNVP	*Deutsch-Nationale Volkspartei*	German Nationalist Party
FHA	*Führungshauptamt*	SS Leadership Main Office
FM	*Fördernde Mitglieder*	Sponsoring or supporting 'Members' of the SS
Gestapa	*Geheimes Staats-Polizei-Amt*	Secret State Police Headquarters (in Berlin; origin of Gestapo)
Gestapo	*Geheime Staats-Polizei*	Secret State Political Police
GISASS	*General-Inspekteur der* SA *und* SS	Combined SA and SS Inspector (1930–32)
GmbH	*Gesellschaft mit begrenzter Haftung*	Limited Liability Company (Ltd)
GRUSA	SA *Grundbefehl*	Fundamental SA Order
HIGA	*Hilfsgrenzangestellten*	Auxiliary Border Employees
HSSPF	*Höhere SS- und Polizei-Führer*	Superior SS and Police Leader

I-C		Intelligence Service or Intelligence Officer in German army, Storm Troops (SA) or SS
IMT	International Military Tribunal	Trial of the Major War Criminals before the International Tribunal at Nuremberg
KL	*Konzentrations-Lager*	Concentration camp
KPD	*Kommunistische Partei Deutschlands*	German Communist Party
Kripo	*Kriminalpolizei*	Criminal Investigation division
Lt. a. D.	*Leutnant ausser Dienst*	Lieutenant, retired
MUL	*Mannschaftsuntersuchungsliste*	Mustering questionnaire
NAPOLA	*National-Politische Lehranstalt*	State Political High School
NCO		Non-commissioned officer
NSBO	*Nationalsozialistische Betriebszellen-Organisation*	National Socialist Factory Cell Organisation
NS	*Nationalsozialistisch*	National Socialist, Nazi
NSDAP	*Nationalsozialistische Deutsche Arbeiter-Partei*	National Socialist (Nazi) German Workers' Party
NS-Dienst	*Nationalsozialistischer Dienst*	Camouflaged Storm Troops (SA) in the Sudetenland
NSK	*Nationalsozialistische Korrespondenz*	National Socialist Press Service
NSKK	*Nationalsozialistische Kraftfahrer-Korps*	National Socialist Automobile corps
NS-*Mannschaft*	*Nationalsozialistische Mannschaft*	Camouflaged SS in the Sudetenland
OC	Organisation Consul	Secret assassination (terrorist) band
OKH	*Oberkommando des Heeres*	Supreme Command of the German army
OKW	*Oberkommando der Wehrmacht*	Supreme Command of the German *Wehrmacht*
Orgesch	*Organisation Escherich*	Underground group resisting compliance with Versailles
Orpo	*Ordnungspolizei*	'Order Police', general purpose or regular police

OSAF	*Oberster Sturm-Abteilung-Führer*	Supreme Commander of the Storm Troops
OT	*Ordnertruppe*	'Marshals'
PI-Dienst	*Presse- und Informations-Dienst*	Press and Public Relations Service
PO	*Politische Organisation*	'Political Organisation'; cadre for mobilising political activists (NSDAP)
RAD	*Reichsarbeitsdienst*	National Labour Service
RGB	*'Reichsgesetzblatt'*	*'Reich Law Gazette'*
RKFDV	*Reichs-Kommissar für die Festigung Deutschen Volkstums*	Reich Commissar for the Strengthening of Germandom
RMBliV	*'Ministerialblatt des Reichs- und Preussischen Ministerium des Inneren'*	*'Ministerial Gazette of the Reich and Prussian Interior Ministry'*
RSHA	*Reichssicherheitshauptamt*	Reich Security Main Office
RuS	*Rasse und Siedlung*	Race and Settlement
RuSHa	*Rasse- und Siedlungs-Hauptamt*	Race and Settlement Main Office of the SS
SA	*Sturm-Abteilung*	Storm Troop(s)
SABE	*Sturm-Abteilung Befehl*	Storm Troop Order (from the Supreme Commander of the SA)
SD	*Sicherheitsdienst*	Security Service (secret intelligence unit of the SS)
SGV	*Schriftgutverwaltung des Persönlichen Stabes, Reichsführer SS*	Records Management of the Staff, *ReichsFührer* of the SS
Sipo	*Sicherheitspolizei*	'Security Police'; investigative police for criminal and political matters
SS	*Schutzstaffel*	Guard Squadron
TV	*Totenkopfverbände*	Death's Head units
TWC		Trials of War Criminals before the Nuremberg Tribunals
Uschla	*Untersuchungs-und Schlichtungs-Ausschuss*	Investigation and Conciliation Committee (of the NSDAP)

VDA	*Verein für das Deutschtun im Ausland*	Society for Germandom Abroad
VJHZ	'*Vierteljahrshefte fur Zeitgeschichte*'	
VoMi	*Volksdeutsche Mittelstelle*	Liaison Office for Ethnic Germans
VT	*Verfügungstruppe*	Special Duty Troops (VT) (of the SS)
VVV	*Vereinigte Vaterländische Verbände*	United Patriotic Leagues (of Bavaria)
VWHA	*Verwaltungs-und Wirtschafts-Hauptamt*	Main Office for Administration and Economy (of the SS)
WVHA	*Wirtschafts-und Verwaltungs-Hauptamt*	Main Office for Economy and Administration (reorganisation of VWHA)
z.b.V.	*zur besonderen Verwendung*	On special assignment; temporary duty ('TDY')

LIST OF ILLUSTRATIONS

All illustrations reproduced courtesy of Brian Leigh Davies

15   'Workers – Vote for the front-line soldier – Hitler!' A poster from 1932 demonstrating the Nazis' appeal to the masses.

16,17 These private photographs, found in an SS barracks at the end of the war in Europe, show pre-war General SS men burning Communist banners.

18   Heinrich Himmler, photographed while watching Storm Troop manoeuvres with Hitler.

19   5 March 1933 – early co-operation between the police and the Nazi auxiliaries.

20   Nazi leaders in their first hour of triumph on 5 March 1933. From left: Röhm, Himmler and Daluege.

21   The Nuremberg rally of 1933, a powerful show of force by the paramilitary wings of the Nazi party.

22   Massed ranks of General SS at a Nuremberg rally.

23   Young drummers of the *Hitlerjugend*, which from 1933 incorporated the right-wing *Jungstahlhelm*.

24   The *Leibstandarte Adolf Hitler*, which acted as Hitler's personal bodyguard.

25   Sepp Dietrich (left) with Wilhelm Brückner, Hitler's personal adjutant.

26   General SS troops salute Adolf Hitler and General Karl Litzmann on the occasion of the latter's eighty-fifth birthday. With their pledge of personal loyalty, the SS enjoyed at least the appearance of closeness to the *Führer*.

27   Ernst Röhm, SA Chief of Staff, from Streicher's book commemorating the 1933 Nuremberg rally.

28   Rank upon rank of the SS and SA at Nuremberg, giving some idea of the expansion they carried out in the 1930s.

29   SS-*Obergruppenführer* Eicke, who killed Ernst Röhm in 1934.

30   Participants in and survivors of the June–July purge, pictured at Nuremberg in November 1934. Left to right: Göring (behind), Lutze, Hitler, Hess and Himmler.

31   An early photograph of the new *Verfügungstruppe*, which gradually became organisationally distinct from the General SS.

32   SS officer Reinhard Heydrich in full uniform and loyal Nazi pose.

33   Dressed here in SS uniform, Alfred Naujocks was in fact part of the Gestapo's far-reaching system. He is famous for commanding the covert operation which saw German troops dressed as Poles attack the radio station at Gleiwitz, on the German-Polish border. Giving Hitler his excuse for invading Poland, this was arguably the first act of the Second World War.

34   An early photograph of the Adolf Hitler regiment, with the Death's Head prominent on their banners.

35   Himmler addressing SS officers in Norway. Scandinavians were among the first non-German peoples to be brought into the SS structure, partly because their Nordic background could be held to satisfy the criteria of the Race and Settlement Main Office.

36   An example of the use of the General SS in domestic police duties – here performing crowd control during the celebration of Hitler's birthday.

37   Advancing *Waffen*-SS troops on the Eastern Front.

INDEX